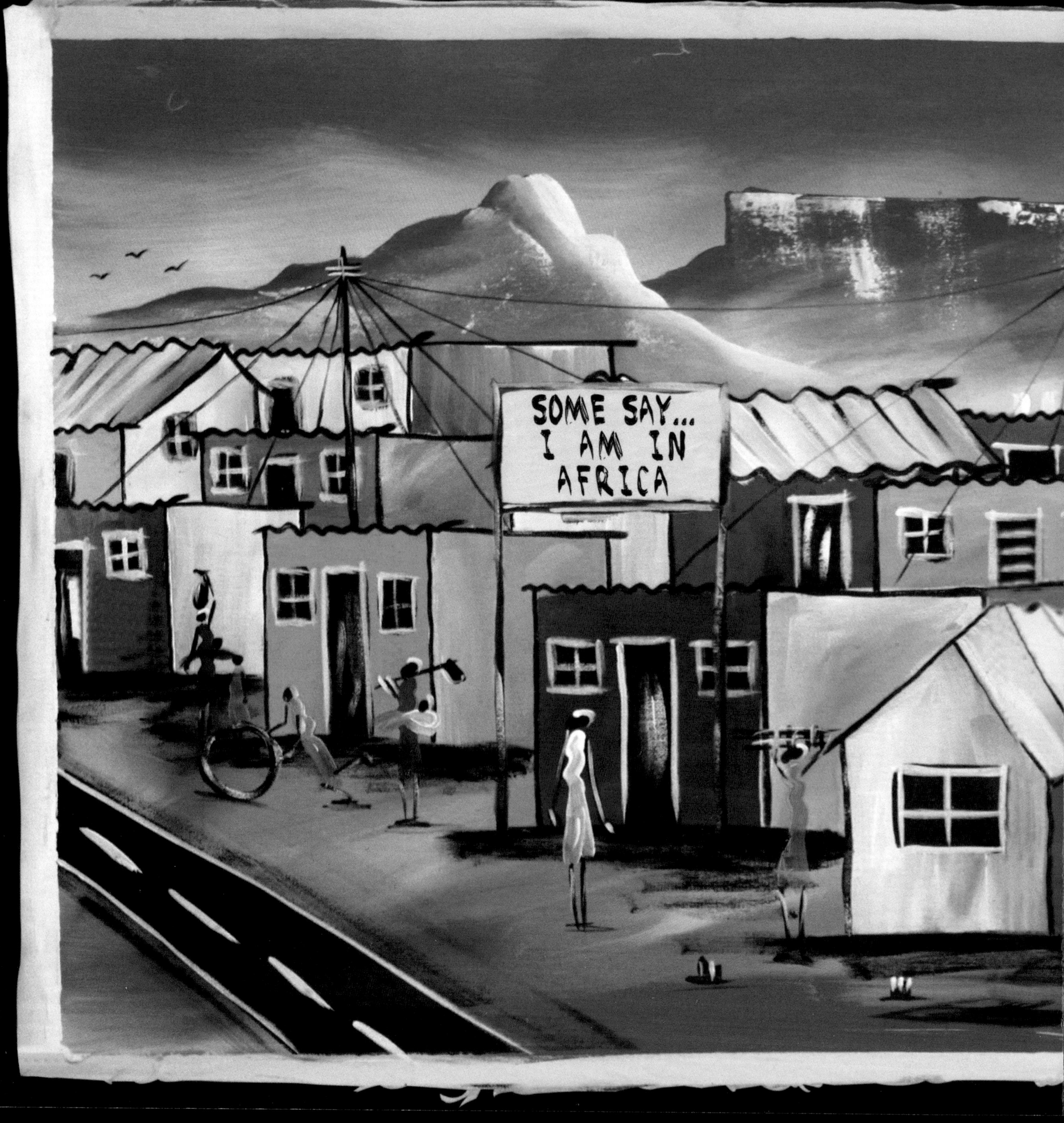
SOME SAY...
I AM IN
AFRICA

THE TRUTH IS...
AFRICA IS
IN ME

MUKANGV
'09

Published by Awesome SA Publishers
info@awesomesa.co.za
Phone +27 (0)82 786 8450
www.awesomesa.co.za
Graphic designer details available on request

Books are available in bulk to corporations and institutions.
For more information, please contact the publisher.

First Edition April 2010
Seventh print run March 2013

Printed and bound by ABC PRESS Cape Town

ISBN 978-0-620-46527-4 (soft cover)
ISBN 978-0-620-48596-8 (hard cover)

Awesome SA Publishers

AWESOME SOUTH AFRICA

Created by
Derryn Campbell

Art Director
Tish Roux

Editor
Siobhan Gunning

Designers
Tish Roux
Kirsty Stirton
Debbie Jayne Holmes
Dylon Levi Dreyer
Lisa Jeanine Meyer
Keshni Naidoo
Andrea Fleuriot

Cover Design
Kirsty Stirton

Research, Writing and Proofreading
Karen Lotter, Mabusi Kgwete,
Brenda Daniels, Dustin Kramer,
Liz Fisher, Warren Haslehurst,
Brenen Nortje, Kendell Mullany,
Richard Swart, Kim Lindeboom,
Steve Kotze, Camille Taboza-Vas
Caryn Fortune, Diana Young,
Lauren O'Brien, Dee Vryenhoek,
Toni Palmer, Julie Hunter,
Claire Campbell.

ABOUT THE BOOK

'The miracle that is South Africa.' This was the expression used by Archbishop Emeritus Desmond Tutu to describe South Africa. How then do you even begin to compile a book that not only encapsulates a country with so many mixed cultures, extreme diversities and a deep-rooted history, but also portrays the magnitude of this miracle? When you stop to think about it, it truly is a miracle and South Africa stands proud as a role model to the rest of the world. What we tend to overlook is that change is not an event but a process and our democracy is still young. Like a teenager growing up needs to work through the challenges of everyday life, so South Africa needs time to develop and mature. Whilst these challenges often dominate conversations and perceptions, let us not overlook the joy and accomplishments of this nation.

The purpose, therefore, of this book is to present a collection of random trivia, facts and fun which provide a light-hearted celebration of this amazing country. The objective of the pages is to enlighten and entertain whilst encouraging an understanding and appreciation for the country, its spectacular beauty and the many cultures which make up this Rainbow Nation.

Max du Preez said, 'I feel strongly that we should know our history with all its warts, but that we should be mature enough to say, 'I will not allow the sins of my forefathers to paralyse me with feelings of guilt and shame'.' This book reveals various sides to the country, touching on the turbulent and the comical. It is not meant to offend and the information contained within will appeal to South Africans' two greatest attributes – their pride and their sense of humour. This is not an encyclopaedia or an academic resource and there is no science behind the selection of topics, their order or preference.

People ask me what made me choose to write a book. The truth is, this book chose me! I am a passionate South African who felt a compelling need to produce a book that incorporates the many facets of South Africa. Together with the team that so willingly and tirelessly assisted me, we have had tremendous fun putting the pages together. I am, however, not a journalist, a historian or a writer and I therefore apologise in advance for any errors which you may come across. Many of the photographs or humorous anecdotes were received via email and the originators are unknown, and I would like to take this opportunity of thanking them for their input. This compilation should be seen as a work in progress. If anyone has additional information, photographs or suggestions or can identify any errors, then I would welcome your feedback and input for future print runs.

So I invite you to indulge yourself in the history, the greatness and the humour that is South Africa.

Enjoy!

Derryn.

derryn@awesomesa.co.za

A SPECIAL THANKS TO my family and friends who always stand by me and support my crazy ideas, I could never have done this without you. I know I have challenged the boundaries of normality on countless occasions and taken unreasonable advantage and I thank you for your patience. Dee, Louis, Mark and Shirls, your input has been wonderful. To my family, Mom, Ashley, Lauren and John, your never-ending encouragement and support is overwhelming. Thanks to Angela for the typing and daily support. A special word of thanks to Di Smith and my fellow Awesome SA colleagues for making this book a reality. Siobhan, Karen, Mabusi and Brenda, thank you for the tremendous amount of work you did in pulling the information together. The design work was a mammoth undertaking, so to Tish and the team of Debbie, Kirsty, Dylon and Lisa – you have done a fantastic job!

And lastly, Wayne, Stuart and Claire, what else can I say, you are the absolute best!

Photo courtesy Loot Eksteen

AWESOME SOUTH AFRICA

This book is about South Africans, for South Africans. South Africa is blessed with diverse, dynamic and determined people who have influenced the country and its people in one way or another. A special word of thanks to those who have contributed by sharing their passion and love for South Africa:

I just love South Africa! I have my whole family here with their children (we have 12 grandchildren), and I am so thrilled that they have chosen to live here and have not moved abroad. What gives me confidence is when I compare South Africa today to what it was like in the 70s and 80s, and early 90s, before Mr de Klerk and Mr Mandela gave us a new breath of life. South Africa has got a great future. We are going through a difficult time very much like young people go through changes in their lives, but I have great hope and confidence for this country.
With very best wishes,

**Raymond Ackerman,
Chairman of Pick n Pay, March 2010**

South Africa is awesome because it is a land that takes enormous pleasure in painting itself (albeit richly) as one clumsy stumble from the abyss. Marooned on the southern tip of the most feared continent on the planet, South Africans simultaneously suffer from an acute inferiority complex and a slightly bewildering sense of self-importance. A land of complication and contradiction, as rich as a potjiekos, as fragrant as braai smoke, yet ultimately elusive to all who are lucky enough to encounter her. In short – if you think you have this country figured out, you're clearly either insane or a foreigner (or both).

**John van de Ruit,
Author of bestselling novel, Spud**

South Africa is awesome because of the unbelievably resilient people whose stories shine a phenomenally bright light upon our land, in spite of all the dark headlines we are sadly famous for. You see, stories in our cultures work as a connection, umbilical cords between our ancestral world and the here and now. Through our diverse stories we touch each others' lives and this way we will finally heal our nation. And our children will dance to new music; not perfect but more honest and alive.

**Gcina M Mhlophe,
Author and South Africa's
favourite storyteller**

I am absolutely passionate about South Africa and wouldn't want to live anywhere else in the world. The soul and spirit of the land and its beautiful people is irreplaceable and the country is vibrant and alive with energy.

Let us remember that it is not our past that defines who we are, but rather the choices we make every day. The future is a creation and we create it with our thoughts, words and actions. My vision for this country is that we 'Keep the Dream Alive', that we continue to break down the barriers of the past whilst building strong foundations for the future. It is in the small, seemingly insignificant moments that healing and transformation take place, so let's continue to celebrate what's great about South Africa and consciously create moments of magic in our interactions with each other.

Don't forget to be AWESOME!

Robin Banks,
International Speaker

CONTENTS

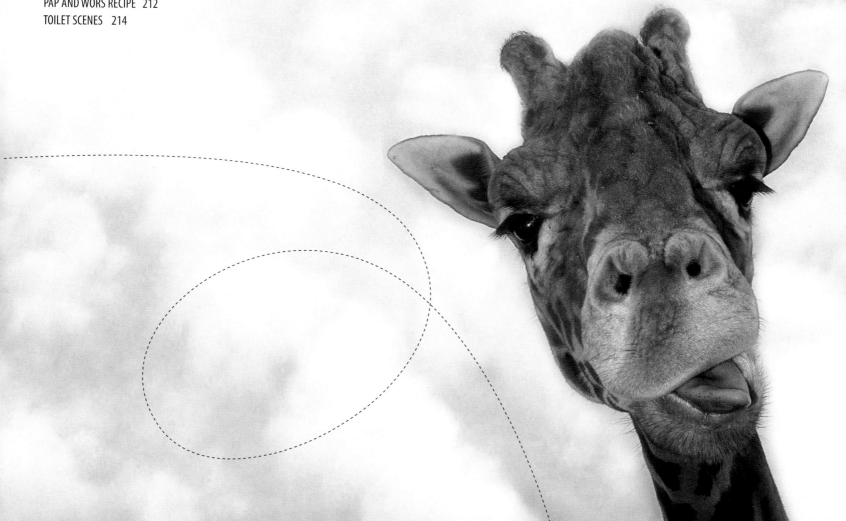

ROAD TO DEMOCRACY

THE FIRST WHITE MAN STAKES HIS CLAIM IN 1488 AT MOSSEL BAY

1808 150 YEARS OF SLAVERY IN THE CAPE COMES TO AN END

EQUALI

1950 RESISTANCE GAINS MOMENTUM WITH THE FIRST NATIONAL DAY OF PROTEST

1948 NATIONAL PARTY COMES INTO POWER AND IMPLEMENTS APARTHEID

FREEDOM CHARTER

FREEDOM CHARTER ADOPTED BY THE **CONGRESS OF THE PEOPLE**

1955 WOMEN SHOW THEIR STRENGTH AS 20 000 MARCH TO THE UNION BUILDINGS

VOTES FOR WOMAN

SOUTH AFRICA STANDS PROUD AS THE RAINBOW NATION

SOUTH AFRICAN FLAG FLIES FOR A UNITED SOUTH AFRICA **1994**

NEARLY 70% OF WHITES VOTE IN FAVOUR OF ENDING WHITE MINORITY RULE **1992**

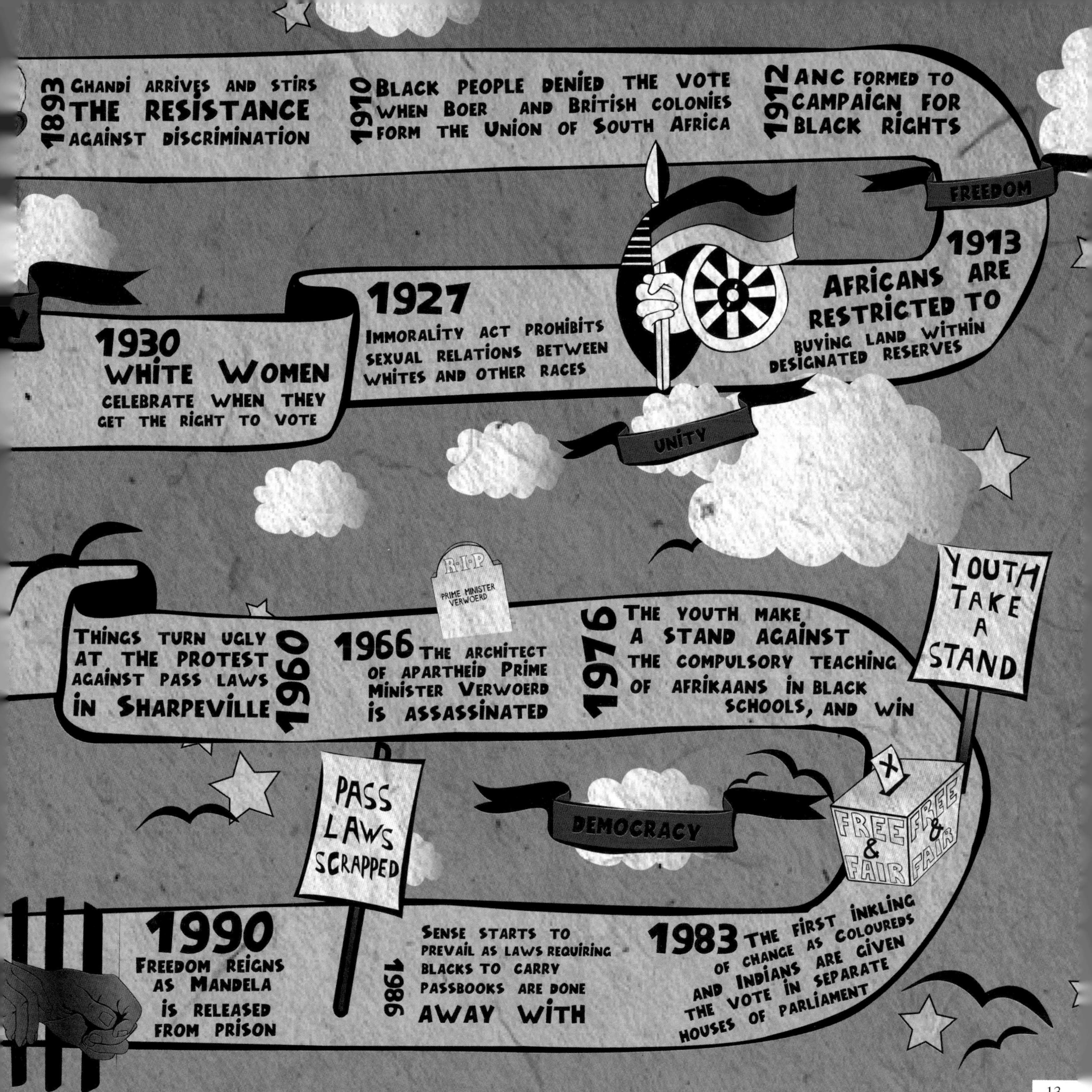

1893 GHANDI ARRIVES AND STIRS **THE RESISTANCE** AGAINST DISCRIMINATION

1910 BLACK PEOPLE DENIED THE VOTE WHEN BOER AND BRITISH COLONIES FORM THE UNION OF SOUTH AFRICA

1912 ANC FORMED TO CAMPAIGN FOR BLACK RIGHTS

FREEDOM

1913 AFRICANS ARE RESTRICTED TO BUYING LAND WITHIN DESIGNATED RESERVES

1927 IMMORALITY ACT PROHIBITS SEXUAL RELATIONS BETWEEN WHITES AND OTHER RACES

1930 WHITE WOMEN CELEBRATE WHEN THEY GET THE RIGHT TO VOTE

UNITY

R.I.P
PRIME MINISTER VERWOERD

1960 THINGS TURN UGLY AT THE PROTEST AGAINST PASS LAWS IN SHARPEVILLE

1966 THE ARCHITECT OF APARTHEID PRIME MINISTER VERWOERD IS ASSASSINATED

1976 THE YOUTH MAKE A STAND AGAINST THE COMPULSORY TEACHING OF AFRIKAANS IN BLACK SCHOOLS, AND WIN

YOUTH TAKE A STAND

PASS LAWS SCRAPPED

DEMOCRACY

FREE & FAIR

FREE & FAIR

1990 FREEDOM REIGNS AS MANDELA IS RELEASED FROM PRISON

1986 SENSE STARTS TO PREVAIL AS LAWS REQUIRING BLACKS TO CARRY PASSBOOKS ARE DONE AWAY WITH

1983 THE FIRST INKLING OF CHANGE AS COLOUREDS AND INDIANS ARE GIVEN THE VOTE IN SEPARATE HOUSES OF PARLIAMENT

seTswana

3.5 million speakers
The Batswana people
are predominantly
from the northwestern
regions of South Africa.
Their ancient stone
settlements date
back to 1600 AD. The
culture is based on
'village democracy,'
holding open meetings
to debate local affairs.

Hello – Dumela
How are you – O kae?
Thank you – ke a leboga
Yes – ee

isiZulu

9.2 million speakers
Zulu origins can be
traced back to 1550 in
KwaZulu-Natal. IsiZulu
is understood by 50%
of South Africans.
The Zulu are ruled by
a monarch and have
strong traditional
beliefs. Singing and
dancing play a major
role in their lives.

Hello – Sawubona
How are you – Unjani?
Thank you – ngiyabonga
Yes – yebo

11 Official languages
11 Amazing cultures

South Africa boasts a rich cultural
and ethnic diversity. The country's
Constitution guarantees equal
status to 11 official languages.

Mother tongue
isiZulu 23,8%
isiXhosa 17,6%
Afrikaans 13,3%
Sesotho sa Leboa 9,4%
English 8,2%
Setswana 8,2%
Others 18.9%

isiNdebele

600 000 speakers
The Ndebele people live
mainly in Mpumalanga
and Limpopo but can
be found throughout
Gauteng. They are best
known for their colourful
homes with geometric
patterns, traditional dress,
ornamentation
and craftsmanship.

Hello – Lotjhani
How are you – Unjani?
Thank you – ngiyathokoza
Yes – Iye

isiXhosa

7.7 million speakers
The Xhosa originated
from the Eastern Cape
region over 300 years
ago. The Xhosa use clay
on their faces for many
purposes. The language
is characterised by
various tongue clicking
sounds, denoted by 'c'
'x' 'q'.

Hello – Bhota
How are you – Unjani?
Thank you – ndiyabulela
Yes – ewe

Stained glass artwork supplied by www.glassescapes.com

Seseotho sa Leboa

3.7 million speakers
Sepedi, the language of the Pedi people of Mpumalanga and Limpopo, is also referred to as Northern Sotho. The Pedi people are known for their rich and varied history of crafting, their unique music and the migrant style kiba dance.

Hello – Dumela
How are you – O kae?
Thank you – ke a leboga
Yes – ee

Sesotho

3.2 million speakers
Sesotho is the language of the people of the Maluti mountains of the Kingdom of Lesotho. They are identified by their straw hats and coloured blankets that are used in ceremonies to denote marital status and identity.

Hello – Dumela
How are you – O kae?
Thank you – ke a leboha
Yes – ee

Afrikaans

6 million speakers
Only 90 years old, it is officially the youngest language in the world. It is the second–most spoken language in South Africa. The name Afrikaans is derived from the Dutch word for 'Africa'. The language evolved from Dutch, French, Malay, Khoikhoi and other influences. Afrikaans is spoken by 60% of white people and 90% of coloured people.

Hello – Hallo
How are you – hoe gaan dit met jou?
Yes – ja
Thank you– baie dankie *
(*famed for its pronunciation as 'Buy a Donkey')

Tshivenda

880 000 speakers
The language of the people of Limpopo, who lived in the area of the Mapungubwe Kingdom from before 1300 AD. Their tribal council meetings (or khoro) play an important role in maintaining their tradition, morals, and respect for each other.
Hello – Ndaa/Aa
How are you – Vho vuwa hani?
Thank you – Ndi a livhuwa
Yes – Ee

English

English is the most commonly spoken language in official and commercial public life - but only the fifth–most spoken home language, representing a mere 8,2% of the population. South African creativity has developed its own version of English, combining the influences of the many other languages spoken in the country. The traditional Oxford Dictionary incorporated many South African words that have become common usage, such as kraal (village of huts) and trek (travel by ox-wagon).

Xitsonga

1.8 million speakers
Xitsonga is spoken by the Batsonga people, also called the 'Shangaans', living in the Limpopo lowveld. Their music is a fusion of their traditional heritage with the drumming and ethnic dancing of the mines in which many of them work.

Hello – Avuxeni
How are you – Ku njhani?
Thank you – ndzi khense ngopfu
Yes – ina

Siswati

1 million speakers
Spoken by a third of the people in Mpumalanga, Siswati is the language of the Swazi people. Famed for their dancing and singing, the amaSwazi celebrate with praise singing.

Hello – Sawubona
How are you – Unjani?
Thank you – ngiyabonga
Yes – yebo

who said?...

Match the name with the quote.

1. I am afraid that this beginning is the most evil and sinister beginning that is possible for any policy of peace and cooperation between white and black in this country in the future... (1925).

2. The challenge of existence is to fall in love with life and come to terms with all its joys and sorrows.

3. We've come a long way, and changing a law is really important. What I've realised is laws change, but you also have to change how people think. And that takes time.

4. Greatness is determined by service and nobody knows that more than South African women.

5. He who covets all will lose all.

6. South Africa is an extraordinary country, poised for tremendous growth and prosperity.

7. Search in your past for what is good and beautiful. Build your future from there.

8. We must find new lands from which we can easily obtain raw materials and at the same time exploit the cheap slave labour that is available from the natives of the colonies.

9. People have turned freedom into licence and forget that freedom has its obverse responsibility and obligation (2006).

10. We refuse to accept that our Africanness shall be defined by our origins. It is a firm assertion made by ourselves that South Africa belongs to all who live in it, black or white.

A   Charlize Theron, Academy Award Winning Actress

B   Anton Rupert, South African Businessman

C   Jan Smuts, South African Prime Minister

D   Desmond Tutu, Archbishop Emeritus

E   Thabo Mbeki, South African President

F   Tokyo Sexwale, Businessman, Politician, former ANC activist

G   Oprah Winfrey, Talk Show Host, Philanthropist

H   Bill Gates, Microsoft Chairperson

I   Cecil John Rhodes, Financier and Statesman

J   Paul Kruger, President of the South African Republic

ANSWERS   1 - C | 2 - F | 3 - A | 4 - G | 5 - B | 6 - H | 7 - J | 8 - I | 9 - D | 10 - E

And I quote...

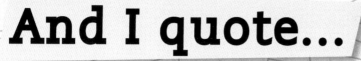

Who were they referring to when they said...

1   **Nelson Mandela** – While many of us have been honoured by countries in every continent with awards including the Nobel Peace Prize, there is one man who has not received some of these, but nonetheless he stands head and shoulders above us all because of his humility and simplicity.

2   **Pieter Dirk Uys** – Without her there would be no rainbow, just many black sashes.

3   **Jan Smuts** – He is the worker and you need him. He is carrying the country on his back.

4   **Mark Twain** – I admire him, I frankly confess it; and when his time comes I shall buy a piece of the rope for a keepsake.

5   **Hillary Clinton** – What you are doing here in South Africa is a testament to what can occur when rage and anger are turned to hope and possibility. The work of reconciliation is to acknowledge history, not to forget it.

6   **Simon van der Stel** – They were civil, polite and talkative...would not sell their children as slaves.

7   **Desmond Tutu** – He is God's gift to South Africa and he is our gift to the world.

8   **Christiaan Barnard** – Given the opportunity, he would have been a better surgeon than me.

9   **Time magazine** – He is the greatest active playwright in the English-speaking world.

10 **Tokyo Sexwale** – He shoots from the hip with his lips and rarely misses.

A   The Truth and Reconciliation Commission

B   All Black South Africans

C   Nelson Mandela

D   Athol Fugard, Playwright

E   Helen Suzman, Leader of the opposition party in the apartheid era

F   Walter Sisulu, Political Activist

G   Cecil John Rhodes, Prime Minister of the Cape Colony 1895

H   The Xhosa people of Southern Africa

I   Hamilton Naki, Gardener and Assistant

J   Archbishop Desmond Tutu

ANSWERS   1 - F   2 - E   3 - B   4 – G   5 – A   6 – H   7 - C   8 – I   9 - D   10 - J

Photograph of storm over Sandton taken by David Maskell

EXTREME WEATHER STATS

Hottest place	Letaba Limpopo Province	Average annual temperature	35,0 °C
Coldest place	Buffelsfontein Eastern Cape	Average annual minimum	2,8 °C
Wettest Place	Matiwa Limpopo Province	Annual rainfall	2004,4 mm
Driest Place	Alexander Bay Northern Cape	Annual rainfall	46 mm
Windiest place	Cape Point Western Cape	Average wind speed	14,1 m/s
Highest 24-hour rainfall	St Lucia KwaZulu-Natal	597 mm Cyclone Domoina, 1984	
Highest temperature	Dunbrody Eastern Cape	50,0 °C in 1918	
Lowest temperature	Buffelsfontein Eastern Cape	-18,6 °C in 1996	

South Africa enjoys one of the world's highest average daily hours of sunshine – 8.5 hours compared with 3.8 in London, 6.9 in New York and 6.4 in Rome.

Johannesburg gets more rain than London, but it rains on fewer than 80 days a year.

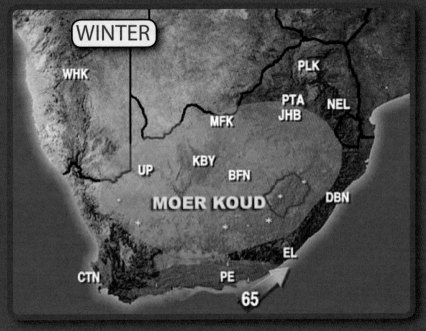

WINTER

WHK   PLK   PTA   JHB   NEL   MFK   UP   KBY   BFN   DBN   EL   CTN   PE

MOER KOUD

65

SUMMER

WHK   PLK   PTA   NEL   MFK   JHB   UP   KBY   BFN   PMB   DBN   EL   CTN   PE

VREK WARM

DAILY TRAFFIC

R4.50
incl VAT
Annual
Subscribers
R3.66

48 PEOPLE PACKED TO THE MAX!

Astonished Port Elizabeth Beeld newspaper photographer, Deon Ferreira, photographed 48 pupils clambering out of a taxi with their rucksacks and school books in May 2009.

SIX LIVE GOATS IN A MAZDA 323

Johannesburg police were busy keeping the traffic flow moving around the Confederation Cup Football Tournament Stadium in 2009. They spotted two men in a blue Mazda 323 driving 'under suspicious circumstances' along Reitz Street. After stopping the men they found, to their surprise, six live goats in the car.

23 PEOPLE - AND ONE GOAT - SPILL OUT OF OVERLOADED TAXI

Photograph taken in Durban by Nash Narrandes as it appeared in The Natal Witness

BAKKIE OVERLOAD

(Right) Traffic policemen tangle with a driver in Krugersdorp, (photographed by Johan Vermeulen and published on News24.com in 2009).

NEWS

One taxi, one driver - and 112 passengers

A NEW SOUTH AFRICAN RECORD

for overloaded minibus taxis was set by a driver from Khayelitsha in Cape Town in June 2009. The driver managed to squeeze 112 passengers into one minibus taxi. Traffic officers, Jaco Strydom and Vernon Johnson, were speechless when they stopped the taxi and counted 105 children and eight adults crammed into a taxi registered to carry only 26 people.

Photograph courtesy: The Independent

DOUBLE TROUBLE

Photo Courtesy: a.j.stuijt@knid.nl

(Left) Taken in Durban - TRAVELLING LIGHT!
This bakkie, photographed by Paul Cowie in Durban, was travelling from Richards Bay to Malawi. It took him two days just to get to Johannesburg, where he was taken off the road!

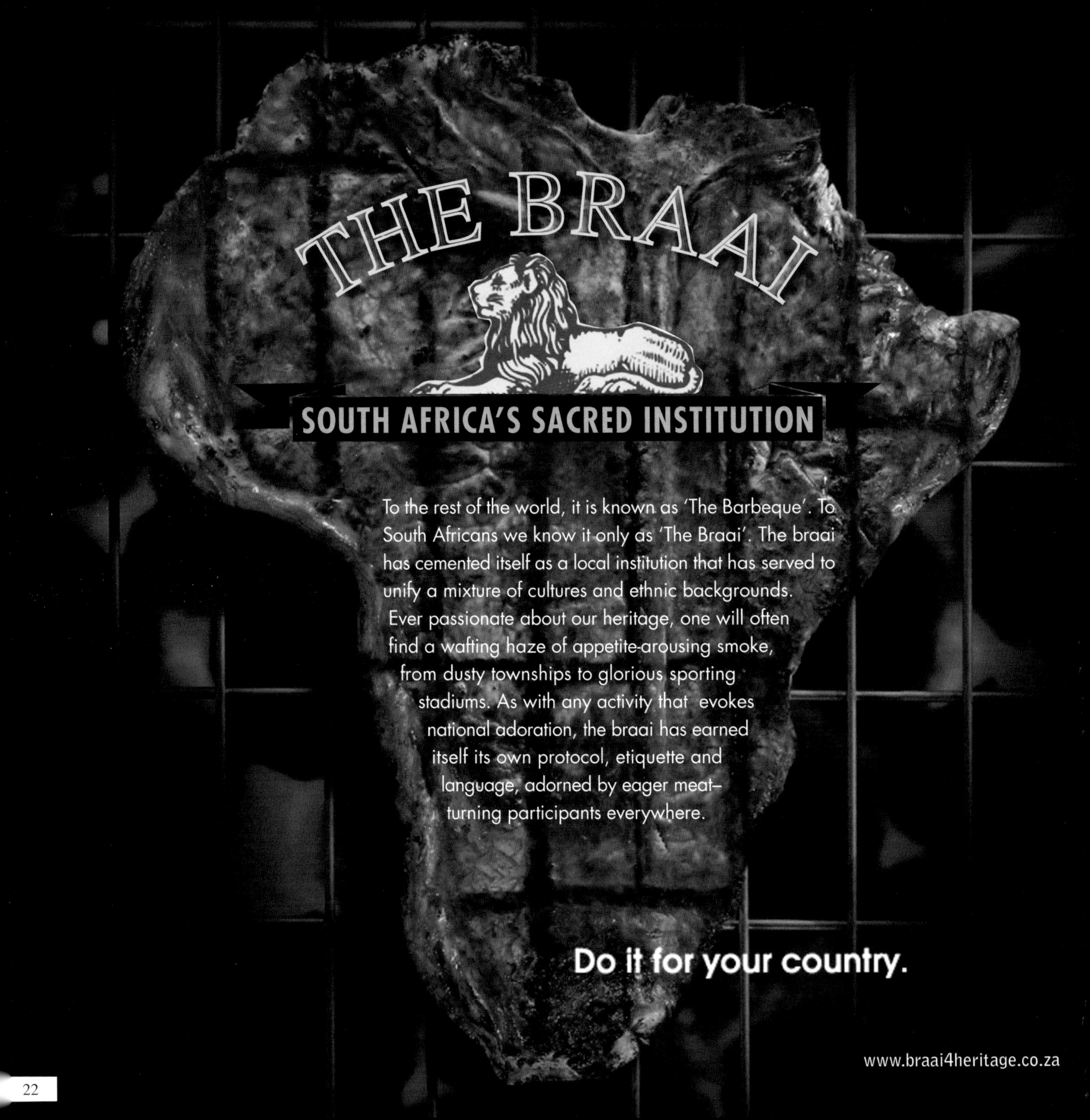

THE BRAAI
SOUTH AFRICA'S SACRED INSTITUTION
To the rest of the world, it is known as 'The Barbeque'. To South Africans we know it only as 'The Braai'. The braai has cemented itself as a local institution that has served to unify a mixture of cultures and ethnic backgrounds. Ever passionate about our heritage, one will often find a wafting haze of appetite-arousing smoke, from dusty townships to glorious sporting stadiums. As with any activity that evokes national adoration, the braai has earned itself its own protocol, etiquette and language, adorned by eager meat–turning participants everywhere.
Do it for your country.
www.braai4heritage.co.za

> Eat more meat. Enjoy each other's company; amid laughter, peace and harmony, with the aroma of braai in the air. Ahh, nothing could be more comforting. **We have 11 official languages but there is only one word for this wonderful institution; it is braai.**
>
> Desmond Tutu

Never use the word 'Barbeque'. People have suffered cruel and intolerable tortures for far less, and a blunder of this proportion will surely earn you a seat in your host's dog kennel. Male hosts need to prepare the fire, which most will agree, is an art form in itself. The braai master has often been known to click his braai tongs together repeatedly between gulps of beer, in a display of Alpha dominance, as he admires the farm style 'wors' browning above the glowing embers of his carefully arranged charcoal. His peers gaze on, beer in hand, all offering sporadic grunts of approval.

At this juncture it is important to point out that whilst it may be frowned upon for any male to ever pour a beer anywhere else but into his oesophagus, there is an exception. It is an unwritten rule that the tong holder may use a small splash of his beer (anything more is just a waste), in an ultimate act of sacrifice, to douse overzealous flames that may be charring the steak, lamb chops or secret recipe chicken.

Legend has it that some wives have told their husbands that they are in fact burning the meat, or that the fire is not of adequate temperature. However, there is little evidence of this as few have lived to tell the tale.

Braai Dictionary

Abbraaiviation	-	A very short braai
Bokdopentjop	-	Bokdopentjop (Bok-dop-en-tjop) - appropriate for a 'bring and braai' - you may bring your bok (babe), your dop (drinks) and tjop (meat of choice)... :-)
Braai Passenger	-	Person/s that arrive for a bring & braai without meat. The 'bring' part of the invitation refers to meat and not to yourself!
Braaiathon	-	A very long braai
Braailiant	-	A well-cooked piece of meat that has been done on the braai. Wow, this steak is lekker boet, it's braaillient!
Braaistard	-	The guy at the braai who steals your drink.

The first recorded mention of a purely social braai was a wartime fund-raising event in 1942

Photo Source: Unknown email distribution

A day off for the ladies...

Braai-ing is the only type of cooking a 'real' man will do. When a man volunteers to do such cooking, the following chain of events is put into motion:

1. The woman goes to the store.
2. The woman fixes the salad, vegetables and dessert.
3. The woman places the meat for cooking on a tray.
4. The woman puts out the necessary cooking utensils.
5. The woman takes the meat to the man, who is lounging beside the grill, drinking a beer.
6. The man places the meat on the grill.
7. The woman goes inside to set the table and check the vegetables.
8. The man takes the meat off the grill and hands it to the woman.
9. After eating, the woman clears the table and does the dishes.
10. The man asks the woman how she enjoyed 'her night off.'

And, upon seeing her annoyed reaction, concludes that there's just no pleasing some women. HAPPY BRAAI-ING!!

Outer Space

A photograph of Comet McNaught taken by Clive Baker, as it appeared over Chapman's Peak in Cape Town in 2007. The comet could be seen clearly with the naked eye by observers in the Southern Hemisphere.

'There is no sign in space saying north should be on top.'

SOUTH AFRICA'S VERY OWN
AFRONAUT

Mark Shuttleworth was the first man to fly the South African flag in space. Mark conducted several science experiments during his ten days in space. After his journey into space he launched the Hip2B² project to inspire a love of maths and science in children.

South African born Mike Melvill made history in 2004 when he became the first civilian to fly a spaceship out of the atmosphere. He also flew the first privately financed manned aircraft (a rocket spaceship) to reach space.

The Southern African Large Telescope (SALT), in Sutherland is the largest telescope in the southern hemisphere (and third largest in the world). It is strong enough to see an image as faint as a candle flame on the moon.

Pretoria resident, Jack Bennett, not only has two comets named after him but he is also the world's only modern skywatcher to make a visual discovery of a supernova.

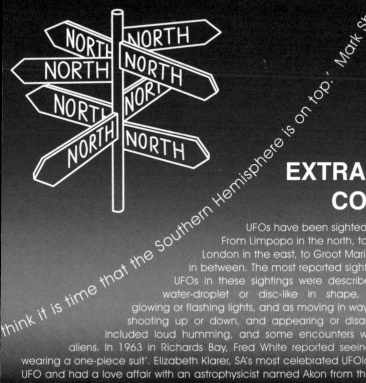

SO THEY CALL THEMSELVES THE RAINBOW NATION!

think it is time that the Southern Hemisphere is on top.' Mark Shuttleworth

EXTRA-TERRESTRIAL COMPANIONS

UFOs have been sighted in South Africa for decades. From Limpopo in the north, to Cape Town in the south, East London in the east, to Groot Marico in the west and everywhere in between. The most reported sightings are in the Klein Karoo. The UFOs in these sightings were described variously as: circular, triangular, water-droplet or disc-like in shape, with: orange, blue, red, white, glowing or flashing lights, and as moving in ways that included: hovering, shooting up or down, and appearing or disappearing with speed. Flight noises included loud humming, and some encounters were accompanied by viewings of aliens. In 1963 in Richards Bay, Fred White reported seeing 'a man with a fair complexion... wearing a one-piece suit'. Elizabeth Klarer, SA's most celebrated UFOlogist, claimed to have travelled in a UFO and had a love affair with an astrophysicist named Akon from the planet Meton. Dr James Hurtak, a futurist and social scientist with two PhDs and extensive experience in UFO research, believes that we could learn from extra-terrestrials who have evolved beyond us. How better to help earth with its environmental and energy problems.

EXPLOSIONS GREATER THAN A NUCLEAR BOMB

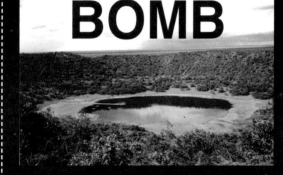

The force which created The Tswaing Crater was over a hundred times more powerful than the nuclear bomb dropped on Hiroshima that vaporised everything in its surrounds. It was caused by a giant asteroid weighing 300 000 kg, moving at 4 000 km/h, which crashed into the earth about 200 000 years ago. The resultant Tswaing Crater, just north of Pretoria, is now a nature reserve rich in local fauna. The Tswaing Crater is a baby compared to the Vredefort Dome, the largest and the oldest known meteor crater on earth, which can be found in the Free State near Parys. The Vredefort Dome is one of South Africa's World Heritage Sites.

REACHING FOR THE STARS

For a school science project, Siyabulela Xuza from Umtata in the Eastern Cape, created an energy-intensive fuel that was safer and more effective than the fuel NASA uses. He then went on to build a rocket that broke the South African Amateur Altitude Record and won top awards at the world's biggest student Science and Engineering Fair. The NASA-affiliated Lincoln Laboratory was so impressed by his achievement that they named a minor planet after him. You will find planet Siyaxuza near Jupiter in the night sky.

49 320 000 TOTAL SOUTH AFRICAN POPULATION

6 165 000 SOUTH AFRICANS OVER 15 YRS OLD WHO CANNOT READ OR WRITE

421 000 BLACK PEOPLE WHO ENTERED THE MIDDLE INCOME LAYER IN 2008

50 000 PEOPLE MOVE FROM THE TOWNSHIPS TO SUBURBS EVERY MONTH

528 HOUSES BUILT EVERY DAY BY THE GOVERNMENT SINCE 1994

53 YEARS IS THE LIFE EXPECTANCY OF MALES (57 FOR FEMALES)

DURBAN IS THE LARGEST PORT IN AFRICA AND ONE OF THE TOP TEN LARGEST IN THE WORLD

STATISTICS

WHILE OCCUPYING 4% OF AFRICA'S LANDMASS, SOUTH AFRICA BOASTS MORE THAN 50% OF THE CARS, PHONES, AUTOMATIC BANK TELLERS AND INDUSTRIAL FACILITIES ON THE CONTINENT

	WEEKLY WORKING HOURS	ANNUAL VACATION DAYS (PAID)
RIO DE JANERO	40	30
PARIS	35	27
JOHANNESBURG	40	21
TORONTO	43	15
HONG KONG	45	9
SEOUL	48	10

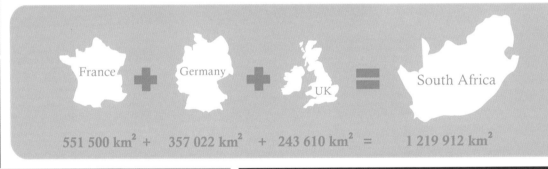

France + Germany + UK = South Africa

551 500 km² + 357 022 km² + 243 610 km² = 1 219 912 km²

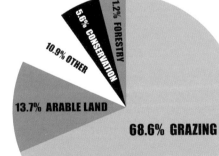

LAND UTILISATION

- 1.2% FORESTRY
- 5.6% CONSERVATION
- 10.9% OTHER
- 13.7% ARABLE LAND
- 68.6% GRAZING

South Africa is the first country outside of Europe to gain Blue Flag status for its coastal management

South Africa accounts for almost 45% of the GDP of the entire African continent, with an economy three times the size of the 2nd biggest (Egypt)

40% of South Africans have a **10%** share of the household income

20% of South Africans have a **62%** share of the household income

800 LANDINGS
every day at South African airports

♦♦♦♦♦♦ **18 000 000** ♦♦♦♦♦
passengers annually

MINERAL RESOURCES	WORLD RANKING	% of WORLD RESERVES
PLATINUM	#1	88%
MANGANESE	#1	80%
CHROME	#1	72%
GOLD	#1	40%
VANADIUM	#1	32%
VERMICULITE	#2	40%
TITANIUM	#2	17%
ZIRCONIUM	#2	19%

Pretoria has the second largest number of embassies in the world after Washington DC

56% of South Africans are churchgoers compared to the world average of 26%

RELIGIONS
80%	Christian
1%	Hindu
1%	Muslim
0.2%	Jewish

Bar chart:
- 58% — Households supplied with electric lighting - 1996
- 80% — Households supplied with electric lighting - 2007
- 62% — Houses within 200 m of a communal tap - 1996
- 85% — Houses within 200 m of a communal tap - 2007
- 52% — Houses with sanitation (flush toilet/soakpit) - 1996
- 72% — Houses with sanitation (flush toilet/soakpit) - 2007

POPULATION

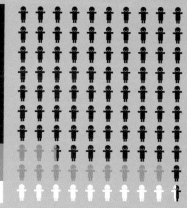

79% Black - 38.6m
2.5% Asian - 1.6m
9.0% Coloured - 4.4m
9.2% White - 4.5m

south africa generates **2/3** of africa's electricity

Percentage of people living below the bread line. **50%**

SPORTING TRIVIA

BEST ALL-ROUNDER
Grant Khomo captained the National Soccer XI, won the SA singles and doubles tennis titles, represented Transvaal in cricket and rugby and captained the SA Bantu Rugby Board first team.

Sport in South Africa contributes more than 2% to the country's GDP.

SOUTH AFRICA HAS HOSTED NUMEROUS INTERNATIONAL SPORTING EVENTS SINCE 1994, INCLUDING:
- Rugby World Cup '95
- African Cup of Nations '96
- IAAF World Cup in Athletics '98
- All Africa Games '99
- Cricket World Cup '03
- President's Cup (Golf) '03
- Women's World Cup of Golf '05 '06 '07 '08
- Confederation Cup (Soccer) '09
- IPL Cricket '09

FORMULA 1 CHAMPION
Jody Schecter won the Formula 1 World Driver's Championship in a Ferrari in 1979. The Italian team had to wait another 21 years for their next driver's title, won by Michael Schumacher.

WATCH HIM FALL BREAKS RECORDS
Matthews Motshwarateu had such an awkward running style that his Sotho nickname was 'Motshwareng o tlawa' (or Loop en Val in Afrikaans) meaning 'Watch him, he will fall'. He became the first black South African to break a world record in 1980 for the 10 km road race.

YOUNGEST OF THEM ALL
Karen Muir, who set 17 world records over a period of 5 years, appears in the Swimming Hall of Fame. She was only 12 years and 10 months, making her the youngest world record-breaker in any sport in the history of organised sport.

WORLD FIRST RECORD BREAKER
Penny Heyns is the only woman in the history of the Olympics to have won a gold medal for both the 100 m and 200 m breaststroke. She set 14 world records and became the first swimmer in history to break five world records in five months.

WINNING IN SILENCE
Terence Parkin has accumulated an astounding total of 29 medals in the Deaflympics during his swimming career.

GOLF
BIG EASY MAKES IT EASY
Ernie Els was the first foreign golfer in 90 years to win the US Open twice, a feat which was repeated two years later by Retief Goosen.

GOLFING ICON
During his career, Gary Player has won 164 tournaments all over the world, jetting an estimated total of 13 million km, more than any other athlete in history.

FROM CADDIE TO HERO
Sewsunker "Papwa" Sewgolum was a caddie at Beachwood Country Club in Durban. He played the game with his hands positioned the opposite way to the traditional grip. He played the British Open, won 3 Dutch Open titles and beat Gary Player in the 1965 Natal Open, the same year as Gary Player's Grand Slam miracle.

GREATEST PRIZE MONEY EVER
When the prize money of $1 million for the golf tournament at Sun City was announced in 1981, it was the largest sum ever offered in the world. In 2000, the Nedbank Golf Challenge became the first golf tournament ever to offer US$2 million to the winner.

TENNIS

A WINNING PARTNERSHIP

Bob Hewitt and Frew McMillan won 57 career doubles titles, including three Wimbledon crowns. After teaming up, they played 45 matches before they suffered their first loss.

GRAND SLAM ENDURANCE

Wayne Ferreira boasted a 6-7 career head-to-head record against Pete Sampras and ended his career having played in a record 56 Grand Slam tournaments in succession.

WORLD TENNIS AWARDS

Amanda Coetzer was ranked #3 in the world and spent 10 years in the top 20. She received 3 awards from the WTA tour – the most ever by a single player in one year.

REFEREES AND UMPIRES

Umpire Rudi Koertzen became the first man to umpire 200 one-day internationals and only the second man to stand in 100 tests.

WORLD ATHLETE OF THE YEAR

Hestrie Cloete was named World Female Athlete of the Year in 2003, after winning 22 of the 26 high jump competitions.

FIRST EUROPEAN WINNER

When Vincent Tshabalala won the French Open in 1976, he was the first black golfer to win a major tournament on the European circuit.

YOUNGEST AMATEUR

Ashleigh Simon was not only the youngest golfer to have won the SA open at the age of 14, but also the youngest golfer to have represented SA in a major competition.

A LIFETIME OF RECORDS

Comrades runner Wally Hayward held the record for the up and down runs, the youngest (21 years) and oldest (aged 80) winner and was the first octogenarian.

STAN CHRISTODOULOU

was inducted into the International Boxing Hall of Fame after he became the first person to referee world title fights in all 17 weight categories.

SHOWING THE WORLD

Wheelchair racer Ernst van Dyk won the Boston Marathon for the eighth time in nine years and shares the record for most wins with Irish woman Jean Driscoll.

JONATHAN KAPLAN

set a world first by becoming the first referee in the history of rugby to take charge of 50 tests.

SPORTS OF MOST INTEREST TO SOUTH AFRICAN ADULTS	
Soccer	78%
Rugby	47%
Cricket	39%
Wrestling	25%
Athletics	22%
Tennis	22%
Boxing	18%
Motorsport	12%
Golf	12%
Netball	11%
Source SABC Markinor 2004	

ON TOP OF THE WORLD

More than 50% of the paragliding world records have been set in South Africa.

IN LIFE AND DEATH

OUR COUNTRY HAS BEEN MOTHERLAND AND HOME TO MANY INFLUENTIAL PEOPLE THROUGHOUT THE YEARS; SOUTH AFRICANS WHO HAVE PLAYED A SIGNIFICANT ROLE IN GETTING OUR NATION WHERE IT IS TODAY. AS A QUIRK OF FATE, SOME OF THEM DIED EITHER AS THEY HAD LIVED OR HAD A POIGNANT IRONY LINKED TO THEIR DEATHS.

STEVE BIKO

Noted anti-apartheid activist, Biko founded the Black Consciousness Movement that would empower the urban black population of South Africa. He is also known to have popularised the phrase: 'Black is beautiful'. Banned during the height of Apartheid, Biko was educated at the University of Natal and spoke fluent English, Xhosa and semi-fluent Afrikaans. For his role in various anti-apartheid protests, including the June 16 Soweto Uprising, he was targeted and eventually arrested at a police roadblock. His head injuries showed strong evidence that he had been severely beaten in police custody, and he died shortly on arrival at the Pretoria prison. His death was met by shock and anger locally, as well as abroad, and his funeral attended by over 10 000, including numerous international ambassadors and diplomats. Today, Biko is a revered anti-apartheid hero and has been honoured at many universities in South Africa and abroad.

GENERAL KOOS DE LA REY

He was a renowned general from the Boer War. In 1914, 'Afrikaans Nostradamus' Siener van Rensburg predicted that De La Rey would die on the fifteenth day of one of the months to come. His prophecy was not taken seriously, and Siener was dubbed a false prophet. However, on 15 September 1914, De la Rey's driver drove through a road block, on the general's instruction, and was fatally shot when the police officer mistook him for a member of the notorious Foster crime gang.

HECTOR PIETERSON

Every year on June 16, South Africans around the country commemorate Youth Day as a tribute to the events of the tragic, yet eventful day in 1976 that changed our country's history. Over 500 students were killed during the Soweto Uprising which was in protest to the imposition of Afrikaans as a medium of instruction in township schools. As the police clashed with protesters, 12-year-old Hector Pieterson was one of the first casualties, and the infamous photograph of a fellow student carrying his lifeless body, with the boy's sister running next to him, haunts many of us to this day. What started as a normal school day for Hector Pieterson ended in tragedy but changed the course of history. The photograph circulated locally and internationally to a response of shock and anger. The results of the uprising saw pressure added on the apartheid government; with thousands more joining the resistance movement, Afrikaans, as a medium of instruction, was dropped in township schools and education generally was uplifted in Soweto.

MIRIAM MAKEBA

Also known as 'Mama Afrika', she was one of the greatest South African songstresses and performers of our time. Stirring songs of the hope for freedom among the oppressed, her music was banned by apartheid authorities. However, after democracy the government fittingly appointed her Goodwill Ambassador of our country. It was after performing at an anti-racism and anti-organised crime concert in Caserta, Italy that Mama Afrika collapsed and passed away, only minutes after she finished singing her final and favourite song.

'I will sing until the last day of my life' – Miriam Makeba

DAVID RATTRAY

Also known as the 'White Zulu', this famous South African historian and storyteller captivated audiences ranging from the Prince of Wales to KwaZulu-Natal locals with his account of the Anglo-Zulu war of 1879.

Fluent in Zulu, Rattray spent most of his life preserving the Zulu culture. He also played a significant role in post-democratic reconciliation, as well as the promotion of tourism and economic development in his beloved country. Late one Friday night, in 2007, Rattray was shot by six intruders at his lodge in Kwa-Zulu Natal. The criminals were subsequently apprehended.

DR HENDRIK FRENSCH VERWOERD

Although not technically the architect of apartheid, HF Verwoerd did take apartheid to new levels. He fervently promoted and justified a policy of racial segregation with religious and intellectual motives. At a press gathering during a state of emergency in April 1960, Verwoerd declared: 'We shall not be killed. We shall fight for our existence, and we shall survive.' Survive he did, at least a first assassination attempt. At this briefing, one David Pratt walked up to the prime minister and shot him at close range. Verwoerd survived and went on to lead for six more years. Despite this unsuccessful attempt, Pratt became a hero and was quoted as saying: 'If you know you must do something and you don't do it, you are not free.' Shooting the epitome of apartheid had apparently set him free. In 1966, Dimitri Tsafendas had similar feelings about the apartheid ruler and stabbed him to death in his seat in parliament.

LUCKY DUBE

In his lifetime, reggae singer Lucky Dube's mission was to make the world a better place by reaching people through his music, which tackled a range of social problems. Despite his Rasta image, Dube neither smoked nor drank alcohol and was known to be shy, gentle and friendly. Having won over 20 awards both locally and abroad, he is the only South African artist to have a record signed to Motown Records, in addition to being the first black artist to be played on a white radio station. Ironically, in spite of his concerns about crime in his lyrics, he was tragically shot dead in the attempted hijacking of his car.

'Do you ever worry about leaving home and coming back in a coffin, with a bullet through your head?'- Lucky Dube. Lyrics from his song 'Crime and Corruption'

NKOSI JOHNSON

Born HIV positive, Nkosi became the youngest hero of our time, making a powerful impact on the world through speaking passionately about the plight of HIV/AIDS sufferers. Nkosi Johnson was given the honour of being keynote speaker at the 13th International AIDS Conference and also received the International Children's Peace Prize. He became the longest-surviving child born with the virus after he succumbed to his illness at the age of 12. Nkosi left a legacy as he and Gail Johnson, his foster mother, formed Nkosi's Haven, a refuge for mothers and children suffering from HIV/AIDS, which still operates today.

'An icon of the struggle for life'- Nelson Mandela, in reference to Nkosi Johnson.

PAUL KRUGER

Also known as 'Oom Paul', he was the face of the Boer resistance against the British during the Second Boer War. Kruger loved his country and instead of rejoicing at the discovery of gold, stated that people should be weeping because it will 'cause our land to be soaked in blood'. Because of his contribution to South African politics and his fight against the British, The Kruger National Park was named after him, as well as the Kruger Rand coin. When the British closed in on Pretoria towards the end of the Boer war, Kruger fled abroad, settling in Switzerland, where he enjoyed the reputation of a Freedom Fighter. He never returned to the country he fought for, and died in exile in 1904.

Animal

LESSONS FROM

Ku dlokodla mfutsu

To poke at a tortoise.
A Tsonga proverb that is used in situations when you want to put someone on the alert.

Impungushe kayivalelwa nezimvu

The jackal is not kept in the same kraal with the sheep.
A Zulu proverb which cautions that it is unwise to put together those things or people that should be kept apart.

Intaka yakha ngoboya bezinye

A bird builds with the feathers of others.
A Xhosa proverb which explains that we are all reliant on each other and must work together to achieve our goals.

Ingwe ikhotha amabala ayo amhlophe namnyama

A leopard licks both its white and black spots.
A Zulu proverb that describes how justice should be administered fairly to all by those in authority.

Ngwana a ka feta gare ga molete wa tau

A child can go through the hole of a lion.
A Northern Sotho proverb which advises that adults should be open to what children say.

Unebhungan' ekhanda

He has a beetle in his head.
A Zulu proverb that is used to describe someone who does strange things or has abnormal behaviour.

proverbs

THE WILD

These words of wisdom were used by our forefathers to give advice and warnings about everyday life.

Iqaqa aliziva Kunuka

The polecat is not aware of its smell
A Xhosa proverb that reminds us that a person is often blind to his or her own weaknesses.

Nala kungekho qhude liyasa

Even when the rooster is not present, day dawns.
A Zulu proverb that is used when a person thinks he is indispensable.

Akunyoka yakhohlwa ngumgodi wayo.

There is not a snake that forgets its hole.
A Zulu proverb which reminds us that there is no place like home and that a person will return there when life becomes hard.

Ku ba ndlopfu hi xibakele

To hit an elephant with a fist.
A Tsonga proverb that describes a situation when a person makes only a very slight impression.

Go diega ga tshwene ke go gadima morago

A monkey will be caught if it keeps looking back.
A Northern Sotho proverb reminding us to let go of the past and move on with our lives.

Ku va ni mahiri ya lampfana

To have the tricks of a chameleon.
A Tsonga proverb that is used to describe someone who is a liar.

HOW SOUTH AFRICA COMPARES TO THE REST OF THE WORLD

DEALING WITH URBANISATION & ENVIRONMENTAL CHALLENGES

Johannesburg ranks second among countries from Asia/Pacific, Middle East and Africa
Mastercard Insights Report

For the past five years, South Africa's tourism industry eclipsed gold as a foreign exchange earner in South Africa

The Rand is the second best performing of the 26 emerging market currencies

CORPORATE TAX RATES

UK	28%
USA	35%
JAPAN	30%
CHINA	25%
BRAZIL	34%
AUSTRALIA	30%
FRANCE	33%
RSA	28%

Cape Town, Johannesburg and Port Elizabeth are voted amongst the world's top 100 Most Liveable Cities

Mercer Human Resource Consulting

BIG MAC INDEX 2010 PRICE IN US$

SWITZERLAND	6.30
EURO AREA	4.84
AUSTRALIA	3.98
CANADA	3.97
BRITAIN	3.67
USA	3.58
JAPAN	3.50
SINGAPORE	3.19
RSA	2.46
CHINA	1.83

BRITISH MAGAZINE, THE ECONOMIST, RATED SOUTH AFRICA AS THE BEST PERFORMING HOUSING MARKET IN THE WORLD OVER THE LONGER-TERM

Consumer Confidence in SA has improved by 43% over the past 5 years

South Africa sold $1.8 billion worth of cars to the US in 2008, ahead of Sweden and Italy as suppliers to the US market

The **University of South Africa (UNISA)** is a pioneer of tertiary distance education and is the largest correspondence university in the world with 250 000 students

Johannesburg is the cheapest city in the world for expatriates – the most expensive are: 1st Tokyo, 2nd Osaka, 3rd Moscow, 4th Geneva, 5th Hong Kong

2
Transparency surrounding budgets – SA is ranked number 2 worldwide, second only to the UK

IMPORTS	FOREIGN TRADE PARTNERS	EXPORTS
GERMANY #1		#1 JAPAN
CHINA #2		#2 USA
USA #3		#3 GERMANY
SAUDI ARABIA #4		#4 UK
JAPAN #5		#5 CHINA

Worldwide Press Freedom Index 2007 ranked SA higher than Japan, Spain, Italy and the United States and higher than any country in Asia, the Middle East or South America

On the Global Gender Gap Index
South Africa is ranked **sixth worldwide in reducing gender disparities**
World Economic Forum

The **rand was stronger** than the US Dollar until March 1982

The strongest historic level was in 1973: **R1 bought US$1.50**

The weakest historic level was in 2001: **$1 bought R13.84**

The American Express Foreign Exchange Holiday Cost of Living Index rated SA as the **cheapest holiday destination** to have a beer, a Coke or a meal for two...even with the wine!

2010 PETROL PRICE US$

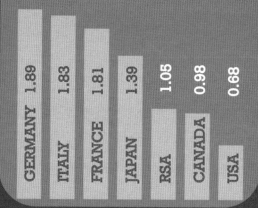

GERMANY	ITALY	FRANCE	JAPAN	RSA	CANADA	USA
1.89	1.83	1.81	1.39	1.05	0.98	0.68

SA is in the top 10% of countries in respect of Real GDP Growth projected for 2010

South Africa's reporting and auditing systems are the second best in the world, with only Hong Kong scoring higher
World Economic Forum

SOUTH AFRICAN MANAGERS EARN DISPOSABLE INCOMES HIGHER THAN DEVELOPED COUNTRIES SUCH AS THE UK, DENMARK, CANADA AND SWEDEN
Haygroup World Pay Report

THE ILLUSTRATIONS ON OUR MONEY
Ⓡ

A REVELATION OF OUR RICHES

The South African Rand is named after the Witwatersrand, the area around Johannesburg where gold was first discovered.

The illustration on the front of each of the five South African notes depicts one of the animals from the Big Five. Big game hunters in Africa coined the phrase 'the Big Five' when referring to the five most difficult animals to hunt on foot: the rhinoceros, the elephant, the lion, the buffalo and the leopard. Many still argue, however, that the hippopotamus and the great white shark should be included in this iconic list.

However, it is the reverse side of each of these notes that represents a multitude of information about South Africa itself.

FISCAL FACTS

According to the Bloomberg's Currency Scorecard, the South African Rand was the best performing currency against the US Dollar between 2002 and 2005.

The rand is the world's most actively traded emerging market currency and is one of only 17 currencies worldwide where forex transactions are settled immediately, lowering the risks of transacting across time zones.

THE LANGUAGE OF MONEY

The plural of rand is rand, not rands.

Like the United States dollar, the rand is colloquially called a buck. This comes from the Afrikaans name for the antelope - bok. The antelope was featured on the one rand coin.

SOUTH AFRICAN NAMES FOR MONEY

Ront

Bucks

Kites

A buffalo

Moolah

Dough

Tom

Marcha

Kroon

Pano

THE R10 NOTE: AGRICULTURE

South Africa is not only self-sufficient in virtually all major agricultural products, but is also a net food exporter. South African agricultural exports increased from 5% in 1988 to 38% in 2007. South Africa is among the world's top five exporters of avocados, grapefruit, tangerines, plums, pears, table grapes and ostrich products. Maize is the most widely grown - followed by wheat, oats, sugar cane and sunflowers.

THE R20 NOTE: MINING

South Africa is the world's leader in mining and minerals. It is ranked as the world's highest producer of alumino silicates, ferro-chromium, platinum, vanadium and vermiculite. South Africa held the position as the world's largest gold producer for over 100 years until 2007, when it was surpassed by China. It is the world's fourth-largest producer of diamonds. Mining contributes 21% of the country's total exports.

THE R50 NOTE: MANUFACTURE

The depiction of an oil refinery speaks of the country's manufacturing industry that has much to boast about. Sasol was the first – and largest – oil-from-coal refinery in the world, providing as much as 40% of the country's fuel and indirectly contributing 4.71% to the national GDP. Another industry which sees South Africa among the world's top ten exporters is that of primary steel, with the Columbus stainless steel factory as well as the Alusaf aluminium smelting factory in Richard's Bay ranking as the largest on the globe.

THE R100 NOTE: TOURISM

The zebra is the icon for the country's thriving tourism industry. Since 2004, South Africa's tourism industry eclipsed gold as a foreign exchange earner in South Africa. Tourism awards consistently place South Africa amongst the top ten tourist destinations in the world, as it outshines other countries in terms of climate, hotels and lodges and its variety of attractions.

THE R200 NOTE: TRANSPORT & COMMUNICATION

As the fourth-fastest growing mobile communications market in the world, the communications industry provides telephony to over 39 million subscribers – almost 80% of the population. South Africa is ranked fourth worldwide among Resource and Efficiency Driven economies in a recent telecommunications connectivity study, scoring ahead of all African countries, as well as Brazil, Russia, India and China. South Africa was the first country in the world to launch prepaid, Please Call Me SMS, free voicemail and invented touchtone dialling.

CENSI

Prior to the 90s South Africa's conservative and apartheid government used censorship to 'protect' society.

*T-Shirt with peace sign on

*Dancing on Sundays was banned in the Orange Free State by the Control of Dancing Ordinance

*Bumper sticker: 'And on the seventh day...God went surfing'

*A greeting card that read: 'Eat S**T'

'ZULU'
THE FILM

Released in 1964, the film Zulu is a story about the 1879 Battle of Rorke's Drift between the British and the Zulus. The film stars Michael Cain and Chief Mangosuthu Buthelezi as King Cetshwayo, being Cetshwayo's actual descendent in real life. The film was not entirely banned for South African viewers, but absurdly enough the government banned Zulus from watching the film, fearful of a Zulu uprising spurred on by events in the film.

GOOD 'OL STEVIE

While Stevie Wonder's 1985 hit song 'I just called to say I love you' won him an Academy Award, at the same time, his music was swiftly banned from all South African radio stations. The songs lyrics were not the problem but rather the fact that when he went up to receive his Oscar, he dedicated it to the then imprisoned Nelson Mandela. The South African Apartheid government would have none of it.

'NKOSI SIKELEL'
iAFRIKA

Composed as a hymn in 1897 by Enoch Sontonga, 'Nkosi Sikelel' has great linkage to the liberation struggle. After the African National Congress (ANC) was banned, it became a criminal offence to sing the song in public! How weird to think that more than 100 years on, adopted as part of the country's national anthem, the song is now synonymous with unity, peace and freedom for all South Africans.

38

Whatever they deemed objectionable or harmful was all banned at some point in time.

*Bumper sticker: 'Apartheid is doomed – Why fight for a dying cause'   *A beer mug with a naked man's figure and the inscription: 'Hers'

*'Is Marriage Necessary', a book written by Dr. Eustace Chesser

*Movies where Red Indians were not the baddies

*Olivia Newton-John's song 'Lets get ph ysical'

A book on playing chess titled: 'Black Queen, White King'

BLACK BEAUTY

The classic children's story book by Anna Sewell, about a notorious friendship between a young boy and a stallion, sold over 50 million copies worldwide, and even went on to become a hit movie. The story's title: 'Black Beauty' didn't appeal to the Censorship Board in the mid 1950s, and was banned from South Africa for a number of years.

SCOPE MAGAZINE

In a once overtly conservative society, the idea of pornography was not only branded as 'communist infiltration' but also heavily frowned upon in the eye of the public. So, in the 1970s and 1980s, when SCOPE - South Africa's first ever 'girlie' magazine - slowly began to evolve their swimsuit wearing centerfolds into busty topless sex symbols, it was no wonder the government upped their efforts to ban such material; including any written material they deemed too provocative or contentious.

FAST FORWARD TO FREEDOM

While the world's commentators focused on the political changes taking place in the freshly christened new South Africa, the nation loosened its collective chastity belt. Johannesburg hosted gay pride parades; Basic Instinct appeared on cinema screens; Nando's ran its famous Tailgunner ad, in which a sweet old couple invite their obviously gay neighbours for supper, 'So, my children tell me you're a tailgunner,' the old man says to his guests. 'I was a military man myself.'

And who would have thought that using a cucumber to demonstrate how to fit a condom would become an act of patriotism?

Text courtesy Sarah Britten

135 YEAR OLD Koko Moloko FROM LIMPOPO

The OLDEST HUMAN being ever to have lived

The birth certificate of Moloko Temo, affectionately called Koko, reflects her year of birth as 1874. Born before records were officially kept, stories from her early years were pieced together to determine her birth date. This is currently being verified by the Guinness Book of World Records and will confirm her as the oldest woman to have lived.

This lady was blind for 56 years. She had eight children, 29 grand children, 59 great grandchildren, even great-great grandchildren and was cared for by her 90-year-old daughter. Her secret, she said, was eating her favourite foods – moroho (spinach), meat, sweets and drinking Coca Cola. Her advice to others on how to live a long and happy life – 'Trust in God and respect your parents.'

She died in June 2009, aged 135, still lucid and delightful. One of her greatest days was celebrating her 134th birthday with a visit from Nelson Mandela to whom she sang a song with the words:

… "Happy, happy, happy. You promised to marry me and I waited Sunday, Monday and Tuesday."

THE LIFE OF

YEAR	AGE	
1876	2 yrs	Diamonds were first discovered at Kimberley
1879	5 yrs	The Anglo-Zulu War rages at Isandlwana and Ulundi
1881	7 yrs	Kimberley gets the first electricity power plant
1883	9 yrs	The last surviving Quagga dies
1884	10 yrs	Koko sees Imvo, the first 'black' newspaper
1886	12 yrs	Koko hears of the discovery of gold in Johannesburg
1889	15 yrs	The first permanent hospital in Hillbrow is built
1891	17 yrs	Horse-drawn trams are introduced on the Witwatersrand
1908	34 yrs	The first South Africans compete in the Olympics
1909	35 yrs	Johannesburg is covered with a blanket of snow. Brrr!
1910	36 yrs	The Union of South Africa is born
1912	38 yrs	Koko's party, the ANC, is formed
1914	40 yrs	Koko witnesses South Africa enter World War I
1918	44yrs	Over 139 000 people die in the influenza epidemic
1927	53 yrs	The first supermarket, OK Bazaars, is opened
1929	55 yrs	The first full-length film with sound is screened

LIVING THROUGH CHANGE

ALL IN KOKO's LIFETIME

PEOPLE OF KOKO'S TIME

Living through Anglo-Zulu Wars, Frontier Wars, two Anglo-Boer Wars, two World Wars and one long, infamous freedom struggle.

From horse-drawn transport *to* **space travel**

From candlelight *to* **electricity**

From fireside singing *to* **television**

From no hospitals *to* **heart transplants**

From influenza epidemics *to* **HIV**

From a divided colony *to* **a united democracy**

Moloko Temo	1874 – 2009	aged 135
Winston Churchill	1874 – 1965	aged 91
Paul Kruger	1825 – 1904	aged 79
Mahatma Gandhi	1869 – 1948	aged 79
Albert Einstein	1879 – 1955	aged 76
Adolf Hitler	1889 – 1945	aged 56
Queen Victoria	1819 – 1901	aged 82
Hendrik Verwoerd	1901 – 1966	aged 65
Cecil Rhodes	1853 – 1902	aged 49
Nelson Mandela	Born 1918	

KOKO MOLOKO

Year	Age	Event
1930	56 yrs	Trolley buses arrive in the country
1932	58 yrs	SA experiences the impact of the world depression
1933	59 yrs	Koko is left out when white women get the vote
1939	65 yrs	SA joins forces in World War II
1947	73 yrs	Koko sways to the sounds of Miriam Makeba's first solo
1951	77 yrs	The first VW beetle is produced in SA
1952	78 yrs	As a black woman, Koko must carry a pass book
1954	80 yrs	South Africans get their first taste of Simba chips
1957	83 yrs	SA's first computer is installed
1961	87 yrs	Rands and cents replace pounds, shillings and pence
1967	93 yrs	The world's first human heart transplant in Cape Town
1969	95 yrs	SA's worst earthquake causes deaths in the Cape
1970	96 yrs	The South African mint discontinues 1/2 cent coins
1974	100 yrs	SA's Nuclear Weapons programme is launched
1976	102 yrs	The first television programme is broadcast
1981	107 yrs	Johannesburg sees snow again – in September
1982	108 yrs	The first case of HIV is reported in South Africa
1984	110 yrs	Inflation results in the introduction of a R50 note
1988	114 yrs	Koko receives her first official identity document
1990	116 yrs	Nelson Mandela (her idol) is freed from prison
1992	118 yrs	After 3 decades, SA returns to the Olympics
1993	119 yrs	SA sees its first cell phone company, Vodacom, launched
1994	120 yrs	Koko votes for her country for the first time in her life
1999	129 yrs	SA's first telecommunications satellite is launched
2008	134 yrs	Nelson Mandela celebrates his 90th birthday
2009	135yrs	Koko dies of natural causes

CAPE TOWN

Capetonians refer to the cloud that occasionally covers the top of **Table Mountain** as 'the tablecloth'. The tablecloth appears when the notorious south-easter, that frequently blows in summer, creates a high-pressure system to the west of the city. Legend, however, tells another story. It claims that the tablecloth was caused by a Dutch sea captain, Mynheer Van Hunks, who engaged in pipe-smoking contests with the **devil on top of the mountain.** The contests would go on all summer but came to a halt in winter as Van Hunks, suffering badly from rheumatism, could not climb the **mountain in the cold.** This legend also gives rise to the name of the mountain next to Table Mountain, called Devil's Peak, which was perhaps more appropriately first called **'Wind Mountain'.**

25 000 Daily and Sunday Telegraph readers voted for Cape Town as their 'favourite world city' in the Annual Travel Awards. Source: Telegraph.co.uk 2008

Photo: Jacques Marais

43

WORLD WINNING TRAVEL AWARDS

Magazine readers voted

- Cape Town's Cape Grace as the world's best hotel, gaining the highest score in the history of the awards
- South Africa had the highest score for the greatest variety of attractions in the world
- South Africa outshines the global competition for climate

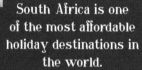

South Africa is one of the most affordable holiday destinations in the world.
American Express Foreign Exchange Holiday Cost of Living Index Survey

The world's leading sustainable tourism project vote went to Bushman Sands in the Eastern Cape

BRITISH GUILD OF TRAVEL WRITERS'

MAROPENG WAS AWARDED THE BRITISH GUILD OF TRAVEL WRITERS' AWARD FOR 'BEST NEW TOURISM PROJECT WORLDWIDE'

TRAVEL & LEISURE WORLD'S BEST AWARDS

THE READERS' POLL VOTED

- Bushmans Kloof Wilderness Reserve voted the 'World's Best Hotel' in 2009
- Singita Sabi Sand took top honours on three occasions for the 'World's Best Hotel'
- Cape Town was voted the 'World's Best City, Africa/ Middle East region'

Voted by over 160 000 tourism businesses

- World's Leading Boutique Hotel for the sixth consecutive year– Saxon Boutique Hotel and Spa
- World's Leading Conservation Company – Shamwari Game Reserve
- World's Leading Safari and Game Reserve – Shamwari Game Reserve for thirteen consecutive years
- World's leading Luxury Train – Blue Train for four consecutive years
- World's Leading Safari Train - Rovos Rail for three consecutive years
- World's leading luxury train - Rovos Rail

World Luxury Hotel Awards

Voting is cast by a select panel of 50 leading tour operators and travel industry consultants.

Luxury Coastal Hotel	–	Arabella Western Cape Hotel and Spa
Luxury Casino Resort	–	The Palazzo Montecasino
Luxury Boutique Hotel	–	Pezula Resort Hotel and Spa
Luxury Lodge	–	Chitwa Chitwa Game Lodge
Luxury Game Lodge	–	Sabi Sabi Private Game Lodge
Luxury Country House	–	De Hoek Country House

And another 16 South African hotels made it to the top 5 shortlist

---

VIP INTERNATIONAL TRAVELLER READERS' AWARD
PEZULA, in the Eastern Cape, won the Most Outstanding Golf Resort Worldwide

---

South Africa's Cape Garden Route

WON

Golf Destination of the Year

Asia & Australasia region

---

guardian

Over 19 000 of the British newspaper's readers voted Bulungula Eco-Lodge, in the Eastern Cape, runner up for the Ethical Travel Awards

---

CAPE TOWN
Boulder's Beach in Cape Town was named 'World's Best Family Beach' - UK Telegraph

---

iExplore.com ranked South Africa second in the category World's Adventure Travel

---

The UK Gap Year Providers named SA as the most popular gap year destination for Brits

the FUNNIER side of that four letter word...

RACE

In the past, South Africa was infamous for its racial prejudice and laws of segregation. Today, our cultural diversity is celebrated, and our mutual love and passion for our country bonds us together. Another thing we share is our unique South African humour. We've found that one of the best ways of dealing with our dark history is to look the demons in the eye and laugh. Here are some of the funny situations or comments people have made over the years. Enjoy.

'..we share a common destiny, regardless of the shapes of our noses..'

Thabo Mbeki, South African President

Dear white fella
Cupla tings you orta no:
Firstly, wen I was born I'm black
Wen I grow up, I'm black
Wen I go out ina sun, I'm black
When I'm cold, I'm black
And wen I get scared, Jeez, I'm black
And wen I die I'm still black...
But you white fella, you...
Wen you born, you pink
Wen you grow up, you white
Wen you sick, you green
Wen you go out ina sun, you go red
Wen you git cold, you go blue
And wen you scared, you go yellow
And wen you die, you go purple...
And you got the cheek
to call me coloured!

An American tourist at the hotel was gazing out one day at the beach and the sea beyond.
'Is that the Indian Ocean?' he asked the waiter who brought him a drink. 'Oh no, sir' the waiter replied. 'That's the European ocean. The Indians use the next beach over there.'

The Immorality Act (1950-1985) was one of the first apartheid laws in South Africa. It attempted to forbid all sexual relations between whites and non-whites so when Cape Town magistrate Josephus Ferrreira was charged under the Immorality Act in 1968, he was ordered to undergo two years psychiatric treatment!

'Get this John Blackman out!' Shane Warne urged his teammates while Makhaya Ntini, still nursing a fragile knee, was batting during the 2005/2006 test series against Australia. Ntini, annoyed by what he interpreted as a racist remark, said 'Less of the black please!' It turned out that Warne was actually referring to the Australian television actor John Blackman, who had played a character called Dicky Knee.

'Be nice to whites. They need you to rediscover their humanity.'

Archbishop
Desmond Tutu

Too many South Africans in service industries today live by the rule 'If you fail, blame it on the computer. When all else fails, blame apartheid'

'The liberation struggle of our people was not about liberating blacks from bondage, it was about liberating white people from fear.'

Tokyo Sexwale, businessman, politician and ANC Activist

Remember the mad old bad days of apartheid when Japanese were honorary whites but Chinese weren't? A Pretoria bus driver was hauled before a disciplinary committee after refusing to stop for a Japanese man as he thought he was Chinese!

During the apartheid era when the Board of Censors determined everything South Africans read and which theatre productions and movies we saw, few of us realised the extent of their reach and the powerful propaganda they practised. Amongst other things, they banned all movies that did not portray Red Indians as 'baddies' and those in which the cops were black and villains white.

'Pigmentocrats' Term applied to Afrikaners

'It is no longer a pigment of the imagination.'

Pieter Dirk Uys, satirist on Apartheid

In apartheid days, when blacks were called 'Non-Europeans', Jan Smuts Airport was forced to change its signage in 1959 to 'Whites' and 'Non-Whites' because the Europeans and Non-Europeans confused the foreigners. Apparently, the Americans kept trying to use the Non-European exits.

COCKTAILS & SHOOTERS

Whether it's sipping a Shling overlooking the beach, downing a Springbok around a camp fire or braving the Sowetan Long Drop, South Africa has a unique and favourite cocktail or shooter for EVERY occasion!

Township Speciality

City Sophistication

Best enjoyed from the Oyster Box Terrace

The Sowetan Toilet (or Longdrop)

Dribble Nachtmusiek® into banana liqueur.

Brandy and Cream

Shake together 1 tot brandy, ¹/₂ tot Amarula® and 1 tot fresh cream. Pour over ice.

Umhlanga Shling

Blend together 1 tot cane, mango juice, fresh pineapple juice, a dash of soda and crushed ice. Add a hint of freshly grated ginger and 1 tablespoon of sugar syrup.

Mountain magic

A touch of the bushveld

Month-end Bergie Bomb

Forget the Jaeger Bombs! Rather than drop a shot of Jaegermeister into a glass of Red Bull, substitute the Jaeger for Old Brown Sherry and the Red Bull for a Black Label beer.

(*Bergie - Slang for Cape Town street vagrant)

South African ALL-TIME favourite

Cape Snow

Blend together 30 ml of brandy and 30 ml of Van der Hum® liqueur with vanilla ice cream.

Brown Elephant

Shake together 2 tots milk, 2 tots Coca Cola® and 1 tot Amarula®. Mix gently and serve with ice.

Springbok Shooter

Pour Amarula® over peppermint liqueur.
LEKKER!

TO LET
HOLIDAY FLAT
MEL 083 421 4580

Ndebele Splendour

Tuscany in Africa

There's no place like Home

2m

Fisherman's Cottage, West Coast

Traditional Rondawel

Hospitality in Alexandra Township

Cape Dutch

Cape Malay in Bokaap

Trolley awards: Car, Dance, Child: Independent Newspapers. Race; Anton Jordaan, www.scpsphoto.com . Security; George Veltchev. Chickens; Paul Williams. Braai; Email distribution, source unknown.

TROLLEY AWARDS

1 Who needs a tow truck when you have a trolley?
2 Trolley Races at Stellenbosch University
3 Security on a break
4 Giving a new meaning to selling fresh produce
5 Providing a ride to the school matric dance
6 A means of escape when times are bad
7 Ensuring a perfect braai

THE SOWETO EXPERIENCE

heartbeat of the nation

Soweto is infused with the history of the Struggle against apartheid and abuzz with the energy of the City of Gold. It's a place of friendship, vibrancy and contrast.

Rows of tin shanties abut luxurious mansions; piles of garbage and pitted roads offset green fields and rustic streams. With over four million residents, Soweto is the most populous black urban residential area in the country, setting trends in politics, fashion, music, dance and language.

Soweto is an acronym for 'South Western Townships'. Back in 1904, the township was created to house mainly black mine labourers. In the 1950s, more black people were relocated there when they were forcibly removed from Sophiatown, just outside the city of Johannesburg.

Thereafter, Soweto's growth was phenomenal - but unplanned. Despite government attempts to curb the influx of black workers to the cities, waves of migrant workers moved from the countryside to live in Soweto and look for employment in the fast-growing city of gold. Today, Sowetans exude a sense of cosmopolitan sophistication.

One in five international tourists visits Soweto, and it is fast becoming a favourite among local Johannesburg residents for corporate events and outings.

The winds of change

In the past four years, four major shopping centres have opened in Soweto, revolutionising the retail trade. The biggest, Maponya Mall, is over 65 000 m².

Almost 50% of the R10 billion annual spending power of Soweto residents is now spent within the confines of Soweto, with nine out of ten residents supporting the shopping centres.

'the townships are diverse, dynamic, and lively places. drive down any street and kids are running around, neighbours are having animated conversations over the fence. men are sitting outside and enjoying cold ones amid lots of chitchat and laughter.

it's kasie fabulous, brother!'

— Ndumiso Ngcobo

Soweto's top 10 attractions

- **Mandela and Tutu's original home in Vilakazi Street**, the only street in the world inhabited by two Nobel Prize Winners
- **Freedom Square,** where the Freedom Charter was proclaimed
- **Soccer City Stadium**
- **Chris Hani Baragwanath Hospital**, the largest hospital in the world
- **Bungee or base jumping** from the cooling towers
- **The Hector Pieterson Memorial**
- **The Apartheid Museum** at Gold Reef City
- **The Soweto Golf Course**
- **Maponya Mall**

WanDies place

Boasting celebrity patrons such as Richard Branson, Evander Holyfield, Jesse Jackson, Quincy Jones and the All Blacks, Wandies Place is a favourite with both international tourists and local South Africans. Started as an illegal shebeen 30 years ago, Wandies today is a thriving restaurant offering traditional meals such as mutton curry with pap.(mielie meal), umqushu (samp & beans) and chakalaka salad.

shebeen

In South Africa, a shebeen refers to an unlicensed bar in the township. During the apartheid era, laws prohibited non-whites from consuming any alcohol except traditional sorghum beer, and illegal taverns selling alcohol became the centre of social activity. With constant raids, people had to find new ways to hide drink. When a plumber's job was completed, all the shebeen keeper had to do was turn on the hot water-tap for brandy and the cold-water for wine. The shebeens provided an atmosphere that contrasted with the rigours of daily life. They were warm and hospitable. Today, the shebeen continues to be the heart of the township.

The Grammy Award Winning Soweto Gospel Choir

55

MEDICAL SCIENCE

Despite the epidemics of the past and the present day challenges, South Africa has remained at the forefront of medical innovation. The world's first successful human-to-human heart transplant catapulted South Africa onto the medical stage of the world. South Africa continues to boast significant achievements, from the successful separation of Siamese twins to the first African-developed HIV vaccine to go to trial.

THE RINDERPEST

The rinderpest epidemic of the 1890s swept through Africa and resulted in the death of 80%-90% of the cattle, eland, buffalo, wildebeest, giraffe and antelope. In South Africa, 2.5 million cattle died. This resulted in widespread famine in what was later referred to as 'The year of the Rinderpest.' The attempts to find a remedy, however, resulted in the formation of a research institute in Grahamstown, spurring organised medical research in South Africa.

SMALLPOX

The smallpox epidemic of 1713 wreaked unparalleled havoc in the Cape, reaching pandemic proportions. Approximately a quarter of the white colonial and slave population died. The indigenous Khoisan people, however, had less resistance to the disease and only ten percent of the original Khoi population of the southwestern Cape survived the epidemic. Their indigenous clan names were lost and instead the Khoisan became known by the derogatory term 'Hottentots'.

HIV is the greatest medical, social and economic challenge facing South Africa

TUBERCULOSIS

Tuberculosis (TB) is one of the most seriously neglected and underestimated health, human rights and poverty problems of our era. It accounts for two million deaths a year worldwide. South Africa ranks fifth on the list of high-burden tuberculosis countries in the world. HIV/AIDS patients are particularly vulnerable to the disease and multi-drug-resistant strains hamper efforts to control the disease. TB claims the lives of over 460 000 South Africans each year.

MALARIA

It is estimated that malaria has been directly or indirectly responsible for 50% of all human deaths since the Stone Age. It was initially thought to come from fetid marshes, hence the name 'mal aria' (bad air), until scientists discovered that the parasite is transmitted from the bite of a female Anopheles mosquito. Ninety percent of the one million people who die each year from malaria are in sub-Saharan Africa. South Africa has the disease well under control, and it is mostly confined to the northeastern border with as few as 60–70 deaths annually.

MEDICAL TOURISM

South Africa has over 400 000 medical tourists annually. Medical tourism, or the process of seeking out medical treatment in another country, is a fast-growing industry covering elective procedures and specialised operations.

Most people come to South Africa for cosmetic surgery, but the country's skilled surgeons also provide organ transplants, cardiac, orthopaedic, ophthalmic surgery and dentistry. Tourists could save up to sixty percent on medical bills by choosing South Africa as their medical destination, with standards in South African clinics potentially as good, if not better, than those in their home country.

Over and above the favourable exchange rates, relatively low-cost healthcare and superior medical facilities, the country's beauty and numerous attractions provide an ideal environment for medical tourists to recuperate.

The first person in South Africa to use ether as an anaesthetic was Dr William Atherstone in 1847. He also founded a hospital, a 'lunatic asylum', and the country's first medical research laboratory. However, he is most famous as the man who identified South Africa's first diamond.

South Africa's first caesarean section was performed by Dr James Barry in 1826. Barry had arrived with the British army's medical department. When Barry died in 1865, it was discovered that 'he' was a woman named Miranda Stuart.

The Chris Hani Baragwanath Hospital in Soweto has been listed by the Guinness Book of World Records as the largest hospital in the world.

In South Africa, 84% of the population rely on the government's public health sector and 16% of South Africans are members of private medical schemes.

FACTS ABOUT THE WORLD'S FIRST HEART TRANSPLANT

Dr Christiaan Barnard performed the first successful human-to-human heart transplant in the world in 1967 at Groote Schuur Hospital, Cape Town. Barnard was also the first person to do a 'piggyback' transplant in 1971, and the first to do a heart-lung transplant. The first transplant would have taken place two weeks earlier had a white donor's heart been available.

FROM GARDENER TO HEART SURGEON

When 14-year-old Naki left home to find work, he was employed by the University of Cape Town as a gardener. Ten years later he was moved to the clinical laboratories to care for the laboratory animals on which surgeons practised their transplant operations. Naki, who never formally learnt transplant techniques, said 'I stole with my eyes' and progressed from cleaning cages to assisting with transplant surgical procedures and was soon teaching others. As a black man in apartheid South Africa, Naki was barred from studying medicine or even entering the whites-only operating theatre. Naki became Chris Barnard's assistant and apprentice and made a significant contribution to the development of heart transplant techniques, assisted in the actual transplant operation and provided invaluable training to thousands of student surgeons. Barnard later admitted that Naki, although officially employed as a gardener, probably had more technical skill than he did. Naki operated and gave lectures to medical professors until he retired on a gardener's pension in 1991. He received some recognition for his work after his retirement, including a National Order of Mapungubwe in Bronze in 2002 and an honorary degree in medicine from the University of Cape Town in 2003. Hamilton Naki, gardener, surgeon, South African, died aged 78 in 2005.

TOP 20 CAUSES OF DEATH

Leading specific causes of death, South Africa 2000

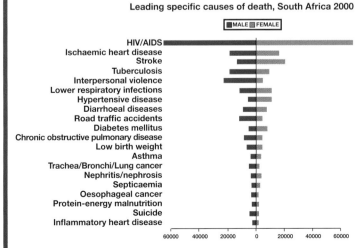

■ MALE ■ FEMALE

- HIV/AIDS
- Ischaemic heart disease
- Stroke
- Tuberculosis
- Interpersonal violence
- Lower respiratory infections
- Hypertensive disease
- Diarrhoeal diseases
- Road traffic accidents
- Diabetes mellitus
- Chronic obstructive pulmonary disease
- Low birth weight
- Asthma
- Trachea/Bronchi/Lung cancer
- Nephritis/nephrosis
- Septicaemia
- Oesophageal cancer
- Protein-energy malnutrition
- Suicide
- Inflammatory heart disease

60000 40000 20000 0 20000 40000 60000

Every morning an impala awakes
knowing that it must outrun the
fastest lion if it wants to stay alive
Every morning a lion awakes
knowing that it must outrun the
slowest impala or it will starve.
It makes no difference if you are
a lion or an impala, when the sun
comes up in Africa you must wake
up running.

THE NATION'S PRIDE

In the collective memory of this country, rugby will always hold a place of pride for the role it played in nation building during those first years of our new democracy.

Nelson Mandela

RUGBY

Let Samoa, Tonga and Ivory Coast know that we are not a Banana Republic. Let Italians realise that we don't eat pizza, but pap and wors. Regarding the French, let's do to them what we do to their polony – eat them. As for the English, Carling their Captain apologised... we don't. But above all, teach the New Zealanders a lesson because, whilst we are a Rainbow Nation, they still go about calling themselves the All Blacks.

Tokyo Sexwale before the opening of the 1995 World Cup

THE SOUTH AFRICAN TROPHY CABINET

| IRB SEVENS WORLD SERIES TROPHY | SUPER 14 TROPHY | FREEDOM CUP | NELSON MANDELA CHALLENGE PLATE | UNITY CUP (2009 LIONS SERIES) | VODACOM TRI-NATIONS TROPHY | THE WEB ELLIS CUP (RUGBY WORLD CUP) |

South Africa winning the 2007 World Cup. Photo courtesy Gallo Images

John Smit is the single player with the most caps as his country's captain in Tests • Fly-half **Jannie de Beer** holds the world record for dropped goals in a test match (5, against England in the 1999 Rugby World Cup) • **Morné Steyn** holds the world record for most points scored by a player who has scored all their team's points. **The International Rugby Hall of Fame** boasts simply 'the best of the best' in the world to have played the game. Those inducted include: **Danie Craven,** who played tests in four different positions - scrumhalf, centre, flyhalf and No.8 – and had doctorates in social anthropology, psychology and physical education • **Naas Botha** scored 3,781 points in a career of 277 first-class matches lasting from 1978 to 1992 • **Frik du Preez** was named South Africa's rugby player of the twentieth century by the country's passionate fans of the game • The movie 'Invictus' says it all for **Francois Pienaar** • When **Morné du Plessis** was elevated to the Springbok captaincy in the 1970s, it was the first time in history that a father and son had both captained their country • **Hennie Muller,** nicknamed 'Windhond' or 'greyhound', introduced a new style of play for a No.8 forward • **Danie Gerber** was a world-class centre in the 1980s, scoring 19 tries in only 24 tests • **Joost van der Westhuizen** redefined the scrum-half's role with his powerful bursts from both set-pieces and loose play • **Bennie Osler** had a controlling influence in an unbroken run of 17 test matches for South Africa between 1924 and 1933

THE CONSTITUTION

ONE OF THE MOST DEMOCRATIC AND PROGRESSIVE CONSTITUTIONS IN THE WORLD!

IT'S MORE THAN A CONSTITUTION - IT'S AN INCENTIVE TO BECOME BETTER HUMAN BEINGS. TO BECOME MORE ENLIGHTENED IN OUR THINKING, TO BE ENLIGHTENED IN OUR ACTIONS, AND TO UNDERSTAND THAT OUR RIGHTS ARE THE SAME AS EVERYONE ELSE'S IN SOUTH AFRICA, WITHOUT PREJUDICE, WITHOUT EXCEPTION. FOR THE SOUTH AFRICAN CONSTITUTION IS STRONGLY INFLUENCED BY THE UNIVERSAL DECLARATION OF HUMAN RIGHTS. IT ACKNOWLEDGES OUR COMMON HUMANITY, OUR LINK TO THE WORLD FAMILY. IT IS NOT JUST THERE ON PAPER, IT IS THERE TO BE HONOURED AND LIVED BY. IT IS OUR GUIDE AND PROTECTOR. IT GIVES US THE PARAMETERS TO OPEN OUR MINDS AND HEARTS TO HUMANS EVERYWHERE, AND TO LIVE, NOT IN JUDGEMENT, BUT WITH RESPECT.

' WE, THE PEOPLE OF SOUTH AFRICA, RECOGNISE THE INJUSTICES OF OUR PAST; HONOUR THOSE WHO SUFFERED FOR JUSTICE AND FREEDOM IN OUR LAND; RESPECT THOSE WHO HAVE WORKED TO BUILD AND DEVELOP OUR COUNTRY AND BELIEVE THAT SOUTH AFRICA BELONGS TO ALL WHO LIVE IN IT, UNITED IN OUR DIVERSITY. ' FROM THE PREAMBLE TO THE CONSTITUTION OF SOUTH AFRICA.

EVERYONE IS EQUAL BEFORE THE LAW AND HAS THE RIGHT TO EQUAL PROTECTION AND BENEFIT OF THE LAW. EVERYONE HAS INHERENT DIGNITY AND THE RIGHT TO HAVE THEIR DIGNITY RESPECTED AND PROTECTED. EVERYONE HAS THE RIGHT TO LIFE. EVERYONE HAS THE RIGHT TO FREEDOM AND SECURITY OF THE PERSON. EVERYONE HAS THE RIGHT TO BODILY AND PSYCHOLOGICAL INTEGRITY. NO-ONE MAY BE SUBJECTED TO SLAVERY, SERVITUDE OR FORCED LABOUR. EVERYONE HAS THE RIGHT TO PRIVACY. EVERYONE HAS THE RIGHT TO FREEDOM OF CONSCIENCE, RELIGION, THOUGHT, BELIEF AND OPINION. EVERYONE HAS THE RIGHT TO FREEDOM OF EXPRESSION. EVERYONE HAS THE RIGHT, PEACEFULLY AND UNARMED, TO ASSEMBLE, TO DEMONSTRATE, TO PICKET AND TO PRESENT PETITIONS. EVERYONE HAS THE RIGHT TO FREEDOM OF ASSOCIATION. EVERY CITIZEN IS FREE TO MAKE POLITICAL CHOICES. EVERY CITIZEN HAS THE RIGHT TO FREE, FAIR AND REGULAR ELECTIONS FOR ANY LEGISLATIVE BODY ESTABLISHED IN TERMS OF THE CONSTITUTION. EVERY ADULT CITIZEN HAS THE RIGHT TO VOTE AND TO STAND FOR PUBLIC OFFICE AND, IF ELECTED, TO HOLD OFFICE. NO CITIZEN MAY BE DEPRIVED OF CITIZENSHIP. EVERYONE HAS THE RIGHT TO FREEDOM OF MOVEMENT AND RESIDENCE. EVERY CITIZEN HAS THE RIGHT TO CHOOSE THEIR TRADE, OCCUPATION OR PROFESSION FREELY.

EVERYONE HAS THE RIGHT TO FAIR LABOUR PRACTICES. EVERYONE HAS THE RIGHT TO AN ENVIRONMENT THAT IS NOT HARMFUL TO THEIR HEALTH OR WELLBEING; AND TO HAVE THE ENVIRONMENT PROTECTED, FOR THE BENEFIT OF PRESENT AND FUTURE GENERATIONS. NO-ONE MAY BE DEPRIVED OF PROPERTY EXCEPT IN TERMS OF LAW OF GENERAL APPLICATION, AND NO LAW MAY PERMIT ARBITRARY DEPRIVATION OF PROPERTY. EVERYONE HAS THE RIGHT TO HAVE ACCESS TO ADEQUATE HOUSING. EVERYONE HAS THE RIGHT TO HAVE ACCESS TO HEALTH CARE SERVICES, FOOD, WATER AND SOCIAL SECURITY. NO-ONE MAY BE REFUSED EMERGENCY MEDICAL TREATMENT. EVERY CHILD HAS THE RIGHT TO A NAME AND A NATIONALITY FROM BIRTH; TO FAMILY CARE OR PARENTAL CARE, OR TO APPROPRIATE ALTERNATIVE CARE; TO BASIC NUTRITION, SHELTER, BASIC HEALTH CARE SERVICES AND SOCIAL SERVICES; TO BE PROTECTED. A CHILD'S BEST INTERESTS ARE OF PARAMOUNT IMPORTANCE IN EVERY MATTER CONCERNING THE CHILD. EVERYONE HAS THE RIGHT TO A BASIC EDUCATION, INCLUDING ADULT BASIC EDUCATION, AND TO FURTHER EDUCATION. EVERYONE HAS THE RIGHT TO USE THE LANGUAGE AND TO PARTICIPATE IN THE CULTURAL LIFE OF THEIR CHOICE. PERSONS BELONGING TO A CULTURAL, RELIGIOUS OR LINGUISTIC COMMUNITY MAY NOT BE DENIED THE RIGHT, WITH OTHER MEMBERS OF THAT COMMUNITY, TO ENJOY THEIR CULTURE, PRACTICE THEIR RELIGION AND USE THEIR LANGUAGE; AND TO FORM, JOIN AND MAINTAIN CULTURAL, RELIGIOUS AND LINGUISTIC ASSOCIATIONS AND OTHER ORGANS OF CIVIL SOCIETY. EVERYONE HAS THE RIGHT OF ACCESS TO ANY INFORMATION HELD BY THE STATE; AND ANY INFORMATION THAT IS HELD BY ANOTHER PERSON AND THAT IS REQUIRED FOR THE EXERCISE OR PROTECTION OF ANY RIGHTS. EVERYONE HAS THE RIGHT TO ADMINISTRATIVE ACTION THAT IS LAWFUL, REASONABLE AND PROCEDURALLY FAIR. EVERYONE HAS THE RIGHT TO HAVE ANY DISPUTE THAT CAN BE RESOLVED BY THE APPLICATION OF LAW DECIDED IN A FAIR PUBLIC HEARING BEFORE A COURT OR, WHERE APPROPRIATE, ANOTHER INDEPENDENT AND IMPARTIAL TRIBUNAL OR FORUM. EVERYONE WHO IS ARRESTED FOR ALLEGEDLY COMMITTING AN OFFENCE HAS THE RIGHT TO REMAIN SILENT; TO BE INFORMED PROMPTLY OF THEIR RIGHTS; TO BE BROUGHT BEFORE A COURT AS SOON AS REASONABLY POSSIBLE. EVERYONE WHO IS DETAINED, INCLUDING EVERY SENTENCED PRISONER, HAS THE RIGHT TO BE INFORMED PROMPTLY OF THE REASON FOR BEING DETAINED; TO CHOOSE, AND TO CONSULT WITH A LEGAL PRACTITIONER, AND TO BE INFORMED OF THIS RIGHT PROMPTLY; TO CHALLENGE THE LAWFULNESS OF THE DETENTION IN PERSON BEFORE A COURT AND, IF THE DETENTION IS UNLAWFUL, TO BE RELEASED; TO CONDITIONS OF DETENTION THAT ARE CONSISTENT WITH HUMAN DIGNITY. EVERY ACCUSED PERSON HAS A RIGHT TO A FAIR TRIAL.

MONOPOLY

World votes

For top cities in Global Monopoly edition and Cape Town wins third place!

28th August 2008

2008 - the first-ever World Edition Monopoly Board Game is released and pays tribute to some of the greatest cities in the world. Over 5.6 million people from over 70 countries put forward their choice of top cities for the Monopoly Board Game. Cape Town was voted third, far ahead of great cities such as Paris, Sydney, London, New York, Barcelona, Tokyo and Hong Kong, making it one of the most expensive and desirable cities on the World Edition Game board in which to own property.

GO DIRECTLY TO JAIL

ZERO TOLERANCE ON CRIME

The most played commercial board game in the world

More than 5 billion of the tiny green houses have been produced

TATA CHA

RIGA
1st SPOT

MONTREAL
2nd SPOT

MARS SPACE STATION

CAPE TOWN WINS 3rd SPOT

PARIS
4th SPOT

MON

CHANCE

YOU ARE CAUGHT BRIBING A TRAFFIC COP

Go back to begin

?

CHANCE

YOUR FRAUD IS EXPOSED

Go directly to jail

?

CHANCE

GET OUT OF JAIL FREE

This card may not be sold or used for bribery

?

2008

CLIFTON
R20 000
R20 million

OR Tambo
JOHANNESBURG INTERNATIONAL

TATA CHA

MONOPOLY

THROUGH THE AGES...

A celebration of how the South African game of monopoly has changed over the years, from the first edition in 1963 to the second edition in 2002 and finally the international edition in 2008.

Over 200 million copies sold in 80 countries, in 26 languages

During World War II the International Red Cross distributed a special edition for prisoners. Hidden inside were maps, compasses and real money for escaping

There is more Monopoly money printed daily than there is by the US Treasury

1963

COMMUNITY CHEST

YOUR BEE RATING IMPROVES

Advance to begin

COMMUNITY CHEST

ADVANCE TO FREE PARKING

Tip the car guard R5

COMMUNITY CHEST

CREATE A SHELTER FOR STREET KIDS!

Advance 10 paces

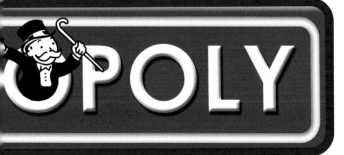
OPOLY

MUSGRAVE RD
R60

Now this would have been a good investment.

ELECTRICITY

Rather invest in solar power

BLOEMFONTEIN STATION

No longer First Class Travel for whites ONLY.

WEST STREET
R100

Dr Pixley Kasame Rd

SMITH STREET
R100

Anton Lembede St

SANDTON
~~R15 000~~

R1 million

HILLBROW
~~R15 000~~

R2.5 million

PORT ELIZABETH

Still the friendly city!

2002

MANY PEOPLE DEDICATED THEIR LIVES TO A FREE AND DEMOCRATIC SOUTH AFRICA. HERE ARE JUST A FEW OF THEM.

FREEDOM FIGHTERS

1.

ALBERT LUTHULI

Dr. Albert Luthuli's Christian beliefs acted as the foundation for his non-violent political life, earning him the honour of being Africa's first winner of the Nobel Peace Prize. He was president of the ANC.

'The main thing is that the government and the people should be democratic to the core. It is relatively unimportant who is in the government. I am not opposed to the present government because it is white; I am opposed to it only because it is undemocratic and repressive.'

2.

HELEN SUZMAN

Helen Suzman, as member of the opposition party, was the sole parliamentarian unequivocally opposed to apartheid. The outspoken English-speaking Jewish woman, when accused by a minister of asking questions in parliament that embarrassed South Africa, replied:

'It is not my questions that embarrass South Africa, it is your answers.'

'I hate bullies. I stand for simple justice, equal opportunity and human rights. The indispensable elements in a democratic society are well worth fighting for.'

3.

CHRIS HANI

Chris Hani, a charismatic leader of the South African Communist Party, was pivotal in the ending of apartheid. In the last year of his life, he urged militant youth to work towards peace. His assassination and the subsequent reaction persuaded the negotiating committee to fast track a date for the first democratic elections.

'What right do I have to hold back, to rest, to preserve my health, to have time with my family, when there are other people who are no longer alive, when they have sacrificed what is precious, namely life itself?'

4.

WALTER SISULU

Leader of the Defiance Campaign and founder member of the ANC Youth League, Sisulu was an active trade unionist. He was subsequently imprisoned for 26 years on Robben Island.

'The fundamental principle in our struggle is equal rights for all in our country, and that all people who have made South Africa their home, by birth or adoption, irrespective of colour or creed, are entitled to these rights.'

5.

OR TAMBO

OR Tambo was one of the founding members of the ANC Youth League and served as the ANC president and national chairperson. He spent 31 years abroad mobilising the opposition to apartheid.

'We have a vision of South Africa in which black and white shall live and work together as equals in conditions of peace and prosperity.'

6.

FW DE KLERK

As state president and one of the architects of the negotiated settlement, de Klerk played a leading role in the negotiating process, converting his government from a racially based government to a non-racial one. Together with Nelson Mandela, he was the joint recipient of the Nobel Peace Prize.

'The new era which is dawning... will lift us out of the silent grief of our past and into a future in which there will be opportunity and space for joy and beauty – for real and lasting peace.'

7.

STEVE BIKO

Steven Bantu Biko was one of South Africa's most significant political activists and a leading founder of South Africa's Black Consciousness Movement. His death in police detention led to his being hailed as a martyr of the anti-apartheid struggle.

'The power of a movement lies in the fact that it can indeed change the habits of people. This change is not the result of force but of dedication, of moral persuasion.'

What's in a name?

Afrikaans origins

One has to wonder what they were thinking. Translating animal names from Afrikaans to English doesn't always give you what you expect.

English Name	Afrikaans Name	Translation back to English
Sombre Bulbul	Gewone Willie	Plain Willie
Giraffe	Kameelperd	Camel horse
Forest Buzzard	Bosjakkalsvoel	Bush jackal bird
Red-chested Cuckoo	Piet-my-vrou	Peter my wife
Leopard	Luiperd	Lazy horse
Striped Polecat	Stinkmuishond	Smelly mouse dog
Porcupine	Ystervark	Iron pig
Common Slug Eater	Tabakrollertjie	Tobacco roller
Hippopotamus	Seekoei	Sea cow
Hedgehog	Krimpvarkie	Shrunk pig
Sperm Whale	Potvis	Potfish
Praying mantis	Hottentotsgot	Hottentot god
Warthog	Vlakvark	Shallow pig
Kori Bustard	Gompou	Gum peacock
Shrike	Laksman	Executioner
Cockroach	Kakkerlak	Glue shitter
Cheetah	Jagluiperd	Hunting lazy horse
Small Baboon	Bobbejaantjie	Our star rugby players

The Afrikaans word for a small baboon is **bobbejaantjie** - giving us a good laugh when our star rugby players Gcobani Bobo and Conrad Jantjes are photographed together.

African origins

Crocodile	– ingwenya	meaning 'champion fighter'.
Eland	– impofu	meaning 'the humble one'.
Elephant	– indlovu	meaning 'the unstoppable one'.
Hyena	– impisi	meaning 'the cleaner' due to its ability to make things orderly.
Lion	– ingonyama	meaning 'the master of all flesh', hence its reputation as the king of the beasts.
Leopard	– ingwe	meaning 'pure sovereignty', symbolising all that is noble, honourable and courageous.
Baboon	– imfene	meaning 'to resemble', referring to the resemblance to human beings.
Wildebeest	– inkonkoni	meaning 'the leader', explaining how this animal is held in such reverence. This is also the name given to the wisest traditional leader in a community and the best footballer in any township is also called inkonkoni.
Hippopotamus	– imvubu	meaning 'to combine', giving the animal the reputation of being known as 'the mixed-up creature' because it is unable to make up its mind whether it is an elephant or a rhinoceros.

Greek origins

Hippopotamus – Greek '(h)ippo', meaning horse, and 'pot-amus', meaning flowing river: a river horse.

Leopard – Greek word 'pardus' for panther and 'leo' for lion, shortened to leopard from leopardus.

Porcupine – Greek word 'porcus', meaning pig and 'spina', meaning species, direct translation 'spined pig'.

The poor hippopotamus

- in Greek   a river horse
- in Afrikaans a seacow
- in Zulu   a combination of elephant & rhinoceros.

No wonder the poor animal is called the mixed-up creature!

The Wikipedia list of collective nouns

A coalition of cheetahs

A parade of elephants

A tower of giraffe

A prickle of porcupines

A crash of hippos

A clan of hyenas

A rank of impala

A skulk of jackal

A leap of leopards

A troop of monkeys

A business of mongoose

A stubbornness of rhinos

An implausibility of wildebeest

A zeal of zebras

A congregation of crocodiles

A parliament of owls

A shiver of sharks

A cauldron of bats

A committee of vultures

An alliance of male dolphins

A party of female dolphins

A mob of meercats

Photo courtesy N Wolmarans

Photo courtesy www.earthtouch.com

69

BEER

UMQUOMBOTHI IS TRADITIONAL BEER MADE FROM MAIZE, SORGHUM AND YEAST.

AN OLD ZULU SAYING, 'UTSHWALA BUQINISA UMZIMBA', MEANS 'BEER STRENGTHENS THE BODY.'

THE WORD 'SHEBEEN' COMES FROM THE ANGLO-IRISH WORD SIBIN, MEANING BAD ALE.

BEER WAS A PART OF EVERYDAY LIFE LONG BEFORE THE INFLUENCE OF THE EUROPEANS REACHED THE COUNTRY. BEER WAS BREWED FROM GRAIN, CORN OR FRUIT.

THE ZULU KING CETSHWAYO DESCRIBED IT AS THE 'FOOD OF THE ZULUS' AND EVERY WOMAN IN THE TRIBE WAS EXPECTED TO KNOW HOW TO BREW GOOD AND NOURISHING BEER.

NOT ONLY FOR MALES
BLACK WOMEN IN SOUTH AFRICA OUTDRINK THE ENTIRE WHITE BEER MARKET

The Zulu Kingdom of KwaZulu-Natal has its own beer route showcasing a number of breweries. These include: The Congella United National Breweries and South African Breweries in Durban; Firkin Hophouse Micro Brewery & Pub in Westville; The Nottingham Road Brewery and the Wartburger Brauhaus in the Natal Midlands; The Farmers' Brauhaus and The Ijuba-United National Breweries in the Battlefields of Dundee and the Zululand Brewing Company in Eshowe.

Whether it's in a rural community, a township shebeen or a sports stadium, beer is enjoyed and is one of South Africa's everyday pleasures

CALCULATE THIS ON A BEER MAT!

A study conducted by Wits University found that the average South African walks about 1 200 km a year. Another study by the South African Medical Association found that South Africans drink, on average, 100 litres of alcohol a year.

This means South Africans get about 12 km to the litre!

DID YOU KNOW ?

- SAB Miller produces 240 million hectolitres of beer and 47 million hectolitres of soft drinks per annum. That's 28 700 000 000 litres a year!
- South African Breweries is ranked as the world's second biggest brewery company, supplying China with around half its needs.
- The SAB World of Beer was officially judged South Africa's top tourist attraction in 2009
- Carling Black Label and Sarita won Gold awards at the 2008 Beer Awards.
- Six SAB Miller brands are in the world's top 50 beer brands.
- Carling Black Label is South Africa's favourite beer, followed by Castle Lager and Hansa Pilsener.

TAXI

For a truly African experience, and for those on a tight budget, minibus taxis (or just taxis, as they are more frequently referred to) are the first choice to get around town quickly (too quickly for some) and bring you up close to the country's VIBRANT mix of cultures and people. 65% of public transport commuters rely on them daily.

CAUTION!!
I learned to drive on my playstation

CA 835-227

TAXI SPARE PARTS

WIRE
STRING
GLUE
MASKING TAPE
SCOTCH TAPE

ZAPIRO

For more Zapiro cartoons, visit www.zapiro.com

In the city of Soweto, black taxis or minibuses have become known as Zolas after the athlete Zola Budd.

PROUDLY SOUTH AFRICAN

The FUNKY colourful graphics give the taxi a brand of its own. Taxi themes based on Hollywood, Bollywood and music stars fill up quicker and give their operator a unique identity. Examples of taxi names include: God's Gift, Only God Knows or Snoop Dogg.

This proudly South African tradition has been adopted by other countries across the continent.

ONLY GOD KNOWS
GODS GIFT
SNOOP DOGG

THE TAXI ADVENTURE

TO CALL A TAXI -
Step out into the road with the appropriate hand signal.

WHILST DRIVING -
Bob your head to the pumping Kwaito or hip hop beats.

SOCIALISE -
Take in the latest gossip from the regulars.

TO STOP -
Shout 'stop!' 10 seconds before required and the driver will make a plan, irrespective of the surrounding traffic. Alternatively, to stop after a traffic light, shout in a deep loud voice 'after robot!' (pronounced uf-dah robot). If the light is red, you're expected to get off there and then.

TAXI RECAPITALISATION

The government has initiated a taxi recapitilisation programme to ensure safe, effective, reliable taxi operations. R7.7-billion has been allocated to replace up to 80% of the country's taxi fleet by 2010. The intervention encourages the scrapping of old taxis and assists in obtaining new taxis that meet compulsory safety and comfort requirements. Taxis that are part of the programme are white in colour with the South African national flag on the sides.

JOHANNESBURG
HAND SIGNALS USED TO HAIL A TAXI

To travel further north
- all five fingers like a high-five

To stay in the general area
- downwards-pointing index finger

To head to Fourways
- hold out four fingers with thumb tucked in

To go to Diepsloot (which has bumpy roads)
- make a wave-like motion

To go south or west
- upwards pointing index finger

WHEN THINGS GO WRONG

OUR COUNTRY HAS SEEN MANY CONFLICTS AND STRUGGLES THROUGHOUT THE AGES. WE USUALLY LEARN ABOUT THE TRIUMPHS, BUT HEAR LITTLE OF THE LOSING SIDE. IN THESE INSTANCES, UNFORTUNATE CIRCUMSTANCES COST THE 'LOSERS' DEARLY. HAD THINGS BEEN OTHERWISE, HISTORY WOULD HAVE TAKEN A VERY DIFFERENT COURSE.

THE XHOSA FAMINE

It was 1857 and the Xhosas, desperate to drive the Europeans from their lands, took the advice of a fourteen-year-old girl named Nongqawuse who was believed to be a prophetess. She stated that spirits had instructed the Xhosa people to destroy all their crops and kill their cattle, which would result in the unwanted settlers being driven into the sea, and the Xhosa's losses being replaced by an even better crop and livestock.

WHAT WENT WRONG? The entire nation followed the prophecy. They sacrificed all their crops and more than 400 000 cattle.

THE OUTCOME: Forty to fifty-thousand Xhosas starved to death, and the rest migrated to other areas. By the end of 1858, their population dropped from 105 000 to less than 27 000 due to the resulting famine, and many Xhosas resorted to cannibalism. The British found that those Xhosas who survived proved to be docile and useful servants. What the British Empire had been unable to accomplish in more than fifty years of aggressive colonialism, the Xhosas did to themselves in less than two years.

SHAKA ZULU

The most legendary figure in South Africa's history was born illegitimate in the 1800s, rose from difficult circumstances and became a military genius. Shaka was also infamous for his brutality, which would ironically become the reason for his demise.

WHAT WENT WRONG? His appetite for blood worsened when Nandi, his mother, died. He had over 7 000 people massacred, including his mother's maid to 'keep her company', and others for reasons such as 'not crying enough'.

THE OUTCOME: Ironically, he was killed the same way he lived, with violence. He became increasingly unpopular because of his violent actions and was stabbed to death by his half brothers, Mhlanga and Dingane.

CHIEF MAGOEBA

The year was 1895. Chief Magoeba refused to give up his land or allow his people to become labourers. Boer Commandant General Piet Retief hired Swazi and Shangaan mercenaries to assist him in dealing with this 'troublesome chief'. To identify the mercenaries from Magoeba's men, Joubert ordered them to tie a white band around their heads.

WHAT WENT WRONG? Unfortunately, Magoeba's men heard of the plan and also tied white bands on their heads. Chaos ensued resulting in over 400 whites and 3 500 mercenaries fleeing down the mountainside.

THE OUTCOME: Determined not to be defeated, the Swazis then hunted down Magoeba, shot him, cut off his head and carried it back to General Joubert's camp as proof of his death. Joubert was subsequently severely reprimanded by Paul Kruger for cutting off Magoeba's head on a Sunday. And what of Magoeba's 4 000 followers? They were put to work on the 'white-owned' farms in the area. Magoeba's Kloof is named after this brave chief.

FLIGHT OF THE HERERO

This is a tragic story of dreadful death from an unforgiving desert and thirst. The Herero people of South West Africa (now Namibia) originated in Central Africa. They were friendly educated people who could read and write.

WHAT WENT WRONG? After seeing the brutal manner in which the colonising Germans had treated a tribe of Hottentots who resisted, the Hereros chose to 'face the Kalahari Desert, rather than face the Germans'.

THE OUTCOME: This resulted in the deaths of over 13 000 Hereros from thirst and dehydration. Their horrific story is still whispered amongst Namibians today. Dehydration being among the worst ways to die, one wonders whether the Hereros' fate at the hands of the Germans would have been quite so severe.

THE JAMESON RAID

1895 saw British-born Jameson lead about 500 English men in a careless raid against the Boers. The consequences saw the British humiliatingly defeated by President Paul Kruger.

WHAT WENT WRONG? Jameson sent two members of his group to cut the telegraph line to Pretoria. It is alleged that, in their drunken state, they ended up cutting a farmer's fence instead. This resulted in the Boers knowing the details of the plans and whereabouts of the British.

THE OUTCOME: This event become a major factor in bringing about the 1899-1902 Anglo-Boer War.

MAKHANDA

In 1819, Makhanda was a Xhosa chief who spent his younger years living in the veld in solitude, pondering on religion, philosophies and tradition. He was particularly drawn to Christianity which he was exposed to while living on a Christian trekboer's farm. Despite developing close friendships with white missionaries and cordial relationships with British officers, Makhanda soon realised these people believed they were superior to him and he eventually turned against them. Makhanda assembled an army of around 10 000 people, the biggest Xhosa army ever to go into battle. He embarked on a full-on military attack on the British in Grahamstown, something never before contemplated by any indigenous group in Southern Africa.

WHAT WENT WRONG? Makhanda sent one of his warriors to Grahamstown to inform the British he would meet them in the morning. It is believed that this was done in the Xhosa tradition of ensuring a fair fight. This alerted the British and gave them time to prepare for battle, resulting in Makhanda losing as many as 2 000 men. The British lost only three men.

THE OUTCOME: Unable to live with himself due to the high number of Xhosa who had been killed in the battle, Makhanda surrendered four months later. He was sent to Robben Island by Sir Charles Somerset where he was kept as prisoner. It is believed that he drowned at Bloubergstrand trying to escape. To this day, the Xhosa people, including Nelson Mandela, refer to Robben Island as the Island of Makhanda. Had Makhanda not warned the British, he may have stopped the British settler immigrants from further colonisation, thereby changing the course of the country forever.

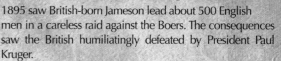

AND THEN THINGS WENT RIGHT

MADIBA, VILJOEN AND THE AWB* (AFRIKANER RESISTANCE MOVEMENT)

Virtually never discussed is how close South Africa actually came to a violent bloodbath right before the 1994 political settlement. Late 1993 saw over 50 000 white conservatives mobilised, armed and ready for a civil race war with SA Defence Force units standing by to join them.

WHAT DIDN'T GO WRONG? A meeting between their leader, the former head of the SADF, General Constand Viljoen and ANC president Nelson Mandela set the foundation for further talks. The general and his team then met with Mandela, Thabo Mbeki and Jacob Zuma. Zuma told them 'We can't go for war – we are from war already! We thought we could destroy each other – we couldn't! Why can't we talk?'

THE OUTCOME: Peace prevailed, war was averted and thus the stage was set for the new Rainbow Nation.

SIENER VAN RENSBURG AND THE BOER WAR PROPHECY

In 1899, Siener, the son of a farmer in the North West Province, became known as the Afrikaner Nostradamus because of a significant vision relating to the Anglo-Boer War. From the age of seven, Siener had seen numerous visions that had come true. In the early 1900s, he was found in the veld in a terrible state, crying and stating that he had seen visions of Boers fleeing over 'blackened earth' and women and children crying bitterly as British soldiers harried them.

WHAT WENT WRONG? Unfortunately, Siener's visions did not go down well with his fellow Boers. He was regarded as a false prophet and ignored.

THE OUTCOME: Two years later, Seiner's vision became a horrendous reality as the British implemented their 'scorched-earth policy', destroying anything that might be useful to their enemy and placing Afrikaner women and children in concentration camps. The Anglo-Boer war turned out to be just as nightmarish as Siener van Rensburg's vision had been.

I'M TOO SEXY FOR MY... FEATHERS!

ADMIRING THE VERY BEST OF OUR FEATHERED FRIENDS.

WHITE-HEADED VULTURE

MARABOU STORK

GREY CROWNED CRANE

GROUND HORNBILL

CRESTED GUINEA FOWL

PIED STARLING

EVITA BEZUIDENHOUT

The sexiest of them all, Evita Bezuidenhout (the character created by satirist performer Pieter-Dirk Uys), is regarded by many as South Africa's favourite 'politician'.

Evita humorously exposed the absurdity of the government's racial policies, ruffling quite a few feathers in the process.

MORE PEOPLE ARE HIV POSITIVE IN SOUTH AFRICA THAN ANYWHERE IN THE WORLD!

AIDS has been ravaging the world since the early eighties, although it was in evidence before that, it had not been officially identified. Formerly marginalised as the 'gay disease', it is, in fact, everybody's disease. Purported to have originated in Africa, it has wreaked its greatest havoc here and decimated generations, leaving millions of AIDS-infected orphans. Like many serious diseases, it could have been contained. And it still can. Informed, each individual can take the correct measures to stay free from HIV. If already HIV-positive, correctly medicated, each individual can enjoy a good quality of life. It's up to each of us, and our government, to be responsible.

ABOUT CIRCUMCISION: Male circumcision reduces a man's risk of becoming infected with HIV by up to **60%**

ARE WE WINNING THE BATTLE?

HIV Prevalence in children aged 2-14 years

2002 - 5.6%
2008 - 2.5%

IN 2001 males 57% females 46%
IN 2008 males 87% females 73%

CONDOM USE

IN 2002 43 deaths from HIV per 1 000 births
IN 2006 31 deaths from HIV per 1 000 births

INFANT MORTALITY RATE IN KAYELITSHA

HIV Prevalence in youths 15-24 years

2002 - 10.3%
2008 - 8.6%

ABOUT CONDOMS

Condoms have a near 100% efficacy but in reality are only 85% effective.

Female condoms are an effective alternative to the more common male condom.

Millions of male condoms which are provided to Africa each year for prevention campaigns are found to be faulty, severely hampering **prevention efforts**.

Condoms are affected by both **heat & light** and can deteriorate if not stored correctly.

BEWARE THE WINDOW PERIOD

After someone is infected with the virus, it takes up to three months before their HIV test shows up as positive. In this three month period, they are still able to transmit the virus to others, even though their tests may have reflected a 'false negative' result.

WHO'S TO BLAME?

25 million people have died worldwide in the past 25 years. AIDS is preventable, so how did the situation get so out of control? Some blame the policies of the Bush administration. Others blame the greed of the pharmaceutical companies and even perhaps the Vatican for condemning the use of condoms. Most blame the South African government for holding back treatment to its people. But all agree, one person has to take responsibility: **YOU!**

HIV is deeply political. It is about how men treat women, how children are treated by society, how rich countries treat poor countries, how corporate drug companies treat consumers, and how private enterprises treat their workers.

(Zackie Achmat)

THE ABC OF STAYING HIV FREE
ABSTAIN
BE FAITHFUL
CONDOMISE

SOUTH AFRICAN HIV STATS

South Africa is home to the world's largest population of people living with HIV.
5,7 million South Africans are infected with the HIV virus.
To date, almost three million South Africans have died of AIDS. There are an estimated 1.9 million AIDS orphans.
HIV prevalance in the age group 20-29 years is twice as high in females compared to males.
Swaziland is the country with the highest rate of infection in the world at 26%, followed by Botswana then Lesotho.

IS THERE LIGHT AT THE END OF THE TUNNEL? South Africa is currently testing two HIV vaccines, developed by the University of Cape Town.

HIV

**HIV AIDS HELPLINE
0800 012 322
www.aidshelpline.org.za
Frightened, confused by Aids?
South Africa's Aids Helpline
offers toll-free, multilingual
assistance from trained
counsellors accessing the
latest data through a
computerised
call centre**

AIDS doesn't discriminate, PEOPLE DO!

THE WORLD RECORD BREAKERS

While the Big 5 capture the interest of most people, South Africa has so much more to experience when it comes to exploring our wildlife.

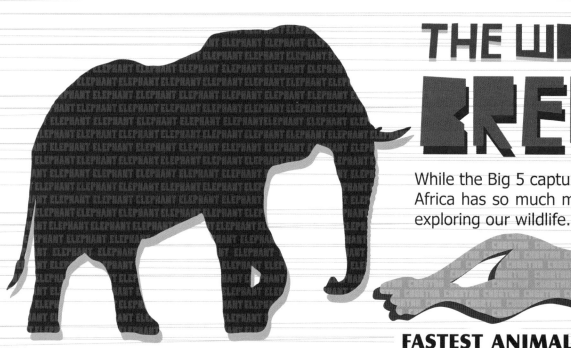

LARGEST LAND ANIMAL

The elephant has an impressive weight of 5 000 kg - more than 5 VW Citi Golfs!

FASTEST ANIMAL

Cheetahs reach a speed of up to 113 km/h. That's 4 times faster than the fastest human.

LARGEST BIRD AND FASTEST 2 LEGGED CREATURE

With a height of 2,75 m and weighing over 155 kg, the ostrich can run at 72 km/h. But unfortunately the ostrich, which is not the cleverest, runs round in circles when alarmed, making it easy prey for attackers.

OLDEST FISH

Dating back over 360 million years, the coelacanth represents an early step in the evolution of fish to the first amphibian creatures that made the transition from sea to land.

TALLEST ANIMAL

A male giraffe will reach as high as 6 m – or to the roof of a two-storey building!

STRONGEST CREATURE

With a length of 60 mm, the rhinoceros beetle can carry 850 times its own weight. That would be equivalent to a human carrying 15 elephants!

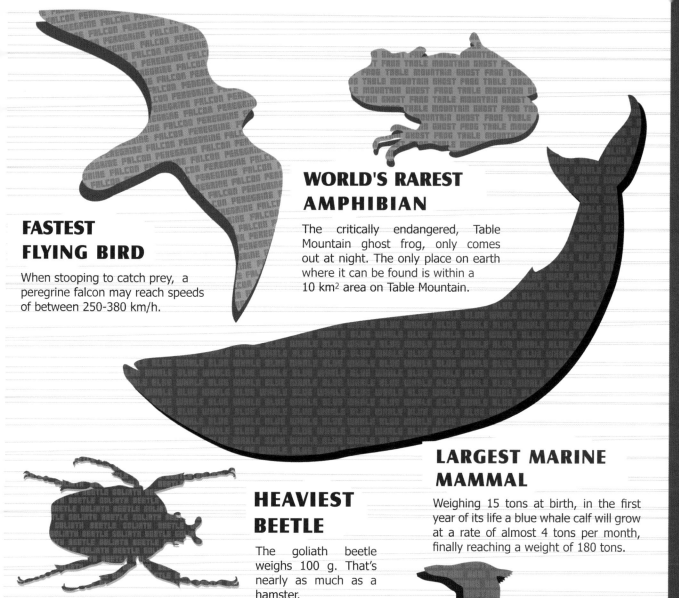

FASTEST FLYING BIRD

When stooping to catch prey, a peregrine falcon may reach speeds of between 250-380 km/h.

WORLD'S RAREST AMPHIBIAN

The critically endangered, Table Mountain ghost frog, only comes out at night. The only place on earth where it can be found is within a 10 km² area on Table Mountain.

HEAVIEST BEETLE

The goliath beetle weighs 100 g. That's nearly as much as a hamster.

LARGEST MARINE MAMMAL

Weighing 15 tons at birth, in the first year of its life a blue whale calf will grow at a rate of almost 4 tons per month, finally reaching a weight of 180 tons.

WORLD'S SMELLIEST ANIMAL

Also called the African striped polecat, a zorilla will put any self-respecting skunk to shame. A squirt of its secretion not only leaves the victim temporarily blinded but the revolting smell lingers for several days.

HEAVIEST FLYING BIRD

Flying can't be easy for the kori bustard with a height of more than 1.5 m, wings that stretch out to 2.6 m and a weight of up to 18 kg.

SOUTH AFRICA'S BIG 12 INSECTS

Giant Dragonfly

Table Mountain Flightless Cockroach

Termite

Bladder Grasshopper

Giant Stick Insect

Giant Preying Mantis

Giant Water Bug

Giant Antlion

Giant Tachinid Fly

Giant Dung Beetle

Mopane Worm

Giant Carpenter Bee

SOUTH AFRICA'S BIG 6 BIRDS

Ground Hornbill

Kori Bustard

Saddle-billed Stork

Lappet-faced Vulture

Martial Eagle

Pel's Fishing Owl

SOUTH AFRICA'S LITTLE 5

Antlion

Buffalo Weaver

Rhinoceros Beetle

Leopard Tortoise

Elephant Shrew

The bushveld is a place
where the human
element indeed shrinks
into utter insignificance,
and grips you and
subdues you and makes
you one with yourself.

Jan Christiaan Smuts,
South African Prime Minister, (1870 - 1950)

With great imagination...

and some strong Ouzo, ancient Greek astronomers drew pictures and created stories of the night sky. More relevant to the southern hemisphere are our own African stories attached to these celestial bodies.

The Xhosa and Zulu people were mainly farmers and used 'Isilimela' (the Pleiades) as the basis for their calendar. The Pleiades are nicknamed the 'Digging Stars' as their appearance in June signals the time to prepare the fields for the season. When they fade again at the end of summer it is time to harvest. Isilimela is actually the Xhosa word for June!

Surprisingly, the constellation of Orion has hunting connotations for both the Greek and African legends. For the Namaqua people, Orion's belt is seen as three zebras and the star of Betelgeuse (Orion's shoulder) as a lion. A man called Aob (part of Taurus) is sent out by his wives (the Pleiades or seven sisters) to hunt. His arrow (Orion's sword) misses the zebra and he is unable to retrieve it for fear of the mighty lion. Too ashamed to face his wives empty handed, he is stuck out in the night sky to suffer from thirst and hunger.

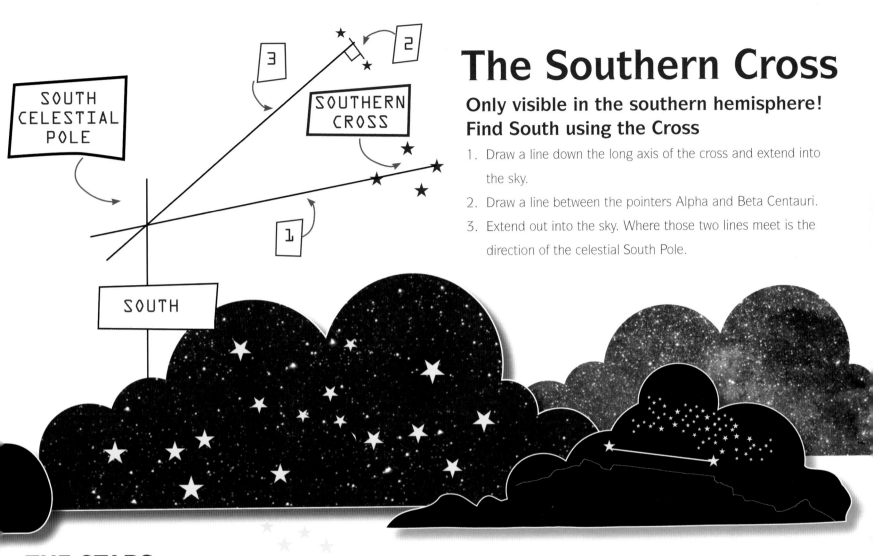

The Southern Cross

Only visible in the southern hemisphere!
Find South using the Cross

1. Draw a line down the long axis of the cross and extend into the sky.
2. Draw a line between the pointers Alpha and Beta Centauri.
3. Extend out into the sky. Where those two lines meet is the direction of the celestial South Pole.

SOUTH CELESTIAL POLE

SOUTHERN CROSS

SOUTH

THE STARS

Fomalhaut: This star may be Ntshuma, the Tswana 'kiss me' star, said to indicate the time for lovers to part before their parents discover them.

Achernar: Called Senakane by the Sotho-Tswana, the dawn rising of this bright star was ill-omened. The Pedi considered this time of the year to be full of danger.

Regulus, Arcturus: Known to the G/wi Bushmen as the 'fire-finisher', which only sets when the firewood has been exhausted.

Canopus: North Sotho villagers traditionally kept an early-morning watch for the first dawn rising of Naka, their name for Canopus, the second-brightest star in the night sky. The man who first saw it was awarded a cow by the chief. The appearance of Naka marked the beginning of the dry season, a time of war, initiation ceremonies, rainmaking rituals and divination.

The constellation Mensa is the only constellation to be named after a geographical feature on planet Earth. Mensa (Latin for 'table') is named after Table Mountain in Cape Town! The cloud-like mass above the table is one of our neighbouring galaxies called 'the large Magellanic cloud'. This resembles the cloud cover we often see over Table Mountain, with Mensa just below.

AN AFRICAN MYTH

A form of moon worship, or reverence, was common in traditional Africa. Amongst the Khoi-Khoi, the moon was the Lord of Light and Life, and new moon was a time of celebration. A Zulu tale tells that meteors result when celestial cattle rush off to better pastures in another part of the sky. Their hooves break through the floor of the sky, creating streaks that soon fill up with mud.

MADIBA
SAYS SOME
WISE
WORDS.

NELSON ROLIHLAHLA MANDELA

Nelson

This name was given to him on his first day at school by his teacher, Miss Mdingane.

Rolihlahla

This is Mandela's birth name, given to him by his father. It is isiXhosa for 'troublemaker'.

Madiba

This is the name of the clan of which Mr Mandela is a member. It was the name of a Thembu chief who ruled in the Transkei in the eighteenth century and is used as a sign of great respect.

EDUCATION is the most powerful weapon you can use to **CHANGE THE WORLD.**

... after climbing a **GREAT** hill, one only finds that there are many more hills to climb.

I hate the practice of **RACE DISCRIMINATION** and in my hatred I am sustained by the fact that the overwhelming majority of mankind hate it equally

There can be no keener **revelation** of a society's soul than the way in which it treats its **children.**

For to be **free** is not merely to cast off one's chains, but to live in a way that respects and enhances the **FREEDOM** of others.

It always seems **IMPOSSIBLE** until it's done.

The **BRAVE MAN** is not he who does not feel afraid, but he who **CONQUERS** that **FEAR.**

To make **PEACE** with an enemy, one must work with that enemy and that **ENEMY** becomes your partner.

REAL LEADERS must be ready to **sacrifice** all for the **freedom** of their people.

People are human beings, produced by the **SOCIETY** in which they live. **YOU ENCOURAGE** people by seeing good in them.

We accord a person **dignity** by assuming that they are **good**, that they share the human qualities we ascribe to **OURSELVES.**

I learned that **COURAGE** is not the absence of fear, but the **triumph** over it.

THE GREATEST SHOAL ON EARTH

23 000 DOLPHINS

100 000 CAPE GANNETS

MILLIONS OF SARDINES

THOUSANDS OF SHARKS

Each year during May through July, a cold northerly current causes millions of sardines to gather in shoals and move north. Visible by satellite, the shoals measuring more than seven kilometres long, 1.5 kilometres wide and 30 metres deep, run up the coast from the Agulhas Bank towards Mozambique, a distance of more than 1 000 kilometres. Inexplicably leaving the nutrient-rich feeding grounds of the Cape for emptier sub-tropical climes, the silvery, swirling swarm becomes fodder for those higher up the food chain. Pursued relentlessly by thousands upon thousands of dolphins, sharks, seals, whales and gannets, these creatures' feeding frenzy spawns the greatest faunal event on earth. As many as 23 000 bottlenose and common dolphins expertly herd the sardines towards shallow waters where the little fish form massive, heaving bait balls measuring up to 20 metres in diameter. Super-pods of dolphins, whales and sharks sweep through the balls, gorging on massive mouthfuls of fish, while voracious seabirds plummet from the skies above like fighter planes, scooping out their victims with ease. Then, almost as soon as it's begun, it's all over and the sea becomes calm and seemingly lifeless once again.

BASIC RULES FOR DRIVING IN GAUTENG

Indicators will give away your next move. A real Gauteng motorist never uses them.

Never, ever come to a complete stop at a stop sign. No one expects it and it will only result in you being rear ended.

IN SOUTH AFRICA, YOU ARE WHAT YOU DRIVE

The faster you drive through a red light, the smaller the chance you have of getting hit.

On average, at least three cars can still go through an intersection after the light has turned red. It's people not adhering to this basic principle that cause the big traffic jams during rush hour.

Remember that the goal of every Gauteng driver is to get there first by whatever means necessary.

If you drive an SUV, it says you're an adventurer, even if it's never been off road in a game park or travelled over a rocky riverbed. So you might need to throw a little mud over it to impress the neighbours. If you drive a BMW, it means you're upwardly mobile, like to push the accelerator to the floorboard and are well on your way to one day owning a Mercedes SLK. That's if your beamer isn't highjacked before you get there.

Under no circumstance should you leave a safe distance between you and the car in front of you, or the space will be filled by two Golfs, a BMW and a Getz putting you in an even more dangerous situation.

Braking is to be done as hard and late as possible to ensure that your ABS kicks in giving you a nice relaxing foot massage as the brake pedal pulsates. For those of you without ABS, it's a chance to stretch your legs.

If you've put mag wheels and a spoiler on your old twin-cam Toyota and loaded its boot with woofers and tweeters, then you're probably a cool Indian guy who's into drag racing, clubbing and chilli bites. And if you drive a Tata Ma Chance double cab with dodgy brakes and no tread on the tyres at 180 kph on the road to Babanango, you're a risk taker and could be heading for the Pearly Gates (or the other place) anytime soon.

WARNING

FASTEN BRASTRAPS AND REMOVE DENTURES VERY BUMPY ROAD

Kosi Bay Bush Camp ↑

072 150 6382

THIS IS A "GO **VERY SLOW** ROAD"

- WATCH OUT FOR **BABY PLOVERS** ! Smaller than a golf ball !
- **TORTOISES** ! The size of a R5 coin !
- **POTHOLES** ! The size of Kimberley se gat !

20

AJUBATUS marine rescue

DRIVING STYLES

In truth, we are defined as much by our driving styles as our accents or the clothing we wear.

Both hands in air gesturing, both feet on accelerator, head turned to talk to someone in back seat – that's Matubatuba .

One hand on wheel, one hand on newspaper, foot solidly on accelerator - that's Sandton.

Both hands on wheel, eyes shut, both feet on brake, quivering in terror – that's Bloemfontein driving in Johannesburg.

One hand on wheel, one hand out of window - that's Durban.

One hand on wheel, one hand on horn - that's Soweto.

One hand on horn, one hand greeting, one ear on cellphone, one ear listening to loud music, foot on accelerator, eyes on female pedestrian, conversation with someone driving vehicle alongside - that's a Diepkloof taxi driver.

ARRIVE ALIVE
www.arrivealive.co.za

SADD
SOUTH AFRICANS AGAINST DRUNK DRIVING
www.sadd.org.za

Road Failure Ahead
Umgwaco Mubi Embili
600 m Ahead

NOTICE
All drivers of 4 x 4s
- Engage 4WD
- Select low range
- Lock all hubs + diff
- Cross your fingers
Everyone else just drive normally.
(Don't worry 4WD is not needed but it helps them justify the cost of buying or hiring one)

GO AHEAD DRINK AND DRIVE

↱  JAIL

↰ HOSPITAL

→ MORGUE

Text courtesy of Sarah Britten. The Art of the South African Insult and James Clarke

WORLD'S LARGEST OPEN WATER SWIM

17 000 swimmers

The Guinness Book of Records officially recognised the **Midmar Mile**, held across Midmar Dam near Pietermaritzburg, as the world's largest open water swimming event.

The **Midmar Mile** captures the true spirit of sport, featuring participants from five to 80 years old, able-bodied and disabled swimmers, amateurs and world-class competitors.

Photo courtesy of SA Tourism

THE BIGGEST

WORLD'S LARGEST ULTRA MARATHON

15 000 runners

The approximately 90 km between Durban and Pietermaritzburg, including five hills, annually test the muscle, sinew and mental strength of thousands of competitors from all over the world. The **Comrades Marathon** epitomises the great warm spirit and genuine camaraderie of all the athletes.

Photo courtesy of SA Tourism

WORLD'S LARGEST INDIVIDUALLY TIMED CYCLE RACE

The Cape Argus
Pick n Pay Cycle Tour
35 000 cyclists

The first event outside Europe to be included in the International Cycling Union's Golden Bike Series, the 109 km route around Cape Town is as spectacular as it is gruelling. It is the world's largest individually timed cycle race.

RACES IN THE WORLD

WORLD'S LARGEST CANOE MARATHON

The Hansa Powerade
Dusi Canoe Marathon
1 400 paddlers

The marathon winds 125 km through KwaZulu-Natal's Valley of a Thousand Hills, to where the uMgeni and uMsundusi rivers meet and compress the water into a churning mass of whirlpools challenging even the strongest of athletes.

I am an African… I owe my being to the hills and valleys, the mountains and glades… to the Khoi and the San whose desolate souls haunt the great expanses of the beautiful Cape. I am formed of the migrants who left Europe to find a new home in our native land… of the Malay slaves who came from the east…of the warrior men and women that Hintsa and Sekhukhune led, the patriots that Cetshwayo and Mphephu took to battle… I am the grandchild who lays fresh flowers on the Boer graves. Being part of all these people, and in the knowledge that none dare contest that assertion, I shall claim that - I am an African. Today it feels good to be an African.

Extracts from Thabo Mbeki's speech delivered on the occasion of the proposal of South Africa's new constitution, 8 May 1996

The rising sun is a symbol of rebirth and the source of life, light and the wholeness of humanity.

The protea is an emblem of the beauty of our land and the flowering of our nation.

The tusks of the elephant symbolise wisdom, strength, moderation and eternity.

The human figures are a testament to our common humanity and heritage. They are greeting each other, symbolising unity.

The secretary bird, symbolising protection of the nation, is a messenger of the heavens that brings grace to the earth.

The spear and knobkierie symbolise defence and authority. They are lying down to depict peace.

The shield shows both identity and spiritual defence.

The ears of wheat are an emblem of fertility that symbolise growth and the development of our potential.

The motto means - Unity in Diversity

The Coat Of Arms, which exemplifies the extraordinary creativity of our people through the ages, inspires our united and diverse nation to shine as brightly as the sun. The words contained within the Coat Of Arms are in the ancient /Xam language of the San people. It calls for the nation to unite in a common sense of belonging and national pride.

To pronounce the three clicks in the phrase **!KE E:/XARRA //KE**

! - Place the tip of the tongue against the gum root in the middle of the mouth and click hard. This is similar to the 'Q' sound in Zulu, for example in Iqanda (egg).

K - Not pronounced and followed by a short 'e' sound, as in rest.

E: - A very long 'e' which is pronounced with a dip in the voice, like a sheep bleating; similar to e'-he'-he-he'.

/ - Place the tongue softly against the root of the teeth in the middle front of the mouth, then click with the middle of the tongue. The sound is similar to the 'C' sound in Zulu, for example in Ucingo (telephone).

X - Similar to the prolonged 'gggg' sound in Afrikaans, leading to 'gggarra'.

// - Another click, this time with the side of the tongue against the palate, similar to the 'X' sound in the word Xhosa. The K is not pronounced.

SURFING LEGEND
SHAUN TOMSON'S TWELVE SIMPLE LESSONS FOR RIDING THROUGH LIFE.

1 I WILL NEVER TURN MY BACK ON THE OCEAN

2 I WILL PADDLE AROUND THE IMPACT ZONE

3 I WILL TAKE THE DROP WITH COMMITMENT

4 I WILL NEVER FIGHT A RIP TIDE

5 I WILL ALWAYS PADDLE BACK OUT

6 I WILL WATCH OUT FOR OTHER SURFERS

7 THERE WILL ALWAYS BE ANOTHER WAVE

8 I WILL ALWAYS RIDE INTO SHORE

9 I WILL PASS ALONG MY STOKE

10 I WILL CATCH A WAVE EVERY DAY

11 ALL SURFERS ARE JOINED BY ONE OCEAN

12 I WILL HONOUR THE SPORT OF KINGS

SURFING THROUGH THE AGES

SOUTH AFRICA WAS INTRODUCED TO SURFING WHEN AMERICAN MARINES STOPPED OFF IN CAPE TOWN DURING WORLD WAR I.

THE FIRST SURFBOARDS WERE BUILT IN SA IN 1964.

IN 1968, BARON STANDER STARTED A DAILY RADIO SURF REPORT FOR DURBAN THAT WAS TO LAST FOR 34 YEARS, A WORLD RECORD.

WORLD CLASS SURF BREAKS

JEFFREY'S, EASTERN CAPE, HOME TO THE RENOWNED SUPER-TUBES, THIS FAST-BREAKING RIGHT HAS OFTEN BEEN HERALDED AS THE BEST WAVE IN THE WORLD!

BRUCE'S, ST FRANCIS BAY, PUT SOUTH AFRICA ON THE WORLD MAP WHEN IT FEATURED IN THE SURFING FILM 'ENDLESS SUMMER' IN THE SIXTIES.

NEW PIER, DURBAN IS A FAST AND HOLLOW TUBE THAT SUCKS OVER SAND STRAIGHT FROM TAKE-OFF.

MDUMBE, WILD COAST, THIS PERFECT POINT BREAK COUGHS UP WAVES THAT RUN FOR 800 M.

SURFER SLANG!

FULLY: AN AFFIRMATION TO A QUESTION OR STATEMENT MADE BY ANOTHER SURFER.

KICK OUT: AT THE END OF YOUR RIDE, YOU KICK OUT OF A WAVE IN A CONTROLLED WAY.

GUN IT: THE ACT OF GAINING SPEED TO MAKE IT THROUGH A TRICKY SECTION.

AMPED: FULL OF ENERGY, INDUCED BY ADRENALIN, FEELING WIRED OR HIGH ON FEAR.

PARK OFF: TO CHILL OUT, SIT DOWN OR RELAX.

BOMB: A POWERFUL OR PERFECTLY SHAPED WAVE.

JOPL: A PARTY OR TO HAVE FUN.

HOWZIT: A GREETING, SHORT FOR HOW IS IT?

JACKING: A SWELL THAT IS PITCHING TOWARDS THE ACT OF BREAKING.

RIDING GIANTS AT
DUNGEONS

LOCATED OFF THE SENTINEL IN HOUT BAY, CAPE TOWN WHERE NATURE CHALLENGES SURFERS WITH THUMPING

RECORD BREAKING

70 FT (20 M) WAVES

GUNNING IT IN
SURFING
SOUTH AFRICA

'Across countries and cultures surfers are connected not by nationality or religion or politics or age or sex, but by their experience riding waves' Shaun Tomson.

PICTURED: GREG LONG RIDING A 65 FT WAVE AT DUNGEONS TO WIN THE WORLD BILLABONG XXL BIG WAVE AWARD.

FOR SALE – POTENTIAL
Mortuary or Fruit Packing/
Meat Processing Facility

200 m² cold room; 100 m² tiled area;
300 m² factory space; 50 m² office space.
Excellent access, plenty of parking.
Central Midlands area.

Telephone 084 573 3911

SITEKI BURIAL SOCIETY

OFF CUTS FOR SALE

VREKGEWERK
Junie   2005   Julie

ONLY IN SOUTH AFRICA

DIAMOND
COLLECTION

 'GENTLEMEN, THIS IS THE ROCK ON WHICH THE FUTURE SUCCESS OF SOUTH AFRICA WILL BE BUILT.'

{ These were the words of Colonial Secretary, Sir Richard Southey, in an address to the Cape Assembly on the 83 carat diamond, the Star of South Africa, found in 1866. }

THE FIRST DIAMOND FOUND IN SOUTH AFRICA

'You have got to be joking. I will never take your hard-earned money for a worthless pebble. Take it. The children, I am sure, will pick up many more,' said Mrs Jacobs in 1867 to a farmer, Schalk Jacobus van Niekerk, who wanted to buy a shining pebble that her children were playing with near Kimberley. He wasn't joking because the pebble turned out to be the Eureka, the first diamond to be found in South Africa.

THE LARGEST ROUGH DIAMOND EVER FOUND

Weighing 3 106 carats, the Cullinan diamond was named after Sir Thomas Cullinan, the owner of the Premier diamond mine near Pretoria, where it was discovered. It was cut into three large parts in Amsterdam. The largest polished gem was called Cullinan I or the Great Star of Africa, weighing 530.2 carats - it is the largest polished diamond in the world. The diamond is mounted in the head of the British royal sceptre. The second largest gem, known as Cullinan II (or the Lesser Star of Africa), weighs 317.4 carats and forms part of the British crown.

THE MOST EXPENSIVE DIAMOND

{ A vivid blue diamond weighing 7.03 carats was extracted in 2009 from the Cullinan mine and sold a year later at a Sotheby's auction for R70 million ($9.5 million), the highest price ever paid per carat for any gemstone. }

THE CULLINAN DIAMOND
is the same size as a 330 ml soft drink can.

THE DIAMOND COMPANY DE BEERS,
founded by Cecil John Rhodes, today markets 40% of the world's rough diamonds.

THE START OF THE BIGGEST MAN-MADE HOLE IN THE WORLD

Rumour has it that Fleetwood Rawstone and his team of prospectors, known as the Red Cap Party, had staked their claim on the Northern Cape farm called Vooruitzicht, in the hope of finding fortune and fame. They had a cook named Damon who was frequently drunk and, as punishment, he was sent off into the hills and told to return once he had found a diamond. Damon returned a few days later, sober as a judge, carrying a few shiny stones. The date was the 16th July 1871. The hill on which Damon found the diamonds became one of the richest diamond mines in the world and is today the biggest man-made hole in the world.

Photo courtesy The Big Hole, Kimberley

THE KIMBERLEY HOLE

The Kimberley Hole is the biggest man-made hole in the world. It is as deep as Table Mountain is high. The 'Big Hole' in Kimberley was closed down as a mine in 1914.

During its 43-year existence, over 25 million tons of soil and rock were excavated and over three tons of diamonds removed – which would fit into three average sized bathtubs.

THE MOST INNOVATIVE WAY TO SMUGGLE DIAMONDS

To smuggle diamonds out of mines you had to be extremely innovative. One smart fellow used a homing pigeon. He carried a small lunch box, containing the homing pigeon; this was never checked at the gates where workers entered.

He attached a harness filled with sizable diamonds onto the pigeon's back and released the bird inside the mine premises. When he arrived home, he found the pigeon waiting, with the diamonds.

TRIVIA

Diamonds were formed at least 990 million years ago, although some are estimated to be as much as 4.25 billion years old, therefore pre-dating life on this planet.

To produce a single one-carat diamond, 250 tons of earth will be mined.

Diamonds are formed at pressures of around fifty thousand times that of atmospheric pressure at the Earth's surface, and at temperatures between 900° C and 1 300° C.

A DIAMOND IS THE HARDEST NATURALLY OCCURRING KNOWN SUBSTANCE ON EARTH.

1. Who sold more concert tickets in the last decade than any other act, topping even Celine Dion, Madonna, U2, Bruce Springsteen and Britney Spears?
Clue: He was born in Johannesburg, attended St Stithians College and left South Africa to avoid compulsory military service.

2. Who is known to South Africans as 'Mama Africa' and was the first black woman to receive a Grammy Award for her album recorded with Harry Belafonte?
Clue: She performed at the Rumble in the Jungle match between Mohammed Ali and George Foreman, sang at President Kennedy's birthday party and performed with Paul Simon on his Graceland tour.

3. Who said 'Gay and lesbian Madonna is only big within white pop. I am beyond pop. I am life!' and was subsequently dubbed 'Madonna of the townships' by Time magazine? Clue: She was also know by millions of fans worldwide as 'MaBrrr'.

4. Which Sophiatown jazz singer and former beauty queen became Africa's first acknowledged international female actor in 1949?
Clue: She became the nation's sweetheart and was known as the South African Billie Holiday and the African Marilyn Monroe. As a measure of her mass support, her name became synonymous with 'all right' or 'okay' in township slang.

5. Who is the only South African artist to have a record signed to Motown Records? Clue: He did not smoke marijuana, cigarettes or drink alcohol and was a man on a mission to make the world a better place. He won 'Best Selling African Recording Artist' at the World Music Awards and his first two albums were the best selling discs ever in South Africa. He was the first black South African artist to be played on a white radio station in South Africa and he shared the stage with international artists such as Peter Gabriel and Sting.

6. Which group is named after their hometown, the colour of their prize goat and the Zulu word for axe which was a reference to the way the group would 'chop down' the opposition? Clue: They have won three Grammy Awards.

7. Which musician, whose albums broke all international sales records in France, Switzerland and Belgium, was made an adopted son of a Zulu chief and has appeared at all four of Nelson Mandela's 46664 Aids Awareness Concerts?
Clue: He faced repeated concert shutdowns and threats because his band angered the then apartheid government.

8. Which double Grammy award-winning group performed at a New Year function for Oprah Winfrey and 200 of her VIP guests, including Mariah Carey, Mary J Blige, Tina Turner, Patti Labelle, Sydney Poitier and Quincy Jones? Clue: Together with Peter Gabriel, they recorded the song 'Down To Earth' for the Disney movie 'Wall-E' and they feature on Josh Groban's latest album 'Collection'. They have also shared the stage with international superstars U2, Celine Dion, Queen and Diana Ross.

1. DAVE MATTHEWS OF THE DAVE MATTHEWS BAND
2. MIRIAM MAKEBA
3. BRENDA FASSIE
4. DOLLY RATHEBE
5. LUCKY DUBE
6. LADYSMITH BLACK MAMBAZO
7. JOHNNY CLEGG
8. SOWETO GOSPEL CHOIR

9. Which group appeared via the direct satellite link-up to the Freddie Mercury tribute in London (to an estimated audience of a billion people) and performed in front of 200 000 people at the Paris 'SOS Racism' concert? Clue: They were the main music theme with the ABC worldwide broadcast of Nelson Mandela's release and later headlined at his inauguration.

10. Which artist sold more than one million copies of her CD in three weeks, becoming the fastest selling CD in the history of South African music? Clue: She received votes from over ten million listeners to win the best local established artist in the 1993 Coca Cola Full Blast Music Show and the OKTV Awards as Best South African Female Artist for the period 1989/1990.

11. Who was Nelson Mandela referring to when he said 'You will always be my Princess of Africa'? He also refers to her as his 'dear daughter'. Clue: As a young performer, she was also the first black child to appear on South African television in 1981.

12. Which performer is a vociferous activist who appeared on the infamous 'Chris Hani death list' and is the great-great grandson of General Louis Botha, South Africa's first Prime Minister? Clue: The musical of his multifaceted life sold 20 000 tickets a month in advance.

13. Which South African opera singer had a permanent appointment at the Vienna State Opera and was awarded both a Medal of Honour for Music by the South African Academy of Science and Art and was bestowed the title of Kammersängerin by the President of the Austrian Republic? Clue: She sang the title role in a Viennese premiere of Die Schweigsame Frau.

14. Who was initially unwilling to record the song 'Moon river', the theme tune of the film Breakfast at Tiffany's starring Audrey Hepburn, because he did not understand the lyric reference to 'my huckleberry friend' but was subsequently convinced after seeing the film? Clue: He went on a 20-city tour of Britain with the Beatles.

15. Who led the Duke Ellington Orchestra in the recording of his masterpiece, 'Mannenberg', acknowledged by most as one of South Africa's greatest musical compositions? Clue: He was christened as Adolph Johannes Brand, was known as Dollar Brand and changed his name when he converted to Islam.

16. Which Grammy award-winning musician has composed soundtracks for 29 Hollywood movies featuring actors such as Will Smith, Nicholas Cage, Denzel Washington and Samuel L Jackson and has worked with Seal, Michael Jackson, Manfred Mann, Tina Turner and Bob Dylan, amongst others? Clue: He was also a member of Rabbitt, South Africa's most successful rock act.

17. Which performer drew a bigger crowd to Sun City than Frank Sinatra did when he opened at the Superbowl? Clue: He would give roses to the women in the front of the audience at all his concerts.

9. MANGO GROOVE
10. REBECCA MALOPE 12. STEVE HOFMEYR 15. ABDULLAH IBRAHIM
11. YVONNE CHAKA CHAKA 13. MIMI COERTSE 16. TREVOR RABIN
14. DANNY WILLIAMS 17. BLES BRIDGES

said like a South....... african.

A SOUTH AFRICAN LOVE POEM

Of course I love you Bokkie
I only smaak you dik
You cook and clean and iron my shirts
And look after me when I'm sick
So your bum is only big hey
But I don't mind a bit of flab
It means that when I'm lekker jags
There's something there to grab
So your belly isn't flat no more
I tell you I don't care
So long as when I druk you
I can get my arms round there
No stukkie who is your age
Has nice round perky breasts
They just gave to gravity
But I know you did your best
I'm not tuning kak now
I never tell you lies
But I think it's lank sexy
That you've got dimples on your thighs
So no matter what you look like
I'll always love you Dear
Now shut up while the rugby's on
And fetch me another beer!

GOOD NIGHT AROUND
THE WORLD

NETHERLANDS : Goeden nagt
AUSTRALIA: Night, mate
USA: Good nite
GERMANY: Gute Nacht
SOUTH AFRICA: Are the doors locked,
are the windows closed, is the car put
away, is the alarm activated and have
you fed the Rottweilers? Sleep tight,
don't worry about the lights, Eskom
will put them out.

WHEN SPEAKING SOUTH AFRICAN

A bathing suit is a 'swimming costume'
A traffic light is a 'robot'
An elevator is a 'lift'
A hood is a 'bonnet'
A trunk is a 'boot'
A pickup truck is a 'bakkie'
A barbeque is a 'braai'
A sausage is 'boerewors'
A felt tip pen is a 'koki'
A baby's diaper is a 'nappy'
A pair of sneakers is 'tackies'

SOUTH AFRICAN SPOKEN BY INDIANS

an' all – at the end of a sentence
meaning 'and everything'
hit a luck - expression, to have met with good fortune
laanie (or larnie) - Smart guy, as in 'well-to-do'
late - used to refer to someone who has died
choon (or tjoon) - to tell someone something
onetime - 'without delay' or definitely
ballie - an older male
laitie - a younger person
pozzy - house or home
ou - a person

FROM ZULU OR XHOSA ORIGIN

ayeye – to express wonder and happiness
fundi - expert
gogga - bug (from Khoikhoi xo-xon, creeping things)
haw! - expression of disbelief
hayibo! - wow! (from Zulu, 'definitely not')
indaba - conference (from Zulu, 'a matter for discussion')
laduma! – soccer cheer when someone scores
(literally: 'it thunders')
shongololo - millipede (from the word 'to roll up')
toyi-toyi - protest-dancing

WHAT TO SAY WHEN ...

You are totally outraged or surprised ... jislaaik
You want to express how nice something is ... lekker
You are not exactly sure how long you will be ... now now
You will be a little longer than 'now now' ... just now
You want to say 'what ever' ... jawellnofine
You hurt yourself ... eina
You need to respond but have nothing to add... izit?
You want to give your statement more effect ... hey
You are not sure what to answer ... ja, nee
You want to say everything is good and in order ... sharp sharp
You want to express surprise or disbelief ... eish!

WHAT TO CALL...

A friend – chommie
A girlfriend – tjerrie
A mate – boet
An older female – tannie
Your father – ou ballie
Your grandmother - gogo
An idiot – moegoe

RING RING RING!

NO-ONE SAYS IT QUITE LIKE AN AFRIKANER

poep - fart
domkop - idiot
ek sê - I say
voetsek – go away, scram
howzit – how is it going? how are you?
kokolol - referring to low-class workers
nooit - never, no way, unbelievable!
jol - to have fun or a party
Babbelas - (abbreviated barbie) a hangover
bliksem – to punch someone or as an expression of surprise
dik bek - grumpy, in a huff (literally: 'thick mouth')
dinges - thingamabob, a wotzit or a whatchamacallit
skelm – suspicious or untrustworthy person

Be

105

www.awesomesa.co.za

Awesome SA is a movement of South Africans who are committed to positively influencing the future. Awesome SA's vision is to create a better life for all through awareness, on a national front, of the initiatives by individuals and business to uplift this country. Through their newsletters and website, Awesome SA encourages South Africans to recognise the good in our country and take responsibility for changing that which is not.

Individual South Africans for a United South Africa!

We often cry 'Why doesn't someone do something about this?' Then we realise we are that someone.

www.homecomingrevolution.co.za

South Africa is a dynamic place where anything is possible and there are many opportunities. The Homecoming Revolution encourages and facilitates South Africans living abroad to return to South Africa. They provide practical information about returning to South Africa, as well as offering companies in South Africa an opportunity to link SA talent with international expertise to help fill the skills gap.

You only feel alive once your head is where your heart's always been!

www.sarocks.co.za

SA Rocks shows the good and positive things emerging out of our great nation. Voted one of South Africa's favourite blogs, SA Rocks finds solutions to the glaringly obvious problems that our country faces, and pushes the people of South Africa to stand up and be counted. SA Rocks reminds us that there are unmistakable beauties present in South Africa, from tourism venues to smiling faces, incredibly gifted and talented individuals and teams.

Love where you live or live where you love. I choose South Africa!

'You may never know what results come from your action. But if you do nothing, there will be no result'
Mahatma Gandhi

www.sagoodnews.co.za

South Africa: The Good News is a news website that highlights the positive developments in South Africa. The news mass-media tend to focus on the bad news and largely ignore the positive developments in this county, creating an 'information imbalance'. The goal of SA Good News is to address this reality/perception gap and showcase South Africa as a country of positive development, excitement, opportunity, interest and a potential travel and investment destination.

We like to stimulate dialogue and debate. We like to offer a fresh perspective!

www.southafrica.info

If you're a South African at home or abroad, or if you're interested in visiting or investing in the country, this site is for you. Updated each day with news and features, the site carries interactive maps, downloads, RSS feeds and photo galleries. SouthAfrica.info is one of South Africa's most popular and informative websites, with more than two million page views a month and 300 000 unique users from all around the world.

Talking about a country that's alive with possibility!

'All movements coming together for good, can create an unstoppable force for change- but it starts with you...' Movement for Good

STOP CRIME SAY HELLO
www.sayhello.co.za

The Stop Crime Say Hello message is simple: by actively respecting and dignifying one another and our environment, each of us can help create a society in which crime does not flourish. Small, positive actions, repeated often, create big change. By using your unique talents and gifts you can help to create a safe, peaceful South Africa. All over the country people are getting involved. Join other South Africans and shift the mind set away from fighting crime towards creating peace.

Do something small - make a big difference!

join the positive vibe!

alien love affair

At the age of 50, KwaZulu-Natal-born Elizabeth Klarer allegedly gave birth to a child whom she named Ayling. Her lover was a man named Akon who had grey eyes, fair golden skin, aquiline features and straight white hair. Akon was an astrophysicist from the planet Meton. The birth occurred during the 1950s when fear of communism was rife and Elizabeth reputedly had a close encounter with Russian cosmonauts who tried to kidnap her when she returned to earth in 1956. Born in the same year that Halley's Comet crossed our skies, Elizabeth had always expressed an interest in things astral. She had her first encounter with a UFO at the age of seven and as an adult worked as a meteorologist. Despite detractors to the theory of UFOs, Klarer is taken very seriously by UFO societies today. She attracted international attention with her story and received correspondence from all over the world, including professors and academic institutes. **Is it possible that Klarer's story may one day be verified by alien visitors?**

the Kalahari's hidden city

In 1885, Gilarmi Farini, an American showman and adventurer, discovered in the Kalahari what he claimed was a Lost City. After travelling through the Kalahari, Farini stopped at Mier and saw the ruins of a 'city of a great nation that existed perhaps thousands of years ago.' Farini reported excavating a pavement made of huge blocks that had once formed what appeared to be a monumental Maltese cross. Farini's claims sparked many expeditions to the area by hopeful treasure hunters looking for the Lost City. German scientist-explorer, Dr Hans Schinz, calculated that during his trek Farini covered the distance of almost 3 000 miles by ox-wagon in sandy terrain in less than 50 days. He would have had to average over 400 miles per week, which was an impossible feat. Despite Schinz's doubts, could Farini's reports of the Kalahari's hidden city be true? **Who knows what may still be lying beneath the constant shifting of the Kalahari sands?**

the tokoloshe

Many urban and rural women use bricks as a protection against the Tokoloshe. That is, they raise their beds on bricks. This is so that the Tokoloshe can't reach them while they are sleeping. The Tokoloshe is the evil creation of a man who murdered nine women in his quest to become a witchdoctor. He is hairy, has the face of a monkey, can make himself invisible and, other than attacking unsuspecting women, is responsible for all sorts of mischief. The Tokoloshe has an exceptionally long penis (which it hitches over its shoulder as it walks) and is, fortunately, a dwarf. **One wonders how much commotion this creature would cause if the African women no longer raised their beds with bricks?**

a giant footprint

Imprinted in solid rock on a hill in Mpumalanga is the perfect outline of a human being's left foot. No ordinary footprint this one – it is two metres in length, making its owner an 11 m tall giant. The rock has baffled geologists and their expert opinions remain inconclusive. Most agree the footprint is too perfect to be the result of natural weathering, whilst others say it is a natural footprint left in sand that has subsequently solidified into rock over hundreds of thousands of years. The local people refer to the owner as the 'Heavenly Princess' whilst others refer to the script in the Judeo-Christian Bible that mentions the time when giants walked on the earth. **One wonders if science will ever reveal the true cause of the footprint.**

FACT

hidden treasure

Legend has it that somewhere below the escarpment lies the buried treasure of the Kruger Millions. Just before the end of the Anglo Boer War, fearful of a British takeover, Paul Kruger was said to have ordered the entire national treasury, made up of coins and gold bullion, to be transported and hidden in the countryside. Kruger subsequently fled to the Netherlands where he died in exile. Most of his faithful generals and aides also died in the war. The rough location of the treasure is rumoured to be in or around the Kruger National Park. **But where is the exact location of the Republic's treasury, totalling billions of Rands in today's money?**

elephant graveyard

Somewhere in the Kaokoveld lies a great cemetery, a graveyard to which dying elephants, guided by instinct, make their way. Other animals steer clear, afraid of this barren stretch of land, filled only with shifting sands, bleached bones and the hush of death. The only humans who reportedly know where Ivory Valley lies are the Herero people. These people, it is alleged, would appear from time to time carrying heavy loads of valuable ivory tusks. Asked how they had come by their valuable finds, their standard reply was: 'We found them in the bush.' They never divulged the whereabouts of their endless supply. Ivory hunters have verified the theory of an elephant graveyard by pointing out that, apart from the elephants they shot or trapped, they never came across elephant remains. The Kaokoveld at one time teemed with elephants and they and their giant spoor were easy to spot. **So where did the dying elephants go? No white hunter, it appears, will ever know.**

Sekhukhune's treasure

In the midst of the 1870s diamond rush, the Pedi people, under the leadership of Sekhukhune, provided much of the labour to the gold and diamond hunters. It is said that Sekhukhune required all the Pedi men who were working on the diggings to bring him back a diamond or a gold pound. He accumulated 'two blesbok skins of sovereigns and a gallon pot filled with diamonds ranging from the size of a pigeon's egg upwards.' Sekhukhune kept the treasure in a secret place high up in the mountains near Lydenburg. A shopkeeper named Dick Silk was one of the few people to see the treasure, consisting of diamonds as big as 30 and 40 carats, which he said 'took his breath away'. Sekhukhune, however, could not be convinced to accept Silk's offer of 1 000 gold sovereigns in exchange for the diamonds. When the British defeated Sekhukhune, they formed numerous groups to search the area for the treasure without any luck. In the meantime, Sekhukhune's successor, Chief Magoto, continued to collect diamonds and gold from the Pedi labourers. In 1908, the Transvaal Treasury and the Department of Mines officially confirmed the existence of the treasure. The treasure is then said to have been handed to Modjadji the Rain Queen who, fearing trouble during the Boer War, sent the diamonds to the malaria-infested lowveld. It is believed the messengers hid the treasure before succumbing to the deadly disease. **Can it be that to this day, the treasure remains hidden somewhere in South Africa's lowveld region?**

or fiction

CONSERVING OUR WILDLIFE

South Africa's national animal is the Springbok. The name of this agile, 80 cm tall, brown and white buck comes from the Afrikaans/Dutch 'spring', meaning to jump, and 'bok', referring to an antelope or goat. This iconic animal is known for engaging in bouts of high leaps (up to 3.5 m) when nervous or excited, in a practice known as 'pronking' from the Afrikaans/Dutch word 'pronk', meaning to show off. Springbok can reach speeds of 80-90 km/h and can jump up to 15 m at a time. The literature from the past reveals stories of animal migrations which the Afrikaners called the 'Trekbokken'. The excerpts below describe herds of Springbok and other animal groups, hundreds of kilometres long and provide an image of our countryside prior to fences, borders, hunters and poachers.

Trader Albert Jackson, the Great Karoo

I slept in the veld during the 1896 migration. Often I put my ear to the ground, and even at night, when the buck were resting, it felt like an earth tremor.

Hunter Gordon Cumming on viewing a springbok migration, the Great Karoo

I stood upon the fore-chest of my wagon for nearly two hours, lost in wonder at the scene. I had some difficulty in convincing myself that it was reality I beheld, and not the wild picture of a hunter's dream. During this time the vast legions continued streaming through the neck in the hills in one unbroken, compact phalanx.

Le Vaillant, the Overberg in 1796

The bonteboks, above all appeared in flocks of two thousand at least. I am persuaded that this day, buffaloes, antelopes of all kinds, zebras and ostriches, I had before my eyes at one time more than four or five thousand animals.

Thomas Pringle, the Overberg

We calculated we had sometimes within view not less than twenty thousand of these beautiful animals. They were probably part of one of the great migratory swarms which, after long continued droughts, sometimes inundate the colony from the northern wastes.

Sir John Fraser, on the antelope migration through Beaufort West in the Karoo during the drought of 1849

We were awakened one morning by a sound as of a strong wind before a thunderstorm, followed by the trampling of thousands of all kinds of game – wildebeest, blesbok, springboks, kwaggas, elands, antelopes – which filled the streets and gardens and, as far as one could see, covered the whole country, grazing off everything eatable before them, drinking up the waters in the furrows, fountains and dams wherever they could get at them; and, as the creatures were all in a more or less impoverished condition, the people killed them in numbers in their gardens. It took about three days before the whole of the trekbokken had passed, and it left our country as if a fire had raged over it. It was indeed a wonderful sight.

Source: Place by Bridget Hilton-Barber & Pat Hopkins

On Red Alert

South Africa has 43 animal species and 16 plant species which are listed as critically endangered, meaning they face an extremely high risk of extinction in the wild. A further 87 animal species and 16 plant species are listed as endangered, thus facing a very high risk of extinction.

- The majestic Blue Crane is South Africa's national bird. Currently, under 25 000 Blue Cranes are left in South Africa, yet a century ago 100 000 used to populate the region.
- Cycads grow very slowly. Certain species take 100 years to grow less than one metre in height. Some cycad colonies have been virtually wiped out by collectors seeking a sample.
- Two of the four critically endangered frog species are the Table Mountain Ghost Frog, which is found nowhere else on earth other than in four streams on Table Mountain, and the Micro Frog, whose only remaining population is in the indigenous vegetation inside Kenilworth Racecourse Conservation area.
- The wild dog is Southern Africa's most endangered large carnivore. Its population fluctuates between 200 and 400 animals.
- The population of Black Rhino has declined by over 90% over the last 60-odd years. With a population of several hundred thousand at the start of the twentieth century, they reached a low of under 2 500 in 1992.
- There are less than 250 Riverine Rabbits in the world. They are not like other rabbits however, as they give birth to approximately four offspring only during their lifetime.
- Of the 1.5 million African Penguin population estimated in 1910, only some 10% remained at the end of the twentieth century.
- The Blue Swallow is one of South Africa's most endangered birds with only 85 pairs remaining in the country.
- There are less than 1 500 Southern Ground Hornbills left in South Africa. The dominant pair only breeds on average every two and a half years and successful fledglings only occur every nine years.
- The Short-eared Trident Bat and Rendall's Serotine Bat are both listed as critically endangered. Bats are an essential part of many ecosystems in Southern Africa. Insect-eating bats can devour up to ten times their weight in insects every night and are the only natural pollinators of the Baobab and Sausage Tree.

Today, Southern Africa's illegal international trade in rare animals is booming, with creatures found locally now available to order on the internet. Trading in mammals, birds and reptiles from species-rich Africa has grown rapidly since the early 1990s, causing fears that endangered species could be lost in many African countries. The industry's worldwide estimated worth is now more than R1 billion (£100m) a year.

'African wildlife is not only the heritage of the African people but also that of the International Community. In light of the pressures of modern society on land in Africa such as population growth, industrialisation and the need for more agricultural land to provide for the increasing human needs, wildlife is under threat on our continent. It is the responsibility of all to ensure the continuation of this precious heritage by ensuring a long-term sustainable environment for wildlife to flourish in partnership with man providing socio-economic benefits and biodiversity integrity. The time to act is now, before it's too late.'

John O'Brien,
Group Ecologist, Mantis Dubai World Africa, recipient of several international conservation awards including 'Leading Conservation Company', *for Shamwari Game Reserve* for 13 consecutive years, at The World Travel Awards.

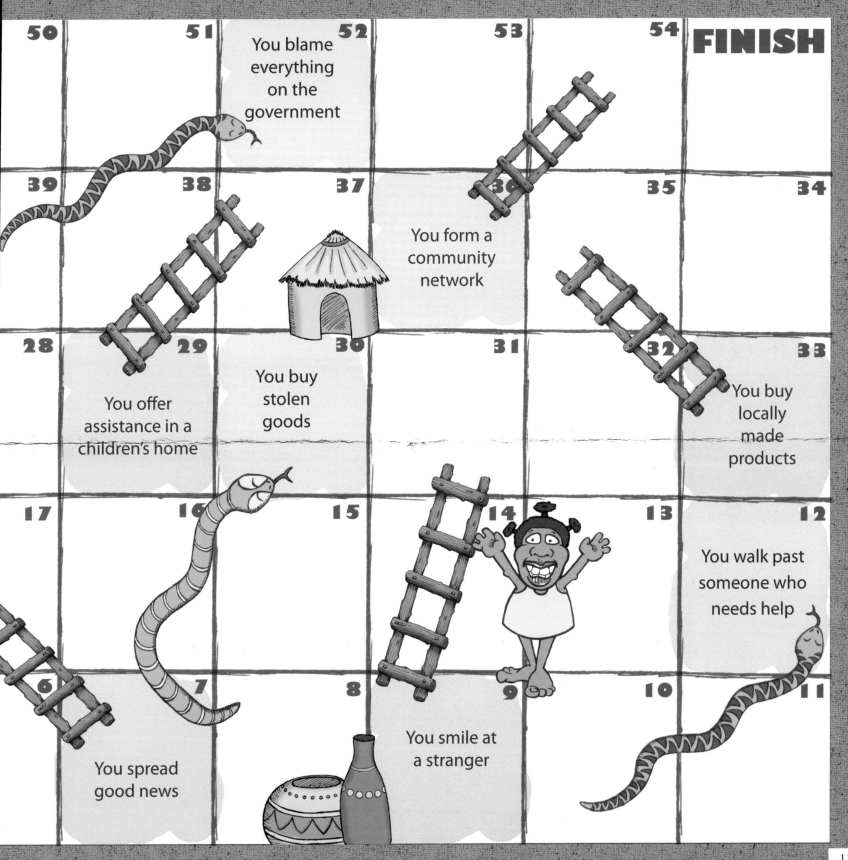

113

Fest

After Edinburgh, the NATIONAL ARTS FESTIVAL in Grahamstown is the SECOND LARGEST in the world

SALON LORRAINE

114

JANUARY

Kleinmond Big
Blue Festival
Cape Town
Minstrel Carnival
Nylstroom
Druiwefees

FEBRUARY

Gauteng FNB
Dance Umbrella
Port Elizabeth
Chillie Festival
Wynberg
Barleycarn Music Festival
Paarl
Cape Country Picnic
Nelspruit
Marula Festival

MARCH

Lambert's Baai
Crayfish Festival
Dullstroom Tonteldoos
Peach Festival
Uniondale
AppleFestival
Cape Town
Jazz Festival
Durban
Time Of The Writer
Rawsonville
Hanepoot Festival
Oppikoppi
Easter Festival

APRIL

Underberg
SplashyFen
Music Festival
Prince Albert Town
Olive Festival
Philippolis
Witblits Festival
Oudtshoorn
Klein Karoo Kunstefees
Nelson Mandela Bay
Splash Fest
Lutzville
Tomato Festival

MAY

Riebeek Kasteel
Olive Festival
The Pietermaritzburg
RoyalShow
Parkview Sasol
Birds And Birding Fair
Knysna
Pink Loerie
Mardi Gras Festival
Franschoek
Literacy Festival
Clanwilliam
Cederberg Kunstefees

JUNE

Robertson
Wacky Wine Weekend
Grahamstown
National Arts Festival
Napier Sweet
Potato Festival
Kirkwood
Wildlife Festival

JULY

Jozi
The Comedy Festival
Knysna
Oyster Festival
Durban
International Film
Festival
Coffee Bay
Bomvu Drum & Dance
Festival
Nelspruit
Innibos Festival
Somerset East
Great Biltong Festival

AUGUST

Northern Cape
Hantam Vleisfees
Magaliesberg
Cellar Rats Wine Festival
Dullstroom
Elandskloof Trout Festival
Greenside
Locust Festival
Northam
OppiKoppi Festival
Durban
SA Women's Art Festival
Hentiesbaai
Visfees

SEPTEMBER

Macufe Mangaung
Magoebaskloof Spring
Festival
Cape Town
Out In Africa SA Gay &
Lesbian Film Festival
Estcourt
White Mountain Folk
Festival
Northern Cape
Gariep Kunstefees
Hermanus
Whale Festival

OCTOBER

Darling
Rocking The Daisies
Dundee
History In Action Festival
Bedford
Garden Festival
Khayelitsha
Khayelitsha Festival
Gansbaai
White Shark Festival
Soweto
The Beer Festival

NOVEMBER

Ficksburg
The Cherry Festival
Nottingham Road
Pink Festival
Johannesburg
Woodstock Festival
Mpumalanga
Frog Festival
Mcgregor
Apricot Carnival
Vredendal
Rittlefees
Umdwebo
Lifestyle Festival

DECEMBER

George
Festival Of Lights
Mosselbaai
Dias Festival
Ballito
Beach Festival
Rustlers Valley
New Year's Gathering
Gonubie
Christmas Fair
Bloubergstrand
Virgin Festival
Pringle Bay
Windgat Festival

Photo © David Olsen

The Legend of the Hole in the Wall

The Wild Coast is Xhosa territory, birthplace of Nelson Mandela and an area steeped in history and stories. The impressive Hole in the Wall has a giant opening carved through its centre by the relentless pounding of the waves. The local Xhosa call this place 'iziKhaleni', which means 'place of thunder' after the thunderous clap of the waves heard sometimes during high tide. According to Xhosa folklore, however, the Hole in the Wall is the gateway to their ancestors. They claim that the Mpako River running through the Hole in the Wall once formed a landlocked lagoon as its access to the sea was blocked by a cliff.

Legend tells the story of a beautiful girl who lived in a village near the lagoon. She would sit on the edge of the cliff and stare out to sea. Unlike her people who were land people and feared the sea, she was attracted to its power and the way in which each wave was different. And so, one night, she went beyond the cliff to the shore of the sea. Out of the waves came one of the sea people. He was as tall as she was, with silky flowing hair like the waves. He had supple wrists and ankles and flipper-like hands and feet. He said he had watched her often and admired her, and now he had come because he wanted her to be his wife.

The girl told her father about the man from the sea but her father would have none of it and shouted 'We do not trade our daughters with the sea people!' and forbade her from ever seeing him again. But the girl slipped away in the dark to meet up with her sea lover and told him of her father's response. Her sea lover said she must wait until high tide to see how he would prove his love for her. This she did, with the suspicious villagers following her. The villagers saw thin willowy sea people on top of the cliff carrying a mighty fish that they used to batter the rock, carving a hole through the centre of the cliff and creating a passage from the lagoon to the open sea. With the force of the tide behind it, a great spout of water gushed through the Hole in the Wall, and on the wave came hundreds of sea people singing and shouting with joy. Riding the wave in front of them was the girl's sea lover. He stretched out his arms and the girl moved to join him. As the wave retreated, foaming and frothing, the girl went with the sea people back through the hole in the rock wall and was never seen again.

According to the Xhosa people, on nights when the tide is high, the sea people can be heard above the roar of the waves as they rush through the Hole in the Wall in their search for a bride.

THE PUBLIC HOLIDAY	HUMAN RIGHTS' DAY 21 MARCH	FREEDOM DAY 27 APRIL	WORKERS' DAY 1 MAY	YOUTH DAY 16 JUNE
IN THE PAST	During apartheid, many people's rights were abused. For instance, black people were forced by white superiors to carry special identification documents called passbooks, without which blacks could be fined or imprisoned. Freedom of expression, of association, of movement and residence – and therefore dignity - was denied to black people.	In 1950 the apartheid government instituted the Group Areas Act. Under this law, non-whites were forced to live in areas separate from whites and from other non-whites. Non-white areas were situated far from the city limits and blacks were not allowed to own land or to vote in national elections.	Workers' Day, celebrated worldwide by socialist and labour movements, is based on the industrial struggle for an eight-hour day. In South Africa, the black nationalist organisations were banned under the apartheid government. Strikes by black workers in 1973 led to the emergence of labour movements and, in the 1980s, the consolidation of trade union power.	In apartheid South Africa, blacks and whites were educated separately. Afrikaans, the language of the ruling National Party, was introduced as the language of instruction in black schools. The Soweto Students' Representative Council organised a march in protest against this policy and poor schooling conditions.
MAKING HISTORY	In 1960, black people in Sharpeville organised a demonstration against the pass laws. 69 demonstrators died and 186 were injured. The carnage made world headlines and the government subsequently banned black political organisations. The Truth and Reconciliation Commission, years later, found the police guilty of gross human rights' violations.	This was the day in 1994 when the first democratic election was held in South Africa – all adults, irrespective of their race, could cast their ballot over a period of four days. On this day in 1997, the new constitution came into effect. This document enshrined many human rights.	Workers' Day became official in South Africa after the first democratic elections in 1994, when the government recognised the role played by Trade Unions, the Communist Party and labour groups who fought against apartheid. The new constitution enshrined labour rights and Workers' Day became celebrated alongside other national days.	In 1976, learners from around the country demonstrated against unfair education conditions in the schools. In Soweto, police opened fire on 20 000 students, killing 12-year-old Hector Pieterson and 61 others. Eight months of violent uprisings across the country ensued.
DRIVING CHANGE	Marked as a turning point in the fight for democracy, this day highlights the value of the rights of all South Africans. The new Bill of Rights was instituted and the Human Rights Commission was officially launched.	Democracy was introduced for the first time with the 1994 election. Exiles returned from abroad and Nelson Mandela became South Africa's first democratically elected president.	Employers and workers are now governed by fair labour practices inherent in the post-1994 constitution. The right to strike is guaranteed by unions.	This protest against unfair education policies came to represent a protest against discrimination and inequalities. It led to the new constitution prioritising children's rights.
CELEBRATION TIME	On this day people celebrate the value in and achievement of the new Bill of Rights. This Bill is now the cornerstone of South Africa's democracy and affirms human dignity, equality and freedom.	On this day people celebrate the end of apartheid and the beginning of democracy in South Africa and recommit to ensuring voting and living equality for all.	This is the day when the achievements of the labour movements are remembered to ensure that future plans continue to entrench equality.	The day is used to mark the valuable contribution of all young people in the establishment of democracy and the role of education in the future of the country.

NATIONAL WOMEN'S DAY 9 AUGUST

Under the apartheid government black people were forced to carry passes (these were special identification documents that curtailed Africans' freedom). In 1952 the pass laws became even stricter, often causing black men and women to be split from their families. Women were affected worst by these and other laws.

In 1956, 20 000 women marched to the Union Buildings in Pretoria to protest against changes to the pass laws. More than 100 000 petitions were left at Prime Minister JG Strijdom's door. The women, white and black, stood in silence before singing the protest song Wathint' Abafazi, Wathint' imbokodo! (You strike a woman, you strike a rock.)

The new constitution stipulated that no-one could be discriminated against on the basis of gender and acknowledged the difficulties and prejudices that women still face worldwide.

Around the country numerous Women's Day events are held in celebration of the contribution made by women to society and the achievements made for women's rights.

HERITAGE DAY 24 SEPTEMBER

In KwaZulu-Natal, this day was known as Shaka's Day, commemorating the Zulu King Shaka, who died in 1828. The Public Holidays bill presented to parliament after 1994 didn't originally include Heritage Day, and the Inkatha Freedom Party, a political party with a large Zulu membership, objected. A compromise was reached by creating a holiday that would forge a new identity for all South Africans.

To create unity from diversity after the dismantling of apartheid, Heritage Day highlights the histories of all racial groups and recognises all the men and women who have contributed to the heritage and culture of the nation.

Freedom of cultural, religious and linguistic expression is now enshrined in the constitution. The term Ubuntu, meaning 'I am because you are', is used to engender respect for other people.

South Africans visit heritage sites, acknowledge the different cultures, and celebrate the various aspects of our culture such as art, music, research and teaching.

DAY OF RECONCILIATION 16 DECEMBER

Prior to 1994, two separate battles were originally commemorated on this day: Afrikaners celebrated the Day of the Vow, remembering when Voortrekkers defeated a Zulu army at the Battle of Blood River in 1838. African National Congress activists commemorated the day in 1961 when it launched Umkhonto we Sizwe, the party's military wing, with the purpose of overthrowing the apartheid government.

The Day of Reconciliation, instead of focusing on past battles, focuses on South Africa's triumph in overcoming the conflicts of the past and building a new nation. Under the apartheid government it was known as the Day of the Covenant to some, and Dingaan's Day to others.

The 1996 constitution recognises South Africans' diversity and Nelson Mandela urged reconciliation between all people of South Africa.

South Africans celebrate their harmony and recommit to continued reconciliation and nation building with an emphasis on equality, mutual respect and a shared future.

SO MUCH MORE THAN A HOLIDAY

NELSON MANDELA DAY

18 July is Mandela's birthday. Although not a public holiday, we celebrate the father of the South African nation. Adopted by the United Nations, Nelson Mandela International Day will be celebrated worldwide, from 2010 onwards, in recognition of the Nobel Peace Prize Laureate's contribution to promoting reconciliation.

Nelson Mandela was politically active for 67 years and around the world, in the workplace, schools and at home, people are asked to commit to spending 67 minutes doing something for the less fortunate within their communities.

Magnificent MIGRATION

Enterprising Eels

FROM MPUMALANGA 1 870 KM TO MADAGASCAR

From the fresh water of Vyfenhoekspruit in the Mpumalanga mountains across the Indian Ocean to the West Coast of Madagascar. 'At the Fireside' editor, Roger Webster, tells the story about the extremely large freshwater eel that travels a staggering 1 870 km journey from the highest part of the Ohrigstad mountains to the west coast to Madagascar. This eel, and others like it, leaves its home upon maturity, heads down the mountain into the Blyde River, the Olifants River, the Limpopo River and then into the sea at Mozambique. The eel pushes on eastwards away from Mozambique until it reaches the west coast of Madagascar. After its journey across the ocean, it stops, mates and spawns, and then sends its young westwards with a mental map of those faraway mountains. The baby eels reach fresh water in Mozambique and swim, against the current – and in one section up a ten-metre waterfall – until they inexplicably reach the Vyfenhoekspruit ponds high up in the mountains – the ponds their parents had left many months earlier.

Messengers of Spring

FROM RUSSIA 20 000 KM AND BACK AGAIN

PARIS 9 294 KM

BERLIN 9 575 KM

SYDNEY 11 642 KM

JERUSALEM KM

NEW YORK 12 541 KM

9 296 KM

Up to three million swallows – that's what you will see gathering as the skies darken over the Mt Moreland Conservancy near Umdloti in KwaZulu-Natal. A familiar twittering and chattering grows louder. Finally, homing in on the reed beds below, millions of Barn Swallows drop to the ground, welcomed by locals and mourned by their counterparts in Europe, Russia and Scandinavia. These tiny creatures had congregated in separate flocks to form one large mass, a month earlier, before embarking on their trip from north to south, a treacherous journey of well over 10 000 kms. Sometimes flying up to 400 kms per day over inhospitable terrain, the birds travelled a specific, innately defined route across Africa. Once here in the warm coastal area of Mt Moreland, the Barn Swallows tear into the local insect population, doing a great job of controlling mosquitoes. Seven months later, they begin gathering on telephone wires, conserving their energy for their long journey north. Large flocks leave one at a time until the end of April. Then they are gone. All is silent and the sky is empty – until their return to the exact same spot the following October.

Jetlag no problem for Nicole

FROM
SOUTH AFRICA
22 000 KM
TO AUSTRALIA

It seems that Nicole undertook her 20 000 km jaunt from South Africa to Australia every year. Nicole, a great white shark measuring 3.8 m, captured the world's attention when she was tracked via satellite from Dyer Island off the Western Cape of South Africa in 2003. Shortly before Christmas she would set off in an easterly direction, travelling an astonishing 4.7 km/h for 99 days before surfacing near the Exmouth Gulf in Western Australia. Barely stopping long enough to catch her breath, Nicole did an about turn (or a tumble turn, if you will) and set off back the way she had come, arriving back at Dyer Island in August of that same year. Nicole, named after actress Nicole Kidman, journeyed mostly at just five metres below the water's surface which indicates that she navigated by tracking celestial markers with her vision – not unlike sailors. When diving to the depths, she probably followed gradients in the earth's magnetic field – similar to that of a compass.

The Leatherback Challenge

CARRYING
500 KG
OVER 7 000 KM

RIO DE JANEIRO
6 055 KM

A leatherback turtle was tracked by satellite for nearly 7 000 km. Weighing up to 500 kg and with a shell of 1.8 m, this marine reptile makes its nesting ground on the shores of the St Lucia Estuary in northern KwaZulu-Natal. In a separate study, it was found that the leatherback turtle holds the record for the longest recorded migration journey in the ocean. A female leatherback turtle was tagged and tracked by satellite for 647 days and covered at least 20 558 km before the signal was lost. She crossed the Pacific from west to east and then part of the way back again. Not only do turtles swim thousands of kilometres, they can also dive to depths of up to 1 200 m. Sadly the leatherback turtle, which has survived for more than a hundred million years, is now facing extinction.

Photo © Radoslav Dechkov

Ubuntu is a word of ancient African origin meaning 'I am what I am because of who we all are'

One of the sayings in our country is Ubuntu - the essence of being human. Ubuntu speaks particularly about the fact that you can't exist as a human being in isolation. It speaks about our interconnectedness. You can't be human all by yourself, and when you have this quality - Ubuntu - you are known for your generosity.

Archbishop Desmond Tutu

A universal truth

A way of life

Antetonitrus, reaching 10 m long, was one of the largest animals ever to have lived on land. Its remains were uncovered more than 25 years ago in the Free State.

Massospondylus was a fairly common dinosaur in South Africa. Its fossils were found in 1853 in the Harrismith area of the Drakensberg and later, in the red-beds of the Karoo basin.

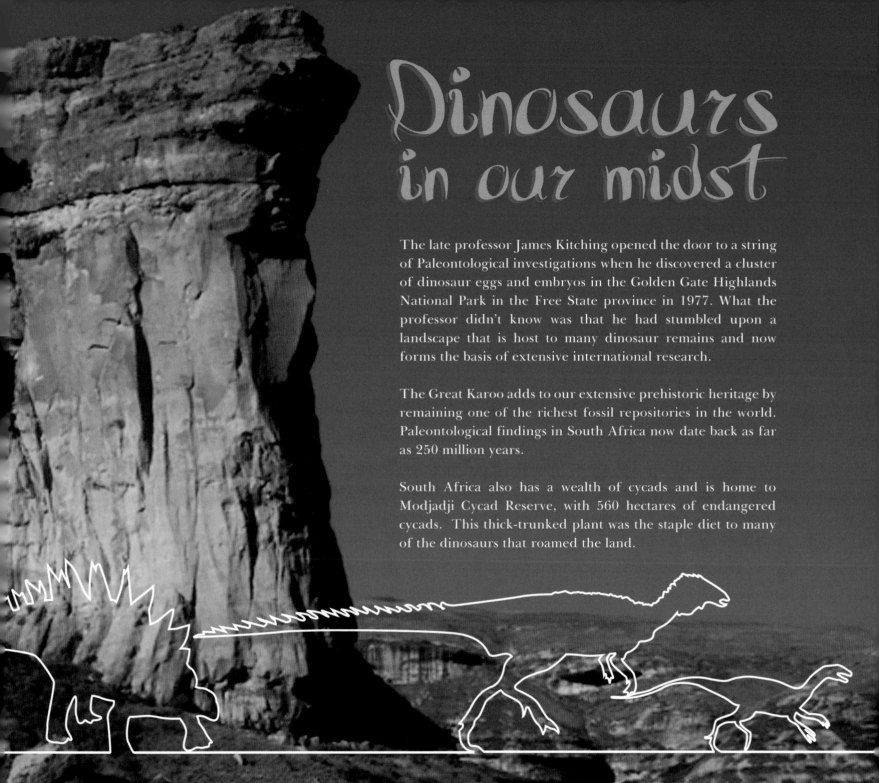

Dinosaurs in our midst

The late professor James Kitching opened the door to a string of Paleontological investigations when he discovered a cluster of dinosaur eggs and embryos in the Golden Gate Highlands National Park in the Free State province in 1977. What the professor didn't know was that he had stumbled upon a landscape that is host to many dinosaur remains and now forms the basis of extensive international research.

The Great Karoo adds to our extensive prehistoric heritage by remaining one of the richest fossil repositories in the world. Paleontological findings in South Africa now date back as far as 250 million years.

South Africa also has a wealth of cycads and is home to Modjadji Cycad Reserve, with 560 hectares of endangered cycads. This thick-trunked plant was the staple diet to many of the dinosaurs that roamed the land.

Paranthodons were first discovered near the Sunday's River in the Eastern Cape in 1845 by Andrew Geddes Bain and William Atherstone.

Lesothosaurus is the oldest genus of dinosaur and was named after the mountain kingdom of Lesotho where it was first discovered.

Nqwebasaurus is named after Nqweba, the Xhosa name for the Kirkwood region in the Eastern Cape where it was unearthed in the 1990s.

Photograph of Golden Gate, Free State Province, courtesy of Robin duBois

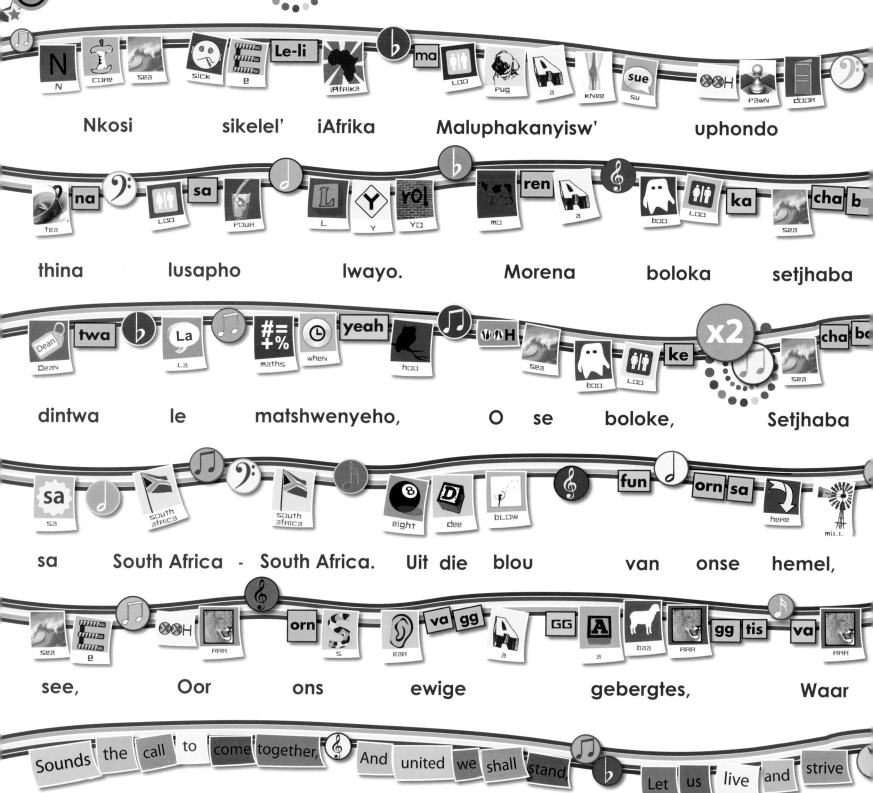

Nkosi sikelel' iAfrika Maluphakanyisw' uphondo

thina lusapho lwayo. Morena boloka setjhaba

dintwa le matshwenyeho, O se boloke, Setjhaba

sa South Africa - South Africa. Uit die blou van onse hemel,

see, Oor ons ewige gebergtes, Waar

Sounds the call to come together, And united we shall stand, Let us live and strive

Nkosi Sikelel' iAfrika

lwayo, Yizwa imithandazo yethu, Nkosi sikelela,

sa heso, O fedise

sa heso, Setjhaba

Uit die diepte van ons

die kranse antwoord gee,

for freedom, In South Africa our land.

The only national anthem in the world that is made up of two national anthems in five languages!

Nkosi Sikelel' iAfrika was originally composed as a Xhosa hymn in 1897. During the apartheid regime, it represented the suffering of the oppressed. Nelson Mandela declared that both 'Nkosi Sikelel' iAfrika' and the previous national anthem, 'Die Stem', be national anthems signifying the dawn of a new era that respected all races and cultures. The isiXhosa and isiZulu of the first stanza flow naturally into Sesotho in the second, Afrikaans in the third and English in the fourth. The harmonious musical bridge created as a result presents a beautiful picture of South Africa's all-embracing new identity, uniting 47 million people.

Nkosi Sikelel'i Afrika translated into English

Lord, bless Africa
May her spirit rise high up
Hear thou our prayers
Lord bless us.
Lord, bless Africa
Banish wars and strife
Lord, bless our nation
Of South Africa.

Ringing out from our blue heavens
From our deep seas breaking round
Over everlasting mountains
Where the echoing crags resound. Sounds the call to come together, and united we shall stand, Let us live and strive for freedom, In South Africa our land.

Page inspired by iBurst

127

ABOUT 80% OF SOUTH AFRICA'S POPULATION DESCRIBES ITSELF AS BEING CHRISTIAN. THE AFRICAN INDEPENDENT CHURCHES WHICH COMPRISE, AMONGST OTHERS, THE ZIONIST CHRISTIAN CHURCH (ZCC) AND NAZARETH BAPTIST CHURCH, PREDOMINATE IN SOUTH AFRICA WITH OVER 10 000 CHURCHES AND A COMBINED MEMBERSHIP OF MORE THAN 10 MILLION PEOPLE. THEIR FAITH IS A UNIQUE BLEND OF CHRISTIANITY AND AFRICAN TRADITIONAL BELIEFS.

THE ZIONIST CHRISTIAN CHURCH

OVER ONE MILLION ZCC MEMBERS MAKE THE ANNUAL PILGRIMAGE TO ZION CITY IN MORIA

ZION CITY IN MORIA, NEAR POLOKWANE IN LIMPOPO PROVINCE, IS HOME TO THE ZCC CHURCH. THE ZCC PILGRIMAGE, WHICH HAPPENS TWICE A YEAR, IS THE LARGEST SINGLE RELIGIOUS GATHERING ON THE AFRICAN CONTINENT. IT IS A TRADITION THAT HAS BEEN LOYALLY OBSERVED FOR MORE THAN 80 YEARS. THERE ARE AN ESTIMATED FOUR TO SIX MILLION ZCC MEMBERS. THE CHURCH HAS A STRICT CODE OF DISCIPLINE AND ITS MEMBERS ARE KNOWN IN THE COMMUNITY AS PEACEFUL, DEPENDABLE AND TRUSTWORTHY.

THE SHEMBE

THE NAZARETH BAPTIST CHURCH (OR SHEMBE CHURCH) WAS FOUNDED IN 1910 AND HAS APPROXIMATELY FOUR MILLION MEMBERS. IT IS SEEN AS A MIXTURE OF ZULU TRADITION AND CHRISTIANITY. IT REVERES ITS FOUNDER, ISAIAH SHEMBE, AS AN AFRICAN MESSIAH AND EMPHASISES THE TEN COMMANDMENTS. THEY ARE SEEN AS PEACE-LOVING PEOPLE WHO HAVE TRANSFORMED THEIR STICKS, SPEARS AND SHIELDS INTO BIBLICAL STAFFS. THE SHEMBE BEGIN EACH YEAR WITH A PILGRIMAGE TO NHLANGAGAZI, THE HOLY MOUNTAIN, ON THE FIRST SUNDAY OF THE NEW YEAR. THE SHEMBES ALSO HOLD A MONTH-LONG CELEBRATION IN JUDEA NEAR ESHOWE EVERY YEAR IN OCTOBER, WHERE UP TO 25 000 MEMBERS GATHER TO RECEIVE THE BLESSINGS OF SHEMBE.

OVER 80 000 SHEMBE PILGRIMS, DRESSED IN SPOTLESS WHITE
ROBES, WALK 80 KM FROM DURBAN UP THE HOLY MOUNTAIN

Cricket

is a simple game really. You have two sides, one out in the field and one in. Each man that's in the side that's in goes out, and when he's out he comes in and the next man goes in until he's out. When they are all out, the side that's out comes in and the side that's been in goes out and tries to get those coming in, out. Sometimes you get men still in and therefore not out. When a man goes out to go in, the men who are out try to get him out, and when he is out he goes in and the next man in goes out and goes in. There are two men called umpires who stay out all the time and they decide when the men who are in are out. When both sides have been in and all the men have gone out, and both sides have been out twice after all the men have been in, including those who are not out, that is the end of the game!

SOUTH AFRICA'S CRICKET TEAM

THE PROTEAS RANKED #1 ODI TEAM IN THE WORLD!

THE DAY OF WORLD RECORDS

Every South African will tell you that there are few encounters that will be savoured more than a victory over our rivals down under. South Africa and Australia both boast proud sporting heritages and there is certainly one match that will be cemented into cricket-loving minds the world over.

DATE:	MARCH 12, 2006
VENUE:	WANDERERS CRICKET STADIUM
TEAMS:	SOUTH AFRICA VERSUS AUSTRALIA
MATCH:	THE FIFTH AND FINAL MATCH, A SERIES DECIDER

SUNDAY MORNING (SA TIME): EARLY EVENING (AUSSIE TIME)

Australia elected to bat and smash their way to an unprecedented 434 in the allotted 50 overs, the first one-day total ever recorded over 400 runs. A new world record was set.

SUNDAY LUNCHTIME (SA TIME): LATE EVENING (AUSSIE TIME)

Australian press, eager to release first edition newspapers before the public woke up, were already hailing Australia's series victory and went to print boasting the string of records that occurred by the close of the first innings.

SUNDAY AFTERNOON (SA TIME): EARLY HOURS (AUSSIE TIME)

South Africa, with no expectations, retaliated. Herschelle Gibbs and Captain Graham Smith posted a formidable partnership of 187 runs bringing South Africa back into contention. Arriving at the final over with 7 required off 6 balls, Andrew Hall, looking set to make history after an emphatic four, was then dismissed. Tail ender, Makhaya Ntini, stepped up to the crease with three balls remaining and, to the exasperated relief of local supporters, managed to edge off a single to tie the match. Mark Boucher sealed the match and a series victory by hitting a 4, with commentator Tony Greig exclaiming, 'One of the greatest one day matches of all time'.

SUNDAY EVENING (SA TIME): EARLY MORNING (AUSSIE TIME)

By the time Australian newspapers, printed earlier, hit the streets, their headlines were already outdated. Later editions of newspapers around the world featured headlines of the new South African world record.

AUSTRALIA		TOTAL	434
GILCHRIST	55	WICKETS	4
KATICH	79		
PONTING	164	OVERS	50
HUSSEY	81	BATSMAN x	9
SYMONDS	27	BATSMAN -	27
LEE	9	PARTNERSHIP	27
MARTYN		RUNS TO WIN	
CLARKE		OVERS LEFT	0
BRACKEN		RATE ACH'D	8,7
CLARK		RATE REQ'D	
LEWIS			
Extras	19		

S AFRICA		TOTAL	438
SMITH	90	WICKETS	9
DIPPENAAR	1		
GIBBS	175	OVERS	49
deVILLIERS	14	BATSMAN -	1
KALLIS	20	BATSMAN x	50
BOUCHER	50	PARTNERSHIP	5
KEMP	13	RUNS TO WIN	
VD WATH	35	OVERS LEFT	1
TELEMACUS	12	RATE ACH'D	8,8
HALL	7	RATE REQ'D	
-NTINI	1		

Mark Boucher is statistically the most successful wicketkeeper the world has ever seen with more than 400 dismissals and 4 000 runs at Test Match level and he is on target to become the only one to complete 500 dismissals • Graeme Pollock was named SA player of the 20th century and had the second highest test average in the world (60.97) for players with more than 20 tests • Barry Richards was the only South African to be included in Sir Donald Bradman's imaginery world team • Barry Richards and Graeme Pollock are the two South African cricketers who have been inducted into the International Cricket Council's Hall of Fame • Jacques Kallis was named world's best batsman by the ICC test batting rankings and he was named Best Cricketer on Planet Earth for 2007 by the prestigious Wisden Almanack • At the age of 16, Darryl Cullinan became the youngest South African to score a test century • Gary Kirsten was the first batsman in the world to score a test century against all nine other test playing countries • Mike Procter shares the world record with CB Fry and Sir Donald Bradman of scoring six first-class centuries in succession. Showing that he was a fine all-rounder too, Procter is the only cricketer in history to capture two all-LBW hat-tricks • When the new 50c coin was launched in 2003, the image of Jonty Rhodes appeared on the coin to commemorate the ICC World Cup Cricket.

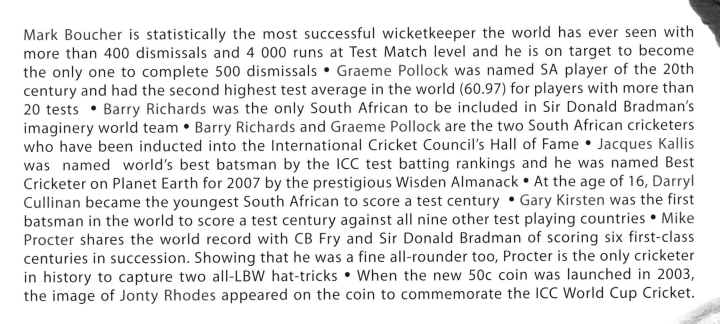

STREET SCENES

South Africans are known for their humour, no matter how bad their circumstances. The jobless, found on street corners throughout South Africa, bring tears, frustration and occasionally smiles to drivers in the hope of small monetary exchange or work. They provided the inspiration to comedian, Leon Schuster, and a fellow actor when, to capture people's reactions for a movie, they were filmed by a hidden camera begging naked during early morning Gauteng traffic.

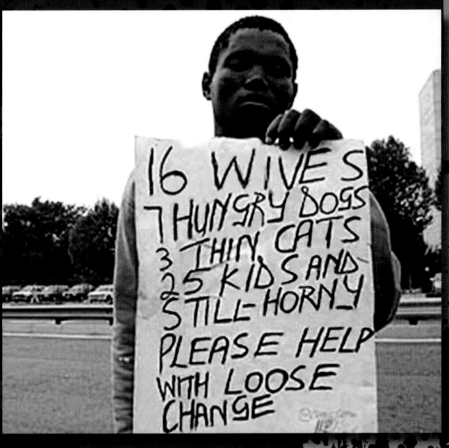

16 WIVES
7 HUNGRY DOGS
3 THIN CATS
25 KIDS AND
STILL-HORNY
PLEASE HELP
WITH LOOSE
CHANGE

VOK DIT!
WERKLOOS.
HAWELOOS.
MOEDELOOS.
KEELVOL.
GAT VOL!
TE DOM OM TE
STEEL.
VRA ENIGE
HULP// A.S.B.
VERSKOON, HOË
AFRIKAANS.
PRYS U VOORBAAT
DANK.

KIDS GONE 2
DISNEYLAND
PORSCHE IN
4 REPAIRS. PLZ
HELP??

ARE YOU GOING TO
GIVE ME MONEY OR
SHOULD I FAKE A LIMP.

*Tjooning you
straight

GOLF IN AFRICA

A unique and astounding experience

THE LEGEND GOLF & SAFARI RESORT

boasts an unforgettable golfing experience. The 18 - hole course, designed by 18 of the world's top golfers, also features the extreme 19th hole. The tee of the extreme 19th is accessed only by helicopter on the majestic Hanglip Mountain, where golfers prepare to embark on the longest par three in the world. The tee stands at a vertical height of 430 m, and plays onto a green that has been shaped to match the shape and contours of the African continent.

AROUND THE WORLD IN 10 HOLES

THE TRIBUTE ten-hole golf course pays homage to some of the world's greatest golf holes ever designed, testing a player's short game. The course is made up of ten world famous holes

1. Pine Valley - 10th
2. Troon - 8th 'The Postage Stamp'
3. St Andrews Old Course - 11th
4. Augusta - 12th 'Golden Bell'
5. Royal Melbourne - 6th
6. Augusta - 16th 'Redbud'
7. Riviera Country Club - 7th
8. An African Redan hole
9. Yale University - 9th
10. TPC Sawgrass - 17th

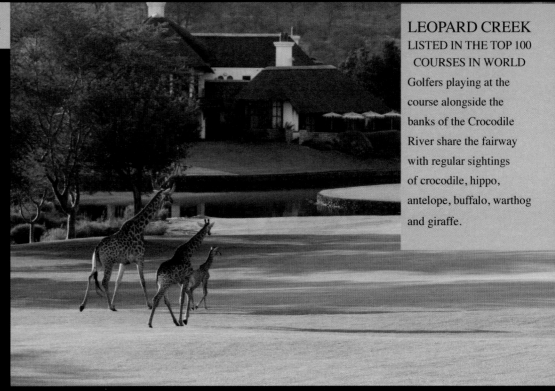

LEOPARD CREEK
LISTED IN THE TOP 100 COURSES IN WORLD

Golfers playing at the course alongside the banks of the Crocodile River share the fairway with regular sightings of crocodile, hippo, antelope, buffalo, warthog and giraffe.

SOUTH AFRICA'S
TOP TEN
courses as ranked
by Golf Digest

1. Leopard Creek - Malelane, Mpumalanga
2. Gary Player CC - Sun City, North West
3. Fancourt Links - George, Southern Cape
4. Durban CC - Durban, KwaZulu-Natal
5. Arabella - Kleinmond, Western Cape
6. Pearl Valley - Winelands, Western Cape
7. Wild Coast - Port Edward, KwaZulu-Natal
8. Royal J&K East - Johannesburg, Gauteng
9. Elements - Waterburg, Limpopo
10. Fancourt Montague - George, Southern Cape

THE LOST CITY GOLF COURSE IN SUN CITY

A pit of crocodiles, measuring over 4.5 m, makes recovering your ball on the 13th a dangerous affair.

135

ENGINEERING FEATS

Bloukrans Bridge, which was completed in 1984, stands 216 m above the Bloukrans River, making it the **highest single span arch bridge in the world**. Its central span is 272 m, with a total length of 451 m. Rumour has it that it is also the third highest bridge in the world.

Orange Fish River Tunnel is an 82.8 km irrigation tunnel which diverts water from the Orange River under the Suurberg mountain plateau to the Great Fish River and the semi-arid areas of Eastern Cape province. It is the longest continuous enclosed aqueduct in the southern hemisphere and the **third-longest water supply tunnel in the world**.

Franz Richter Dam wall is **the largest hand-built stone dam on the African continent**. This feat was accomplished by a group of builders using only two machines.

The Lesotho Highlands Water Project, an ongoing water supply project with a hydropower component, comprises a system of several large dams and tunnels throughout Lesotho and South Africa. It is **Africa's largest water transfer scheme**.

The Drakensberg Pumped Storage Scheme is also known as the Sterkfontein Hydroelectric. On one side of the Drakensberg watershed, the Tugela River carries its waters virtually unused to the Indian Ocean. On the other, the Vaal River flows towards the Atlantic. The Sterkfontein Hydroelectric Power System, therefore, has a dual function, operating as a pumped storage scheme and as a pumping station for water transfer over the Drakensberg. Most of the system is underground, with the surface buildings and access roads built in such a way that they are barely visible in the beautiful natural surroundings of the Drakensberg.

The Dolos is a **South African invention** in which interlocking blocks of concrete are used to protect sea walls and preserve beaches from erosion. They are used throughout the world.

Sasol was formed in South Africa in 1950 to make oil from coal for a country with no large crude oil reserves. Sasol has grown phenomenally into a global force known for providing technology solutions to an energy-hungry world. Sasol is **the only commercial coal-to-liquid plant in the world**.

The Mponeng Mine, situated near Carletonville, is officially the **world's deepest mine**. On 3 February 2009, Mponeng (which means 'Look at me') set a new record when it reached 3 778 m Below Datum. This point is 1 949 m below sea level. By December 2009, the mine had reached 4 200 m. Blasting will continue until 4 500 m is reached.

Woodhead Dam on top of Table Mountain was completed in 1897. It created a reservoir used to supply the nearby city and was built with blocks of stone by Scottish hydraulic engineer Thomas Stewart. He had to overcome the challenges of getting material and equipment up the mountain. Some 110 years later, the masonry marvel that still helps supply water to Cape Town was named ASCE (American Society of Civil Engineers) **International Historic Civil Engineering Landmark**. To date, only 244 projects worldwide have earned this prominent designation, one that illustrates the pioneering spirit of civil engineers. This elite group includes such famous landmarks as the Panama Canal, the Washington Monument, the Golden Gate Bridge, the Eiffel Tower and the Sydney Harbour Bridge.

The Carlton Centre is South Africa's tallest building. When the 51-storey building was opened in 1970 it was the **world's largest reinforced concrete edifice**.

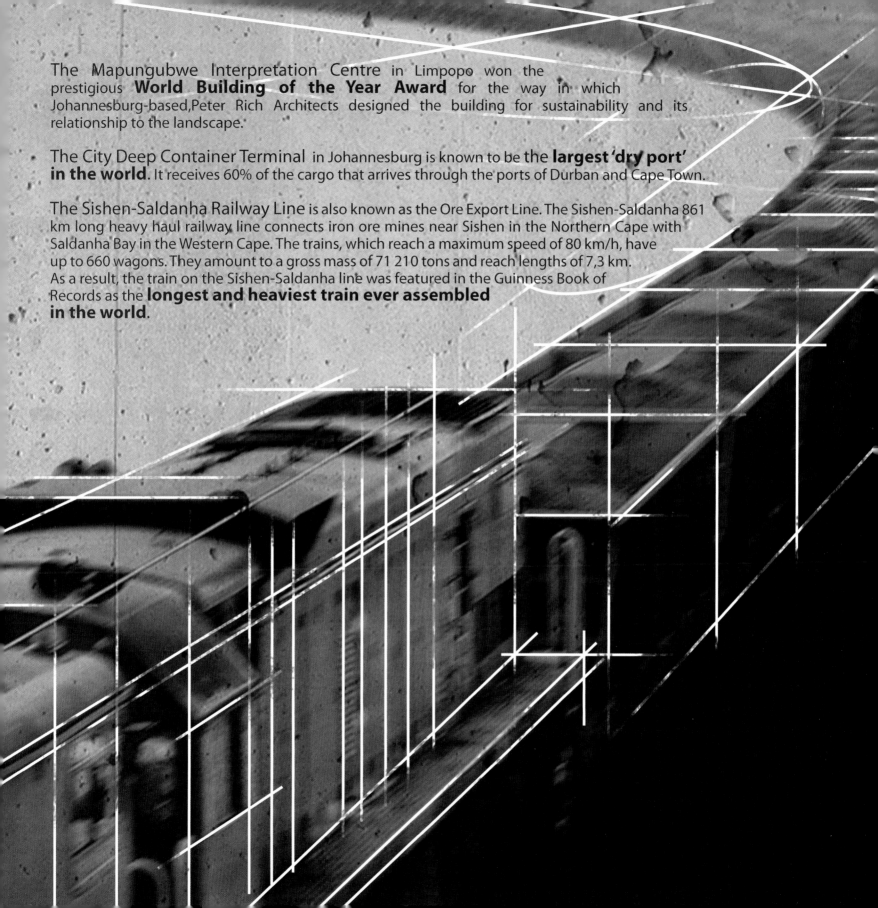

The Mapungubwe Interpretation Centre in Limpopo won the prestigious **World Building of the Year Award** for the way in which Johannesburg-based, Peter Rich Architects designed the building for sustainability and its relationship to the landscape.

The City Deep Container Terminal in Johannesburg is known to be the **largest 'dry port' in the world**. It receives 60% of the cargo that arrives through the ports of Durban and Cape Town.

The Sishen-Saldanha Railway Line is also known as the Ore Export Line. The Sishen-Saldanha 861 km long heavy haul railway line connects iron ore mines near Sishen in the Northern Cape with Saldanha Bay in the Western Cape. The trains, which reach a maximum speed of 80 km/h, have up to 660 wagons. They amount to a gross mass of 71 210 tons and reach lengths of 7,3 km. As a result, the train on the Sishen-Saldanha line was featured in the Guinness Book of Records as the **longest and heaviest train ever assembled in the world**.

Moeggeploegkroeg

Radium Beer Hall
TOP 20 BAR IN THE WORLD

This 'men only' bar from the 1920s spit-and-sawdust era doubled as a shebeen until it had an extreme makeover. Finally women were allowed to join in the foot-tapping live jazz that makes the embossed tin ceiling of this new cosmopolitan Johannesburg bar vibrate.
www.theradium.co.za

Pistols Saloon, Ramsgate
THE WILD WEST ON THE SOUTH COAST

Enter this Western bar through swing doors to listen to live country music or play the old piano. It was named 'Best Pub on the Planet' by the Independent Newspapers' Pub Guide. But be warned, there is R2 payable to the SPCA for anyone caught swearing.

Moeggeploegkroeg at the Hotel in the village of Val. Translation 'moeg -tired; geploeg - ploughing; kroeg - bar'

THE SOUTH AFRICAN BAR

HAVE A DOP SOUTH AFRICAN STYLE

Seaman's Pub, Elands Bay
Getting legless

In this pub, a false leg hangs from the ceiling. The story goes that a railroad chap once left his false leg as collateral for his bar tab. But he never returned. And his leg? Well, that now hangs as a reminder to anyone else that getting legless sure has consequences.

Whether it's a bar, pub, tavern, saloon, inn, cocktail lounge, 19th hole, watering hole or shebeen — try the best and most unusual South Africa has to offer.

Nambitha, Soweto
Trendiest tavern

This elegant landmark is situated a stone's throw away from both Nelson Mandela's and Desmond Tutu's original homes in Vilakazi St. The tavern, which doubles as a gallery for local artists and photographers, was founded by Khulani Vilakazi, the entrepreneurial grandson of the poet and novelist Dr B W Vilakazi. Today, it represents the vibrant and rich Sowetan culture.

Khuwana Tavern, Mandela Village
BIGGEST BEER OUTLET

A typical shebeen that transformed with the changing political climate in the '90s into a thriving, pulsating tavern. Now it's the biggest single outlet of beer in the country. To find the tavern in the informal maze of settlements and tribal communities, north of Tshwane, just listen for the beat of the disco music.
www.kwalata.co.za

The Pig & Whistle, Bathurst
The oldest pub

The favourite place for students who feel a need to prove the merits of the sign outside - 'No thirst like Bathurst'. Dating back 170 years makes the Pig & Whistle in the Eastern Cape the oldest licensed pub in South Africa.
www.pigandwhistle.co.za

Bok Bar, London
LONGEST WALK HOME
There is a small hidey-hole in Covent Garden in London for Saffas (ex-pat South Africans) called Bok Bar. Here any homesick rainbow-nation child will feel his or her heart beating in the six colours of the flag. It is a dream bar with zebra print stools, South African flags, cricket stumps, SA currency on the walls and an atmosphere right out of a plattelandse sports bar. Down a Castle, some Springboks or any other South African 'dop' and brace yourself - it gets hectic when big matches are being played. www.thebokbar.com

The Bokdrol Bar, Dordrecht
MOST (DIS)TASTEFUL BAR
The bar in this sheep farming part of the country is named after an old tradition of drinking brandy and seeing who can spit buck droppings (bokdrols) the furthest, a popular pastime in the region.

The Half
Kimberley
DRIVE-THROUGH PUB
The bar at the Halfway House Hotel dates back to 1875 when Cecil John Rhodes didn't like people to see him struggling back up onto his horse after a few drinks. So he did what powerful people do – he made a law that people could be served drinks on horseback.

Joe Cool's, Durban
Coolest pub
Located on Durban's beach promenade is the coolest bar in town – Joe Cool's. Voted the number one place to watch rugby (out of the stadium, of course), Joe Cool's is famous for being the place where you are most likely to rub shoulders with rugby players after a big game. www.joecools.co.za

Sani Top, Lesotho
Highest Pub in Africa
If you want to get high on beer (literally) then you can do so at 2 874 m above sea level with a glass of homebrew, Maluti Premium, in the highest pub in Africa. Towering mountains, waterfalls, 4x4 treks and crisp mountain air culminate in starry evenings and good company! www.sanitopchalet.co.za

WELCOME TO:-
SANI TOP CHALET
HIGHEST PUB IN AFRICA
2874 meters

The Baobab Tree Bar, Modjadjiskloof
OLDEST BAR IN THE WORLD
It's not often you have a drink inside a baobab tree, and at 6 000 years old, this is most certainly the oldest bar in the world. The bar, that has also appeared on the front page of the Wall Street Journal, is in a natural hollow in the trunk that houses a wine cellar and has the capacity to hold 60 people. www.bigbaobab.co.za

LOST &

Quagga

Recreated with living DNA

Believed to be extinct since the 1880s, the once prolific quagga has been brought back from the dead using an unbelievably minute quantity of one one-hundred-millionth of a gram of DNA. In 1969, Cape Town taxidermist, Reinhold Rau, while remounting a quagga foal (or plains zebra) for the South African Museum, discovered fragments of fleshy tissue and blood vessels adhering to the skin. Although the oddly striped animal had died out more than a century before, methods used on skins at the time did not destroy the genetic make-up of the biological tissue. Ten years later, Rau found molecular biologists willing to work on the tissue and, in 1983, Dr Ryder of the Research Department of the Zoological Society of San Diego, California, officially informed Rau that pieces of the genes of the extinct quagga had been recreated. Originally thought to be a species separate to the so-called plains zebra, it was argued that any attempt at using the DNA specimen to re-breed the quagga would result in an animal that merely looked like the quagga but had no true genetic relationship. Molecular biologists have subsequently found, however, that the quagga and plains zebra belong to the same species and that the quagga was a sub-species. This means that the original gene-pool necessary to re-breed the quagga had always existed in the plains zebra population but in a dispersed and diluted fashion.

Mapungubwe

An advanced ancient African city 'recently' discovered

About 100 km west of Messina in Limpopo Province, lies the ancient citadel of Mapungubwe. Discovered in 1932, carbon dating in 1959 proved that Mapungubwe dated back to the thirteenth century. This advanced African city, we now know, was smelting gold 600 years before Johannesburg was even established. It was probably the first Southern African location to grow cotton and weave it into cloth, and was the first city in the region to have a king. Spurred into trading by Islamic seafarers who ventured inland from the coast, Mapungubwe traded ivory and animal skins. Discovered artefacts include ivory bracelets and bone tools and exquisitely worked gold objects including the Golden Bowl, the Golden Rhino and the Golden Sceptre. But these national treasures have been made public only since June 2000, when the University of Pretoria launched the Mapungubwe Museum. Why the 60-year silence? It seems that the powers-that-were simply could not swallow the concept of an 'advanced' African race. Mapungubwe, it was argued, must have been the result of Egyptian or European influence. In addition, under apartheid, school textbooks dated South Africa's beginning to only the seventeenth century, when Jan van Riebeeck landed at the Cape. They largely ignored the history of the native inhabitants of Southern Africa, thereby keeping one of South Africa's most precious archaeological sites a secret.

FOUND

Strandlopers

An extinct people group still exists today

The remains of an ancient group of people were found dotted along the coast of Southern Africa. Until the latter half of the twentieth century, these human artefacts and human skeletons were attributed to a mysterious group known as Strandlopers. Based on a 1907 study of skulls taken from the South African Museum and elsewhere, the Strandlopers, it was posited, were descended from Boskopoids (or Boskop Man), a more intelligent member of the Neanderthal race. Also known as Watermen, the Strandlopers lived in the Cape coastal area, ate shellfish, birds, seals and whales, and did not keep livestock. By the early 1700s they had virtually disappeared, wiped out it seems, by an outbreak of smallpox. Later studies have disproved both the Boskop-Man theory and the theory that the Strandlopers were a unique race. It now appears that the Strandlopers were a small group subservient to the KhoiKhoi's Cochoqua tribe, a large nomadic group in the Cape that kept animals. Similar to the Bushmen or San who already inhabited the area, the Khoikhoi inhabited the land about two thousand years ago, creating competition for land, marine and food sources. Collectively known as the Khoisan, these two groups live today in small pockets in Southern Africa. Referred to as the First People of Africa, they are the closest surviving people to the original Homo sapien core. However, their non-tribal social structure and hunter-gatherer lifestyle is all but gone.

Coelacanth

'Rediscovered' after 70 million years

On 16 December 1938 Marjorie Courtney-Latimer, curator of the East London Museum, received a call from her good friend, Captain Hendrik Goosen, who had netted a strange fish in the Chalumna River area. Despite her interest in unusual fish, Courtney-Latimer was initially reluctant to go to the harbour and look through a pile of smelly fish. However, she went and returned with a metallic-blue, 57 kg, four-legged specimen. Two months later, Professor JLB Smith clearly identified it as the coelacanth, a prehistoric fish that dated back almost 400 million years and was thought to have been extinct for 70 million years! Despite its 'curious, powerful and penetrating odour,' Professor Smith was keen to study more of the fish and put out a reward of £100 for the capture of a specimen. This amount was increased over the years by other organisations, sparking an interest in catching the fish. The incentive worked and in 1952 a second fish was caught off the Comoro Islands. Unbeknown to the rest of the world, Comoran fisherman had, in fact, seen coelacanths for years but had avoided catching them because of, ironically, their 'strong oily taste and unpleasant odour'. Since 1953, however, 175 specimens have been caught and the celebrated 'living fossil' is now categorised as a 'vulnerable species' and is listed on CITES as 'severely threatened by trade'.

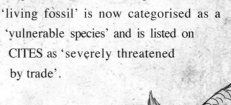

THE BEST ALL-TIME YouTube VIDEOS

#1 TIME MAGAZINE BEST ONLINE VIDEO

Battle at Kruger

With over 27 million views and a National Geographic documentary, 'Battle at Kruger' has received a host of honours, including: Best Eyewitness Video and #1 Most Viewed Animal Video. AOL and Time magazine respectively declared it 'The Best Online Video for 2007' and 'one of the hottest upload(s) in web history'. In Battle at Kruger, a buffalo calf is attacked by a pride of lions as well as two crocs. The buffaloes fight back and the calf, incredibly, survives.

You Tube http://www.youtube.com/watch?v=LU8DDYz68kM [Search]

Isn't nature strange sometimes?

Hippo Saves Impala

In this YouTube video, a young impala falls prey to a crocodile and, inexplicably, is rescued by a hippopotamus. The hippo even tries to resuscitate the wounded animal. Watch it at this link:

You Tube http://www.youtube.com/watch?v=MXR2xZrF5SA [Search]

South Africa's Best

From the southernmost tip of Africa, to the highest commercial bungee jump in the world, to the big five, serene coastlines, majestic mountains and more, dive in and see the best of South Africa at:

You Tube http://www.youtube.com/watch?v=MMP28f1sBG0 [Search]

Huge Predator Hunts Sardines

In the greatest faunal event on earth, millions of sardines gather in shoals and move north pursued by thousands of dolphins, sharks, seals and gannets. In this excerpt, huge Bryde's Whales pierce the swirling bait balls, swallowing hundreds of sardines at a time. View the video at:

You Tube http://www.earth-touch.com/result.php?i=The-largest-sardine-run-predator-makes-an-appearance- [Search]

Use the keywords (or URL address) to search for these must-watch video clips

Leopard Attacks Crocodile

Although leopards are brutal, skilful killers, who would've thought that a croc would fall prey to those ferocious jaws? Watch this short sequence, filmed by Hal Brindley in the Kruger National Park. Visit:

 http://www.youtube.com/watch?v=FF0Lr--K4oo   Search

Animals Get Drunk

Okay, so we're not sure if animals really do get drunk on the famous Marula Fruit. But suspend your disbelief for a moment and watch this clip filmed by the inimitable Jamie Uys. You'll love the swaying ostriches and giraffes, staggering elephants and tripping baboons. Catch it at:

http://www.youtube.com/watch?v=NtPplZnPuMA   Search

Great White Hunts Seal

The Great White Shark is one of the most feared creatures of the deep. In a stunning display of its deadly hunting skills, this, the largest of the predatory fish, hunts a nimble seal off the Cape coast of South Africa. Check out the action at:

http://www.youtube.com/watch?v=La1MbuLx-RE   Search

Surfing Biggest Wave at Dungeons

Dungeons in Cape Town attracts big wave surfers from around the world. Check out these super surfers in the 2008 Red Bull Big Wave Africa Championship. Radical, bru!

 http://www.youtube.com/watch?v=1CeC5ywLOgw   Search

INTERNATIONAL MOVIES SHOT IN SOUTH AFRICA

RACING STRIPES
Whoopi Goldberg
Dustin Hoffman

10 000 BC
Steven Strait
Camila Belle

LORD OF WAR
Nicolas Cage

HOTEL RWANDA
Don Cheadle
Nick Nolte

BLOOD DIAMOND
Leonardo DiCaprio, Djimon Hounsou

INVICTUS
Morgan Freeman
Matt Damon

I DREAMED OF AFRICA
Kim Basinger, Vincent Perez

DISTRICT 9
David James, Jason Cope
Sharlto Copley

RENDITION
Meryl Streep
Jake Gyllenhaal
Reese Witherspoon

PRINCE IT'S SHOWTIME
Vivek Oberoi

JUKSKEI MORABARABA DIKETO
INDIGENOUS GAMES
KGATI NTJOVA KHOKHO DIBEKE

10 MOST COMMON CAUSES OF PLANT POISONING

Syringa fruit · Cycad kernels · Physic kernels · Castor Oil Plant seed · Stinkblaar seed · Oleander leaves · Tung Nut kernels · Wild cucumber fruit · Elephant's Ear leaves · Wild Granadilla fruit

DISHES ENJOYED IN THE PAST

FLAMINGO SUPREME
PORCUPINE CRACKLING
ROAST LEGUAAN
FRIED PYTHON STEAKS
TORTOISE IN JELLY
BAKED OX HEAD

20 RICHEST

1. Lakshmi Mittal (ArcelorMittal Steel) R16 950 mil
2. Patrice Motsepe (African Rainbow Minerals) R14 246 mil
3. Nicky Oppenheimer (Anglo American) R5 359 mil
4. Christo Wiese (Shopright, Invicta) R5 053 mil
5. Ackerman family (Pick 'n Pay) R3 267 mil
6. Elephant Consortium (Telkom) R3 214 mil
7. Rembrandt Trust (Remgro) R3 116 mil
8. Desmond Sacco (Assore) R2 886 mil
9. Stephen Saad (Aspen Pharmacare) R2 422 mil
10. Laurie Dippenaar (RMB Holdings) R1 956 mil
11. GT Ferreira (RMB Holdings) R 1 796 mil
12. Bruno Steinhoff (Steinhoff international) R1 629 mil
13. Bill Venter (Altech, Altron) R1 518 mil
14. Adrian Gore (Discovery Holdings) R1 405 mil
15. Giovani Ravazotti (Italtile) R1 346 mil
16. Tokyo Sexwale (Mvelaphande) R1 162 mil
17. Cyril Ramaphosa (Shanduka Group) R988 mil
18. Guiseppe Zannoni (Italtile) R949 mil
19. Gus Attridge (Aspen Pharmacare) R821 mil
20. Koos Bekker (Naspers) R750 mil

SOUTH AFRICAN OSCAR WINNERS (and selected nominees) * **Charlize Theron** - won an Oscar in 2004 for Best Actress for her role in Monster. Charlize is South Africa's first (and only) woman Oscar winner. ***Ted Moore** - South Africa's first Oscar winner, won an Oscar for Best Cinematography for A Man for All Seasons in 1967. ***Yesterday** - the first-ever feature length Zulu film was nominated for Best Foreign Language Film in 2005. ***Tsotsi** - won the Oscar for Best Foreign Language Film in 2006 – a first for SA. *South African, **Don Edkins**, produced Why Democracy?, the world's largest ever factual media event; ***Taxi to the Dark Side**, one of the documentaries which formed part of the event, won an Oscar for Best Documentary in 2008. ***Dion Beebe** - an Australian who grew up in South Africa, won an Oscar for Best Cinematography for Memoirs of a Geisha in 2006. ***The Soweto Gospel Choir** - nominated in 2009 for Best Motion Picture Song for Down to Earth, their Wall-E duet with Peter Gabriel. ***District 9** - nominated for Best Visual Effects in 2010. ***Alfred Oliver** was part of the Oscar-winning animation team on Happy Feet, 2006. *South African, **Stephen Goldblatt** - Oscar-nominated for Best Cinematography for Batman Forever in 1996 and The Prince of Tides in 1992. ***Celia Bobak** - nominated for an Oscar for her set decoration on Phantom of the Opera (film) in 2004. ***Ronald Harwood** - This South African-born playwright won an Oscar for his screenplay for The Pianist in 2003. ***Wayne Kramer's** The Cooler was nominated for Oscars in 2004. He directed the film.

PROVINCES & POPULATION

10.5 m - Gauteng
10.4 m - KwaZulu-Natal
6.6 m - Eastern Cape
5.3 m - Western Cape
5.2 m - Limpopo
3.6 m - Mpumalanga
3.5 m - North West
2.9 m - Free State
1.1 m - Northern Cape

HOW THEY GOT THEIR NAMES

GAUTENG: 'gauta' is a Sotho word for 'gold'.
MPUMALANGA: 'place where the sun rises'.
KWAZULU-NATAL: 'KwaZulu' means 'place of the Zulu people'. 'Natal' is Portuguese for 'Christmas', the day the sailors reached the bay of Durban in 1497.
CAPE: Portugal's King John II named the 'Cape of Good Hope' in the 15th century.
LIMPOPO: After the 1 800 km Limpopo River.
FREE STATE: Originally called Orange Free State upon gaining independence from the British.

TOP 10 RECOGNIZED OVERALL BRANDS

Coca Cola
SAB
Nike
Vodacom
PicknPay
Eskom
Nokia
MTN
Toyota
BMW

PEOPLE STATS

TALLEST (OR LONGEST) PATIENT
Gabriel Monjane 2,42 m at the Sandton Clinic in 1987

LONGEST PENSION 51 YEARS
Herbert Ross Roberts, who died aged 106 in 1971, had been drawing a pension since 1920

WORLD'S FIRST SURROGATE TRIPLETS
Paula, David and Jose Ferreira-Jorge were born by Caesarean section in 1987 to their grandmother, Mrs Pat Anthony of Tzaneen

WORLD'S FIRST SEXTUPLETS
Susan Rosenkowitz gave birth at Groote Schuur Hospital, Cape Town in 1974 to David, Nickie, Jason, Emma, Grant and Elizabeth

FIRST WHITE SOUTH AFRICAN
Wijlant Barentz in 1652

NOBEL PRIZE WINNERS

2003 JM COETZEE: LITERATURE
2002 SYDNEY BRENNER: PHYSIOLOGY OR MEDICINE
1993 FW DE KLERK: PEACE
1993 NELSON MANDELA: PEACE
1991 NADINE GORDIMER: LITERATURE
1984 DESMOND TUTU: PEACE
1979 ALLAN CORMACK: PHYSIOLOGY OR MEDICINE
1960 ALBERT LUTHULI: PEACE
1951 MAX THEILER: PHYSIOLOGY OR MEDICINE

TOP TEN PANTRY FOODS

Tastic
Huletts
Ace
Koo
White star
Joko
Albany
Iwisa
Five roses
Frisco

TOP 20 WEBSITES

1 News24
2 IOL News
3 IOL
4 Hotmail (ZA)
5 Bidorbuy
6 Webmail
7 iMWEB
8 Mybroadband
9 Vodacom4me
10 SuperSport Zone
11 Yellow pages
12 Vodacom4me
13 Mail & Guardian online
14 Times LIVE
15 Heatlh24
16 Sport24
17 fin24
18 Beeld
19 Football365
20 Autotrader

8 MSN(ZA)
Junkmail

145

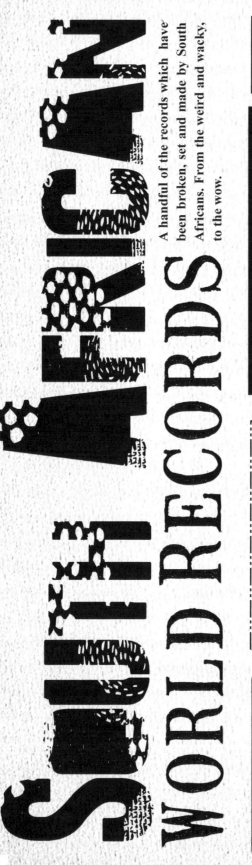

SOUTH AFRICAN WORLD RECORDS

A handful of the records which have been broken, set and made by South Africans. From the weird and wacky, to the wow.

188.9 litres of blood

Maurice Creswick donated 336 units of blood for 59 consecutive years between the ages of 18 and 77.

27 hours 400 pages

LONGEST LEGISLATIVE SPEECH IN HISTORY

Chief Mangosuthu Buthelezi's speech to the KwaZulu Legislative Assembly lasted 27 hours, was 400 pages long and was delivered over 11 days.

780 000 VENOMOUS SNAKES

Bernard Keyter personally milked 780 000 venomous snakes obtaining 3 960 litres (871 gal, 1,046 US gal) of venom over a 14-year period.

He was never bitten.

DEEPEST FRESHWATER CAVE SCUBA DIVE

In 1996, Nuno Gomes dived in Bushmansgat cave, a sinkhole with vertical sides, to a depth of **282.6 m**

The Chappies Little League is listed as the largest football tournament in the world.

FASTEST TEST MATCH HALF-CENTURY

The fastest test match half-century was made from **24 balls** by Jacques Kallis playing against Zimbabwe in 2005

FIRST LADY OF MORE THAN ONE COUNTRY

Graca Machel was married to Mozambique's state president, Samora Machel, until his death in 1986. In 1998, she married President Nelson Mandela.

HIGHEST (and scariest) BUNGEE

Veronica Dean performed 19 bungee jumps in one hour at Bloukans River Bridge, the world's highest commercial bungee jump!

216 m drop!

SHORTEST WOMAN

Madge Bester of Bloemfontein is 65cm (25 in) short and weighs 38 kg. Her mother, Winnie is 70 cm tall

BIGGEST BABY EVER BORN *

10.2 kg

Sithandiwe Simane weighed 10.2kg (22 pounds, 8 ounces). Born by Caesarian section in Sipetu Hospital in Transkei.

OTHER INTERESTING RECORDS:**

Largest Marimba Band to Play Simultaneously

1 164 - most pregnant women under one roof

1 000 kg x 2.6m diameter - largest bowl of cereal

111 m - longest sausage roll ever made

287 bikini clad women - largest bikini parade

24 m - largest football sculpture

12 511 - people blowing vuvuzelas simultaneously

103 - most surfers riding the same wave

Fastest 1 000 Mile Relay Run

Records supplied courtesy of Guinness World Records Limited

Records may not have been verified/approved by Guinness World Records Limited

---

Mossel Bay has the second most moderate climate in the world, second only to Hawaai.**

FASTEST ROUND OF GOLF **

(provided that the ball comes to rest before the next shot is played)

397 m Woodhill Golf Estate in Pretoria.

26 MINUTES AND 37 SECONDS

MOST STEEL CANS COLLECTED IN ONE MONTH

2 122 238 Cans

weighing

66 319.95 kg

by Collect-a-Can in October 2009

---

3 Marathons in **3** days**

South African Johan Oosthuizen completed three consecutive marathons in 8:10:70 at Lake Tahoe, California

---

Records listed on other pages**
Baragwanath Chris Hani Hospital - World's largest hospital
Johannesburg - World's biggest man-made forest
Midmar Mile – World's largest open water swimming event
Anglo Boer War – costliest war
Sishen - **Saldanha** railway train - longest and heaviest train ever assembled

The world's best land-based

whale-watching spot is

located in Hermanus in the

Western Cape.

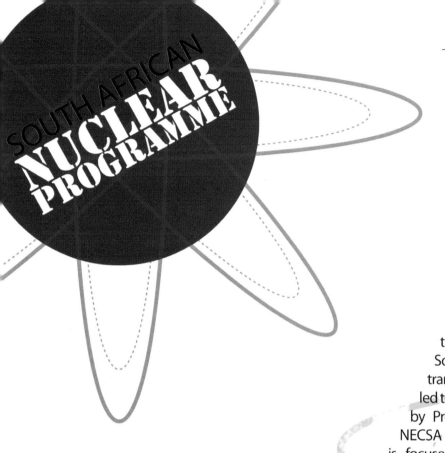

SOUTH AFRICAN NUCLEAR PROGRAMME

WEAPONS OF MASS DESTRUCTION

South Africa's nuclear weapons programme began after World War II and spanned nearly two decades. A uranium enrichment plant was built at Pelindaba in the North West Province and became the new home to the Atomic Energy Board. South Africa was a great fighting nation with an arms capacity matching that of some of the most advanced in the world. Its isolation from the international community, however, meant its nuclear programme was shrouded in secrecy. The improvement of South Africa's security situation, resolution of regional conflicts, along with the collapse of the USSR and threats of Cold War, and political changes in South Africa that demanded greater transparency from the emerging democracy, led to the termination of the nuclear programme by President FW de Klerk in 1991. Today the NECSA (originally the Atomic Energy Corporation) is focused on commercially driven projects and supplies a wide range of innovative hi-technology products and services to South African and foreign market sectors. This research reactor at Pelindaba, SAFARI-1, is the most commercialised nuclear reactor in the world earning millions in foreign revenue for the country.

INTERNATIONAL OUTCRY OVER SECRET TESTING

On Sunday 7th August 1977 an unmarked United States aircraft flying low over the Kalahari Desert in the Northern Cape took pictures of strange structures on the desert floor. This was the sight of a secret nuclear test that was scheduled to take place deep underground. While Atomic Energy Officials say that a 'cold test' (without uranium) was planned, the Soviet and Western Governments were convinced that South Africa was preparing for a full-scale nuclear test. The French foreign minister warned of 'grave consequences' for French-South African relations if the testing continued, implying that France would cancel its contract to provide South Africa with the Koeberg nuclear power reactors that it needed. Once the test site had been exposed, its immediate shutdown was ordered. However, one of the shafts was reopened in 1988 in preparation for another test. This was simply a strategic move to strengthen South Africa's negotiating position during talks to end the war with Angola and Cuba.

In September 1979, US satellites detected a double flash over the Indian Ocean, typical of a nuclear explosion. It was suspected that this was part of a nuclear test collaboration between South Africa and Israel, though no official confirmation of this has been made. For several years thereafter, South Africa continued to deny possession of nuclear weapons.

NUCLEAR WEAPONS IMPLICATED IN BOEING CRASH

On November 28th 1987 at seven minutes past midnight, South African Airways Boeing 747, The Helderberg, crashed into the Indian Ocean off the coast of Mauritius. All 140 passengers and 19 crew were killed. The aircraft lost control following a fire in the main cargo deck compartment and crashed into the sea. Various lines of inquiry were opened in order to determine if The Helderberg was carrying nuclear weapons in its cargo hold, but there has been no proof to either confirm or reject this. However, a later transcript from the cockpit's voice recorder included some details that were not revealed in the original report. The pilots refer to 'Boy George' being on board and are later heard saying 'we fly in their bomb'. Another theory is that while weapons-grade chemicals ignited and caused a fire, Pilot Dawie Uys was instructed to put the fire out and fly on, rather than have illegal cargo discovered. Sadly, it seemed, the fire re-ignited. Many believe that passengers aboard the plane died of smoke inhalation and that the pilot was ordered to fly on instead of landing with an aircraft full of corpses. Others believe that the plane was shot down by the South African Air Force, eliminating the risk of exposure of the nuclear weapons programme.

POWERING A NATION

Koeberg Power Station is the only nuclear power station in Africa. Located 30 km north of Cape Town, it is owned and managed by Eskom, South Africa's national electricity supplier. Koeberg supplies power to the whole of the Western Cape region and is responsible for producing six percent of the country's power requirements. Construction of the plant began in 1976. Both reactor containment buildings are made from concrete that is one metre thick and are lined with steel. Not even an earthquake or a direct hit can break through them. When it comes to safety, Koeberg outranks more than three quarters of the USA's power stations, which are among the best run in the world. (The Institute of Nuclear Power Operations)

SOUTH AFRICA IS THE ONLY COUNTRY IN THE WORLD TO VOLUNTARILY ABANDON ITS NUCLEAR WEAPONS PROGRAMME

152

TOO CLOSE FOR COMFORT!

1. Real life, unedited photograph taken in 2008, Hluhluwe Game Reserve, KwaZulu-Natal by David Plumb.

2. Real life, unedited photographs taken in 2009, Umfolozi Game Reserve, KwaZulu-Natal by Les Dedekind and Pippa Fuller.

3. Photographs courtesy www.emailjokes.co.za, source unknown.

Surviving South Africa's DEADLIEST

SHARK

Since 1990 there have been 112 attacks in South Africa, 13 of them fatal. Seal Island in False Bay holds the record for the highest number of shark attacks in the world.
But before you panic, the number of people who drown along the South African coast outnumbers fatal shark attacks by around 17 to 1.

BEST ADVICE
Swim only within the shark nets.

AVOID
River mouths, fishing areas, swimming after dark.

FACT
Sharks smell one drop of blood in a million drops of water.

IF ATTACKED
Scratch at the eyes and punch at the gills.

CROCODILE

Crocodiles kill their victims by dragging them under water and drowning them with a manoeuvre called the death roll.

BEST ADVICE
Run away if you see a crocodile.

AVOID
Getting closer than 4.5 m from a crocodile. Although they can run 17 km/h they tire easily and will not pursue you.

FACT
The crocodile's bite is stronger than any other creature with a force of 5 000 pounds per square inch.

IF ATTACKED
Punch the crocodile in the nose, poke him in the eye or even better, ram your arm down his throat.

SNAKE

A bite from the black mamba, the largest and most poisonous, can be lethal within 20 minutes. But it is the puff adder who is responsible for the most fatalities.

BEST ADVICE
Wear protective clothing and boots and carry a walking stick.

AVOID
Trying to suck the venom out from the bite.

FACT
In South Africa, the number of deaths from being struck by lightning are ten times higher than those caused by snake bites.

IF BITTEN
Stay calm and walk (not run) for help. Try to identify the snake.

LION

The hunting machine of pure power, speed and agility won't attack unless you look like easy prey.

BEST ADVICE
Stay close to your friends and make yourself look scary by screaming, snarling and showing your teeth.

AVOID
Turning or running away, and never crouch, kneel or play dead.

FACT
The male lion is lazy and the lioness does more than 90 % of the hunting. The male will devour as much as 34 kg of meat at a kill.

IF ATTACKED
Fight back, throw stones, wave clothing and make a noise.

#3 KILLER
HIPPOPOTAMUS

They look slow, clumsy and really cute but don't be fooled. Hippos are responsible for more deaths in Africa than all the Big Five combined. A hippo can open its mouth wide enough to fit a 1.2 m tall child inside. It has been known to bite a crocodile in half.

BEST ADVICE
Keep well away.

AVOID
Getting close and never place yourself between a hippo and either the water or her calf.

FACT
A hippo can run 48 km/h - that's even faster than an Olympic gold medalist, so running is a futile exercise.

IF ATTACKED
Close your eyes and say a prayer.

#2 KILLER
MOSQUITO

The female Anopheles mosquito causes more than one million deaths worldwide each year, 90% of these in sub-Saharan Africa. Fortunately, South Africa is a relatively low risk area but, with over 1 600 deaths in the past ten years, it is still a cause for concern.

BEST ADVICE
Take anti-malaria tablets when visiting a malaria area.

AVOID
Being bitten. Sleep under a net, cover yourself with clothing and use an insect repellent.

FACT
Mosquitos are attracted to perfume and bright coloured clothing.

IF BITTEN
Seek medical attention if you develop a fever or flu-like symptoms within 6 weeks of being in a malaria area.

#1 KILLER
MAN WITHOUT A CONDOM

BY FAR THE MOST DEADLY
There are 5.7 million South Africans living with HIV, resulting in 370 000 deaths a year with an estimated 2.5 million accumulated deaths from AIDS.

BEST ADVICE
Know the HIV status of both yourself and your partner and take necessary precautions.

AVOID
Unprotected sex and multiple sexual partners.

FACT
Condoms are not 100% safe. Using oil-based lubricants will weaken the condom. When buying condoms, check the 'sell by' date.

IF EXPOSED
First get yourself tested, then seek medical advice and professional counselling.

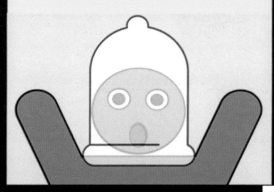

uKhahlamba Drakensberg Park

The majestic uKhahlamba (meaning 'Barrier of Spears' in Zulu) or Drakensberg mountains are breathtakingly beautiful. This cultural and natural heritage site in KwaZulu-Natal covers 230 000 hectares and stretches 150 km. Once home to the San people, it is filled with their rock art, the largest collection in Africa. The site's diversity of habitats protects a high level of endemic and globally threatened species, especially birds and plants.

Robben Island

Robben Island, off the coast of Cape Town, represents South Africa's triumph of democracy and quest for freedom. Although the island is more commonly known for its maximum security prison for anti-apartheid activists, including prisoner 46664, Nelson Rolihlahla Mandela, it has a history that spans centuries. It was a leper colony, a World War II base, a mental hospital and a jail for Dutch colonists as long ago as the 1600s.

8 WONDERS

The Cradle of Humankind

The Vredefort Dome

Sterkfontein, called the Cradle of Humankind, is the richest site in the world for fossils of Australopithecus, a lineage of hominid which appeared over four million years ago. It is also the world's longest sustained excavation ever carried out at an ancient hominid site. Findings include people's earliest-known mastery of fire, and 40% of all the world's human ancestor fossils. Most famous is the discovery of Mrs Ples, the Australopithecus africanus (now believed to be a Mister Ples) and Little Foot, an almost complete ape-man skeleton.

The oldest and largest meteorite impact site in the world was formed around 2 000 million years ago and is estimated to have been 250 - 300 km in diameter. The huge meteorite, larger than Table Mountain, caused a thousand megaton blast of energy, vaporised about 70 km^3 of rock and may have increased the earth's oxygen levels to a degree that made the development of multicellular life possible. The inner circle forms the beautiful range of hills near the town of Vredefort, whilst the outer wrinkle forms the Braamfontein Ridge in Johannesburg.

Mapungubwe National Park

Mapungubwe is South Africa's first kingdom, dating back to between 1050 AD and 1270 AD. Its highly sophisticated people traded gold and ivory with China, India and Egypt prior to any European colonisation. The remains of the palace sites and the settlement area present an unrivalled picture of social and political structures over some 400 years. Mapungubwe, in Limpopo Province, also boasts a beautiful landscape rich in animal and bird life.

Cape Floral Kingdom

The smallest but richest of the world's six floral kingdoms, Table Mountain National Park in the Western Cape has more plant species in its 22 000 hectares than the British Isles or New Zealand. It represents less than 0,5% of the area of Africa, but it is home to nearly 20% of the continent's flora, of which 68% are endemic, occuring nowhere else on earth. The Fynbos vegetation is unique to the Cape floral region.

THE WORLD HERITAGE SITES

Heritage is our legacy from the past, what we live with today, and what we pass on to future generations. Our cultural and natural heritage is an irreplaceable source of life and inspiration. The United Nations Educational, Scientific and Cultural Organisation (UNESCO) has declared eight South African world heritage sites which represent outstanding value to humanity.

Photography courtesy of SA Tourism

Richtersveld Cultural and Botanical Landscape

This spectacular mountainous desert of 160 000 hectares is the home of the nomadic Nama people, descendants of the Khoisan who inhabited the area hundreds of years ago. The Khoisan were made up of the Khoi people, known as Hottentots and the San people, referred to as Bushmen by the Europeans. Ownership of the land was returned to the Nama people, ensuring the conservation of both their thousand-year-old way of life and the succulent Karoo vegetation.

iSimangaliso Wetland Park

'Isimangaliso must be the only place on the globe where the oldest land mammal (the rhinoceros) and the world's biggest terrestrial mammal (the elephant) share an ecosystem with the world's oldest fish (the coelacanth) and the world's biggest marine mammal (the whale).' - Nelson Mandela.

As Africa's largest estuary, the 280 km St Lucia coastline in KwaZulu-Natal has magnificent coral reefs, beaches, coastal forests, plains and woodland areas and is home to hippopotamus, crocodiles, the highly endangered Gaboon adder, and Leatherback turtles.

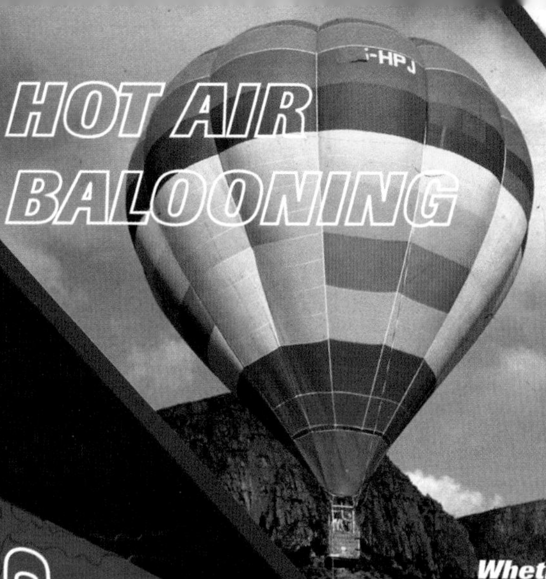

HOT AIR BALOONING

Whether floating above the winelands or game viewing, what better way to experience the beauty of the landscape than floating in a hot air balloon?

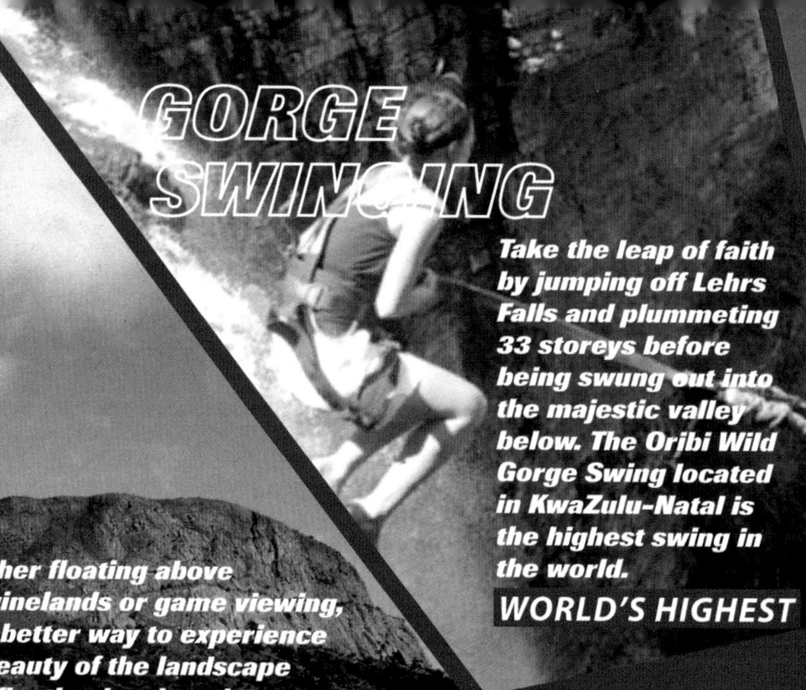

GORGE SWINGING

Take the leap of faith by jumping off Lehrs Falls and plummeting 33 storeys before being swung out into the majestic valley below. The Oribi Wild Gorge Swing located in KwaZulu-Natal is the highest swing in the world.

WORLD'S HIGHEST

KITE

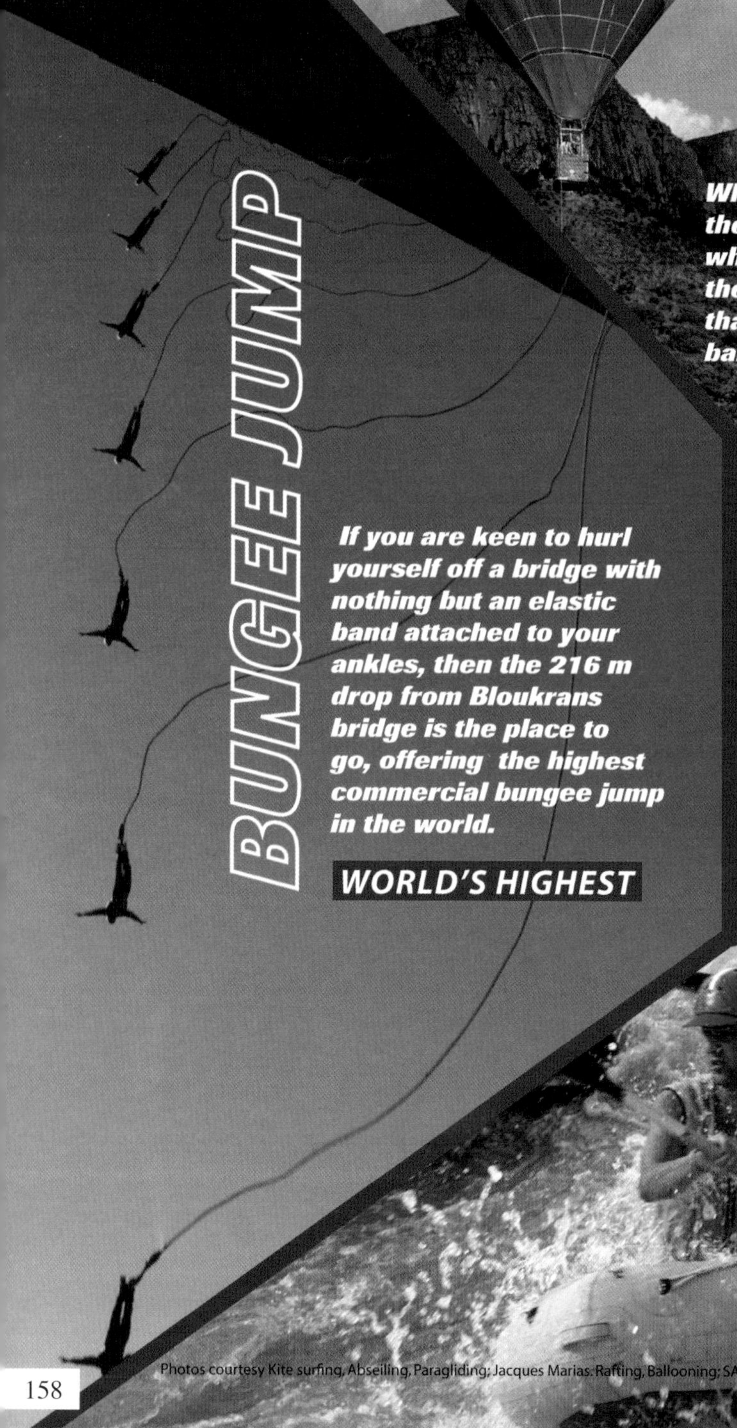

BUNGEE JUMP

If you are keen to hurl yourself off a bridge with nothing but an elastic band attached to your ankles, then the 216 m drop from Bloukrans bridge is the place to go, offering the highest commercial bungee jump in the world.

WORLD'S HIGHEST

ADRENALIN RUSH In South Africa we say

AMP

meaning full of energ

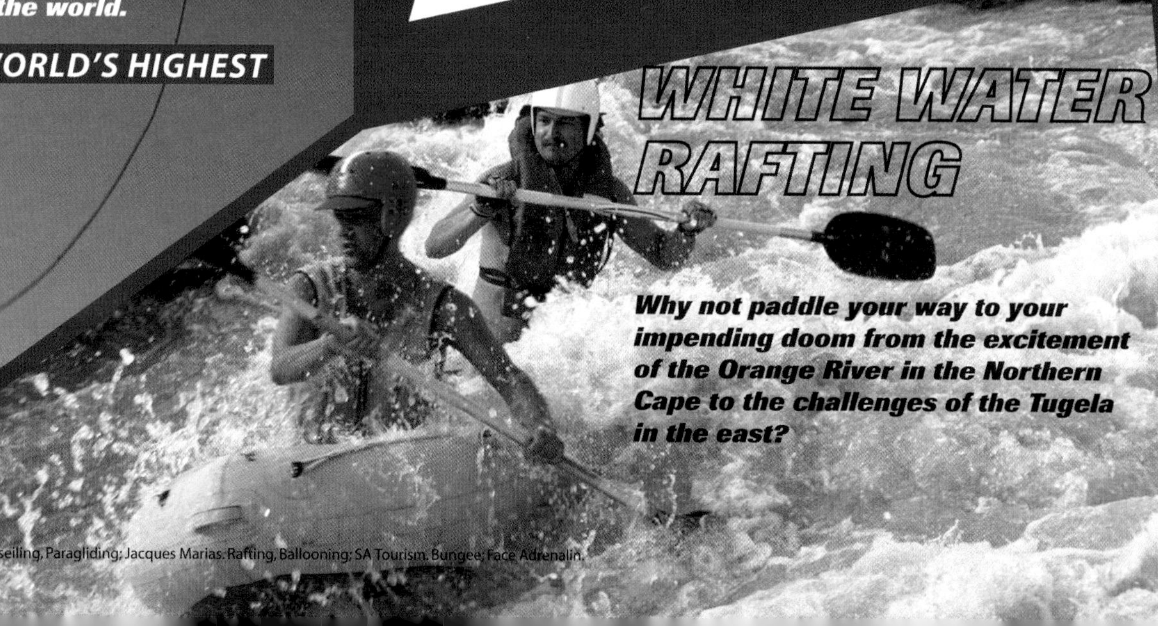

WHITE WATER RAFTING

Why not paddle your way to your impending doom from the excitement of the Orange River in the Northern Cape to the challenges of the Tugela in the east?

BASE JUMPING

Photos courtesy Kite surfing, Abseiling, Paragliding: Jacques Marias. Rafting, Ballooning: SA Tourism. Bungee: Face Adrenalin.

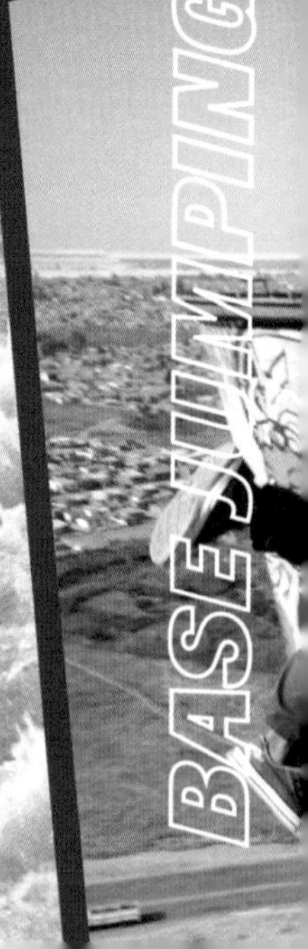

SURFING

If it looks easy - don't be fooled. But with an abundance of waves, water and wind, who wouldn't want to leap hundreds of metres at a time through the air! Langebaan is regarded as one of the top kitesailing venues in the world.

TOP VENUE

If you're brave or mentally impaired enough to take part in adventure sport then you're spoilt for choice. If hurling yourself off obscenely high landmarks or playing with killer sharks is for you, you've found the right place.

PED!

sually induced by adrenalin, feeling wired or high on fear

ABSEILING

With 112 m of rock face below, you will find ample time to loosen your grip and suck in the breathtaking views. The Table Mountain 'Long Drop' is the highest commercial abseil in the world.

WORLD'S HIGHEST

From Soweto's infamous cooling towers, you are spoilt for choice. You can choose between a bungee jump and swinging down 100 m into the darkness of the cooling towers. But to earn the 5 star rating, you need to take the base jump from the top.

PARAGLIDING

When looking for a place to catch some good thermals in South Africa be sure to visit... well, almost everywhere really.

FAMOUS BATTLES OF

BATTLE	WHEN	WHERE	OPPOSING FORCES	TACTICS
Grahamstown	1819	Grahamstown, Eastern Cape	10 000 Xhosa men attacked 450 British, helped by 82 Khoi Khoi troops.	Xhosa prophet-warrior Nxele and his men attacked the Grahamstown British military base by rushing up to the cannon and the barricades, but were unable to break through.
Blood River / eNcome	1838	Dundee, KwaZulu-Natal	15 000 Zulu warriors fought against 464 well-armed Voortrekkers.	The Zulu warriors used the 'bull-horned' battle formation, but could not match the muzzle loading guns and cannons of the Boers, led by Andries Pretorius.
Ndondokusuka	1856	kwaDukuza, KwaZulu-Natal	Two brothers, Cetshwayo kaMpande with 20 000 warriors against Mbuyazi kaMpande's 7 000 plus a small band of white mercenaries.	Mbuyazi kaMpande relied on the guns of John Dunn's mercenaries but Prince Cetshwayo kaMpande had both numbers and intelezi (war medicines).
Isandlwana	1879	Nqutu, KwaZulu-Natal	1768 British troops against 20 000 Zulus.	Zulu commander Ntshingwayo, concealed within 8 km of the camp, surprised Brevet Colonel Henry Pulleine and his men.
Rorke's Drift	1879	Nqutu, KwaZulu-Natal	4 000 Zulu warriors facing 139 redcoat soldiers.	Lt Chard used sacks of food and biscuit boxes to defend the hospital and medical depot against Prince Dabulamanzi kaMpande and his men.
Majuba	1881	Newcastle, KwaZulu-Natal	405 British redcoats, including 171 Gordon Highlanders in kilts, against 450 Boer commandos.	General Colley unsuccessfully held the high ground overlooking the Boers who made steady progress up the side of Majuba mountain.
Mome	1906	Nkandla, KwaZulu-Natal	2 000 white colonial British troops with 900 'loyal' Africans facing over 1 000 Zulu rebels.	Nkosi Bhambata Zondi's Zulu rebels moved into the Thukela Zulu forest gorge but were trapped by Col McKenzie's troops.

SOUTH AFRICAN HISTORY

WINNERS AND LOSERS	SIGNIFICANCE	OUTCOME
The British volleys of musket shot into the tightly packed regiments of warriors resulted in at least 1 000 Xhosa being killed. Only three British troops died.	Nxele's defeat led to the 1820 settler scheme, which ultimately eroded African land quicker and brought about further suffering.	The frontier was no longer preserved and Xhosa independence was imperilled.
The Zulus were unable to dislodge the Voortrekkers from their cunningly devised laager. Boer weapons caused about 3 000 deaths that turned the Ncome River red with blood. No Voortrekkers died.	A sacred vow became the foundation of the belief that the Christian God gave a divine blessing to the Afrikaners in South Africa. It was seen as religious justification for a future white minority rule of the country.	One of the historic legends central to apartheid.
Mbuyazi's men were helplessly pinned against the banks of the flooding Thukela river by Cetshwayo's men. Almost 6 000 were killed, including women and children.	Prince Cetshwayo waited a further 16 years to take over his father's reign, making unwise alliances and dubious agreements which led to the British invasion of 1879 and his defeat.	South Africa's single bloodiest day of violence.
Of the 800 white troops who saw the start of the battle, 727 were killed along with 52 officers and 471 of the African contingent on their side. The Zulu victory came at a cost of over 2 000 warriors.	Zulu regiments, armed with spears and shields, cemented their position as one of Africa's greatest military nations, casting themselves in the symbolic role of warriors for eternity.	The largest defeat of British soldiers in colonial warfare outside of Europe.
After 12 hours of fighting and the burning of the hospital, more than 1 000 warriors died while 17 of the enemy were killed.	The defence and successful evacuation of more than 30 patients has made Rorke's Drift synonymous with bravery, resulting in the death of hundreds of heroic Zulu.	The most highly decorated battle in British history with 11 Victoria Crosses awarded.
The Boers killed General Colley and inflicted terrible casualties on the Highlanders, resulting in 92 British dead and 134 wounded. Only one Boer died.	The British relinquished their claims to the Boer territory, regretting it five years later when the world's greatest deposit of gold was found near Johannesburg.	British humiliation far outstripped the number of dead.
The courage of the rebel forces was no match for the technological advantages of the colonial troops. Hundreds were killed or wounded, and Nkosi Bhambata's head was cut off as a trophy.	This battle marks the last act of armed resistance by Zulu warriors against colonialists. The military tradition established by King Shaka had ended - except on re-enactments for tourists.	Should be regarded as an act of war crime.

Text: Steve Kotze

161

✸ Oscar Pistorius - Changing the rules of the Olympics

Known as 'the Blade Runner' or 'the fastest man on no legs', Oscar Pistorius is an athletics world record holder. Born without a fibula in both legs, Oscar's lower legs were amputated before his first birthday. Despite this, he participated fully in sports at school and in 2004 became the 200 m double-amputee running champion at the Athens Paralympics. Also the 100 m, 200 m and 400 m paralympic record holder, Oscar achieved times qualifying him to compete against able-bodied athletes. With his sights set on the 2008 Beijing Olympics, Oscar was, however, banned from competing by the IAAF on the grounds that his running prosthetics gave him an unfair advantage over athletes competing with their natural legs. Not one to wallow in self-pity, Oscar appealed the decision and months before the competition, the ruling was overturned. Although too late to give him sufficient time to train for 2008, the ruling has significant implications for 2012, not only for himself but for other disabled athletes as well. Oscar's contribution towards the wellbeing of disabled athletes was recognised by the Presidency of South Africa when, in 2007, he received The Order of Ikhamanga in Bronze. Nevertheless, Oscar's achievements in able-bodied athletics inspire all athletes, whether disabled or not.

INSPIRING THE

You're not disabled by the disabilities you have. You are enabled by the abilities you have   (Oscar Pistorius)

✸ Sibusiso Vilane - Reaching the top again and again

Only a handful of people in this world can claim to be members of the Seven Summits Club. Six of those are South African. And on 13 June 2008, Sibusiso Vilane, a game ranger from Limpopo, became the first black African to join the club. After being the first black African to summit Everest in 2003, Sibu seized the opportunity to promote this remarkable sport among Africans by aiming for the top - the seven highest peaks on the seven continents. These are: Kilimanjaro in Africa (which Sibu climbed in 1999), Everest in Asia (2003 and 2005), Aconcagua in South America (2006), Elbrus in Europe (2006), Carstensz Pyramid in Oceania (2006), Vinson in Antarctica (2006) and finally Denali/McKinley in North America (2008). This last mountain was also Sibu's most difficult. But his determination, hard work and his belief that mountains are merely a metaphor for challenge and success helped him conquer this physically torturous peak. A hero amongst his colleagues, and recognised by the Presidency of South Africa in 2006 with the presentation of the Order of Ikhamanga in Bronze, Sibu's achievements touch ordinary South Africans. 'Always strive for the top,' says Sibu. 'Whatever you do, be the best you can be.'

Photo © Stefano Mattana, Italy

✳ Lewis Pugh – Calling on world leaders to make change

When Lewis Gordon Pugh swam the waters of the North Pole in 2007 wearing only a swimming costume, a cap and a pair of goggles he captured the world's attention. His body used 'anticipatory thermogenises' to survive the freezing water. The first person to swim across this patch of icy water, and the only person in the world to have completed a long distance swim in every ocean of the world (in temperatures ranging from 30°C to -1.8°C), Lewis is not simply a pioneer swimmer. He is a hands-on, act-now activist who observes first hand the alarming effects of global warming. So, combining extreme swimming with his legal skills (as a maritime lawyer), Lewis calls on the decision-makers of this world to make changes. And those changes have already been seen. It is often reported that Lewis was the catalyst that persuaded Prime Minister Gordon Brown to enact legislation to cut carbon emissions in the UK. A month after Lewis met with Brown, whilst the adventurer was kayaking near thinning ice in the sea north of Spitsbergen, the UK enacted the Climate Change Act, obliging it to cut its carbon emissions by 80% by 2050. A number of other nations have followed suit.

We need to tread very lightly on this earth
(Lewis Gordon Pugh)

WORLD

✳ Natalie Du Toit – The first athlete to qualify for the Olympics and the Paralympics

The tragedy of life does not lie in not reaching your goals. The tragedy of life lies in not having goals to reach for

(Natalie Du Toit)

Natalie became the first-ever person in the world to qualify in both the Olympics and the Paralympics.
As a young girl, South African swimmer Natalie Du Toit had one goal. To compete in the Olympic Games. Her swimming career looked promising when in 1998, at the age 14, she represented South Africa at the Commonwealth Games, and two years later nearly qualified for the 2000 Sydney Olympics. Olympics 2004 was a distinct possibility but an accident in 2001 changed everything. Or did it? Yes and no. Losing her left lower leg as a result of a traffic accident only served to strengthen this young woman's resolve. In 2004 she not only won five gold medals at the Paralympics but in 2008, became the first and only athlete in history to qualify for both the Olympics and the Paralympics. Natalie's feats have not only raised the profile of disabled athletes, more importantly she has shown each and every South African the power of the human spirit. Awarded the Whang Youn Dai Achievement Award in 2008 for her contribution to the Paralympic Movement, Natalie's participation in both disability and open races has created a greater understanding between disabled and able-bodied athletes.

We are born to win
(Sibusiso Vilane)

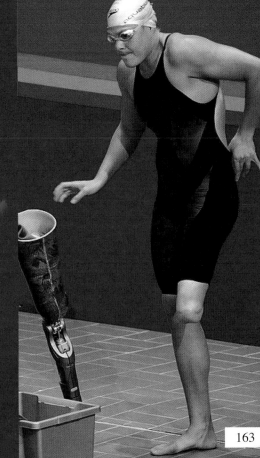

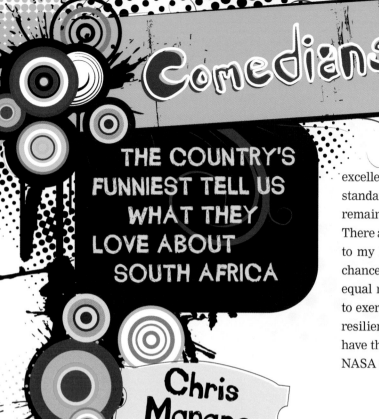

Comedians

THE COUNTRY'S FUNNIEST TELL US WHAT THEY LOVE ABOUT SOUTH AFRICA

John Vlismas

There are many reasons why I love SA. We are spoiled by the sense of space we have grown up with, an abundance of sunshine and our beautiful coastline. Our cities are cosmopolitan and our infrastructure is excellent. Our government is maturing and levels of corruption are reaching international standards. We're in a good position to provide a bridge between Africa and the West, while remaining open to visits from dictators and despots, so we have a low risk of terror attacks. There are no major fault lines below us and, being situated in Johannesburg, I look forward to my Dunkeld flat being beachfront property one day when global warming has had a chance to show us what it can do. We have a constitution that theoretically gives us more equal rights than any other equal rights in the world, provided we survive long enough to exercise them, as our average life expectancy keeps dropping gently. Our currency is a resilient fellow, who does the odd bungee jump, just to keep us on our toes. We also must have the best cell phone systems in the universe as we pay more to phone each other than NASA does to send a fax to the International Space Station. www.whacked.co.za

Chris Mapane

South Africa has what we call 'the politically correct way of saying things'. So you can't say someone is black or white or Coloured. The politically acceptable way of referring to 'black' people is 'Human beings in the absence of light', and 'white' people 'Human beings in the extreme presence of light'. And with Coloured people, well no one seems to care. What's cool about SA is the commitment of SA citizens when coming to service delivery; when you visit government buildings, there are people, outside, doing the same job that they are doing inside. At Home Affairs, there is a brother standing at the corner promising to get you your ID or passport quicker than they will do inside, and at half the price. At the Department of Trade and Industry, there is someone who will register your company and reserve the name later. And it scares me to think I might go to the hospital one day and find a brother waiting for me outside with an injection or a heart ready to do a transplant, saying I don't need medical aid. SA is a very democratic country. I mean, this is the only country where an 18-year-old can drive alone to the traffic department, park inside, close the door, get inside and book a learner's test. That's awesome South Africa right there.
www.chrismapane.co.za

Kedibone Malaudzi

South Africa is a great country. Great weather, great people, great everything. I love everybody, Black people, Coloured people, Indian people and White people. I love Indian people. I just love the way they do auctions. I went to Mr Naidoo's Auction a while back. The first item to be auctioned was a Plasma Screen HD TV. Mr Naidoo: 'The first item on the list is this HD TV. The bidding price starts at R1 000. Do I hear R800? R800 to the lady in a red top. Do I hear R500? R500?'

I love white people. I just love the way they do funerals. It'll be like 20 of them and not even one person is crying. Not us black people. Our funerals are always sold out and we have different styles of crying.

First style: People that were hired to come cry. It's normal crying. Second style: The widow of the deceased. She's crying tears of joy - the poor dude left her with R2 million worth of policies and insurance. Third style: Group of guys that are owed money by the deceased. They are crying, rolling on the floor. It's just a mess. **www. sowetocomedyfestival.net**

Barry Hilton

Living in South Africa is funny because... We have as many prostitutes as criminals ... so, either way, you get screwed. We tell people to tighten their belts in times of crisis, then the ex-finance minister buys a top-of-the-range BMW for R1.5 million and it wasn't even 'manuel'.

We have a quota system in sport so the South African rugby team has got to be demographically representative amongst all the populace of South Africa – The SA Rugby 15 will comprise eight black okes, three white okes, two Coloureds, three quarters of an Indian and a one-eyed black lesbian in a wheelchair. Our soccer team is called Bafana Bafana because you have to tell them twice. It's not what you think - the coach is Portuguese.

Overseas people ask us if we have fast food here. It's clear that if you are not fast, you are food. We have the best taxi system in the world, it's free and fair - if you have opposition, you just shoot them. I saw a taxi for sale – 'E20 taxi great condition, indicators never used, needs new hooter, comfortably sits 48 big adults, balance of traffic fines negotiable.'

If all the people in the government actually worked for the government, we might actually have a government. I find it strange that the leader of our communist party flies Business Class.

But all in all and with all the nonsense, I just love being here, coz after all you can't buy sunshine! On that note, I would like to tell you that I, Barry Hilton, am staying in South Africa! **www.barryhilton.co.za**

KEVIN PERKINS
A.K.A. MICHAEL NAICKER

The weather, the scenery, the culture – I love South Africa. It has to be one of the best places to live in the world. It's not all sunny skies and braais though. Life is tough but rewarding. We start our week watching Carte Blanche on a Sunday night, the frightening investigative journalism TV programme which exposes negative aspects of our lives. This is why the Australian Embassy is busiest on a Monday morning. By Wednesday, things are looking more positive and by Friday, all is well. The weekend lies ahead – friends, ice-cold beers and great sports. Monday traffic beckons and South Africans endure the office environment. Your boss is a 'doos.' (Any normal person can become a doos, a label foisted on those who make our lives unpleasant.) Some people cannot control acting like a doos; their condition is terminal. To hide their embarrassing ailment and rapidly degenerating intellect, they are forced to seek out like-minded individuals and usually go into politics.

Fortunately dooses are a minority and are equally represented among all race groups which leads me to my final point: **People** make South Africa great! Once you are South African, you will **always** be South African. It's the reason Johnny Clegg's 'Scatterlings of Africa' will always bring a tear to South African expatriates and why we roar in support of our national rugby team. South Africa is in your soul and no matter where you are – around South Africa, or around the world – it will always be with you. Nkosi Sikelel' iAfrica! **www.michaelnaicker.com**

Bevan Cullinan

South Africa is a very funny place to live in and I wouldn't trade the experience for anywhere else. There are so many different flavoured fruit in this mad fruit bowl. We love to laugh, because life is good and every person who lives here is funny by proxy. You can't avoid it. There are so many different backgrounds interacting with each other that there is bound to be a laugh point once every second, somewhere in South Africa, just by circumstance. As comedians we just watch and wait for it. I've seen many foreign comedians and quite frankly, they just have nothing real to talk funny about. There is nothing funny about 'regulation', the scourge of the First World. There are only so many jokes you can make about the weather!

If I'm going to make funny, I want to make funny about something that has substance. In order for comedy to work, there has to be some percentage of pain to the gag and so I'd like to thank all the clowns that have influenced this country's path over the last 100 years, from wars to pass laws to beetroot. Without you, comedians wouldn't have been able to make a living ... and make living in South Africa such a great experience.

Be Cool!

A GRAPE ACHIEVEMENT

HISTORY LESSON

On the 2nd February 1659, the great explorer Jan van Riebeck wrote in his journal: 'Today, praise the Lord, wine was pressed for the first time from Cape Grapes'. The grapes had grown from vines sent to the Cape on request by van Riebeck who was eager to please his workers and make them feel more at home in the newly founded Cape regions.

IT'S *HOW* BIG?

Paarl, in the Cape, is the third oldest town in South Africa, and home to the KWV Cellars – the world's largest wine cellar that covers as much as 22 hectares of land.

ROAD TO PARADISE
ROUTE 62

South Africa has the longest (and arguably the most beautiful) wine route in the World – the R62 wine route is 850 km long, stretching from Cape Town to Port Elizabeth.

FIT FOR A PRESIDENT

AWARD WINNER

First lady Michelle Obama selected a bottle of South African Graham Beck Brut NV for her husband President Barack Obama's celebrations on his election night - the same wine that Nelson Mandela used to toast his inauguration in 1994.

ONLY THE BEST

South African wines trounced the competition in both the red and white single varietal categories, winning top accolades at the prestigious 2009 World Wine Awards.

STARTER KIT

AND THEN THERE WAS WINE

Not only did 2009 mark the 350th year of wine making in South Africa, but it is one of the only countries in the world that can pinpoint – to the day – when wine was first produced in the country.

Photo © Ted Stedman

It feels like God visits

everywhere else

but lives in Africa.

Will Smith
(on his first visit to South Africa)

Foreigners ask the weirdest things. To be read with a sense of humour, these South African responses appeared on the internet, with some extras added to match the real-life photos.

(from the USA)

Q: Can I bring cutlery into South Africa?

A: Why? Just use your fingers like we do!

(from the USA)

Q: Will I be able to see elephants in the street?

A: Depends how much you've been drinking!

(from the USA)

Q: Will I be able to 'speek' English most places I go?

A: Yes, but you'll have to learn it first!

(from Sweden)

Q: Is it safe to run around in the bushes in South Africa?

A: So it's true what they say about Swedes!

PHOTO ON RIGHT

Q: Can I bring my pet along with me?

A: Most definitely, but bring a backpack along if worried about how to transport your goat!

(from the USA)

Q: Please send a list of all doctors in South Africa who can dispense rattlesnake serum.

A: Rattlesnakes live in A-meri-ca, which is where YOU come from. All South African snakes are perfectly harmless, can be safely handled and make good pets!

PHOTO ON RIGHT

Q: In the event of emergency, are there ambulances in South Africa?

A: Yes, but we suggest you bring along some carrots and Red Bull® for the oxen!

(from Germany)

Q: Are there killer bees in South Africa?

A: Not yet, but for you, we'll import them!

(from the USA)

Q: Can you give me some information about Koala Bear racing in South Africa?

A: Aus-tra-lia is that big island in the middle of the Pacific. A-fri-ca is the big triangle-shaped continent south of Europe which does not... Oh forget it. Sure, the Koala Bear racing is every Tuesday night in Hillbrow. Come naked!

PHOTO ON LEFT

Q: Can I charge my iPod in South Africa?

A: No need. Just follow the example of this local KZN resident on how to charge a portable transistor radio with a car battery!

(from the USA)

Q: Can you send me the Vienna Boys' Choir schedule?

A: Aus-tri-a is that quaint little country bordering Ger-man-y, which is... Oh forget it. Sure, the Vienna Boys Choir plays every Tuesday night in Hillbrow, straight after the Koala Bear races. Come naked!

Photo courtesy: Boy, Ambulance: Email distribution, source unknown. Radio; Thabiso Jojo

Anglo Boer Wars
1880-1881 & 1899-1902

Two bitter wars that saw pockets of passionate nationalist defiance clash with the industrious might of imperialist machinery changing South Africa's physical and cultural landscape forever!

A war to change all wars

• The Anglo Boer War (1899-1902) was the first war of the twentieth century and saw the introduction of trench warfare, the first large-scale use of concentration camps for non-combatants, and the most prolonged period of guerrilla warfare by a conquered nation's military against a victorious army.

• Camouflage was first used in battle by the Boers, who used camouflaged trenches and adapted battledress to blend into treeless landscapes.

• The world's first news footage and propaganda films were produced during the Anglo Boer War. Technologically, it saw the first use of a generation of weapons that are still with us today - automatic handguns, magazine-fed rifles, and machine guns.

• The Guinness Book of Records lists the Anglo Boer War as Britain's most costly war outside of the two World Wars.

David faces Goliath

Only 87 000 Boers, all unpaid volunteers, bravely took on 450 000 trained British soldiers who were armed to the hilt, well-paid and extremely well supplied with food and ammunition. The Boers were a nation descended from the Dutch settlers who arrived in South Africa in 1652 and intermingled with French Huguenots, German immigrants, indigenous people and others. The British were a colonising nation with a penchant for conquering other, mostly third world, nations in order to help manage their natural resources.

The British adopted a scorched earth policy and destroyed over 30 000 Boer farmhouses, several towns and slaughtered hundreds of thousands of sheep, cattle and horses. 26 000 Boer women and children perished in concentration camps, some of which were as far afield as India, Bermuda and Ceylon (Sri Lanka). 75 000 lives were lost before the British finally won the war.

'The Boers were the most goodhearted enemy I have ever fought against in the four continents in which it has been my fortune to see active service.'
Winston Churchill,
British Prime Minister

'I have fought against many barbarous kaffir tribes, but they are not so barbarous as the English, who burnt our farms and drove our women and children into destitution'.

Paul Kruger

'The individual Boer, mounted, in a suitable country, is worth four or five regular soldiers. The only way of treating them is to either get men equal in character and intelligence as riflemen, or failing that, huge masses of troops'.
Winston Churchill,
British Prime Minister

Taking Sides

The war between the British and the Boers saw a number of parties sending support. The Anglo Boer War was the first war in which the Commonwealth of Australia fought, sending a contingent of 20 000 men. It was also the first time Canadian troops served abroad, and New Zealand sent nearly 6 500 men with 8 000 horses to fight in the conflict.

The Irish sided with the Boers. In 1899, a staggering 20 000 people, including the famous poet WB Yeats, attended a rally in Dublin to support the Boers.

It is estimated that around 16 000 black Africans died in the concentration camps.

Over 300 000 horses killed in battle

The number of horses killed in the Anglo-Boer War was at the time unprecedented in modern warfare. The average life expectancy of a British horse, from the time of its arrival on South African soil, was around six weeks. Conditions were so bad that horses were consumed as food by the British once the regular sources of meat were depleted.

Writing history at Spioenkop

General Buller's troops fought the battle of Spioenkop on their way to relieve the beseiged British forces in Ladysmith. It was a savage battle and the British were famously beaten, incurring 243 fatalities and 1 250 wounded or captured. A 25-year-old London journalist, Winston Churchill, who had been commissioned as a Lieutenant in the South African Light Horse, under General Buller, acted as a courier between Spioenkop and the British HQ.

Remarkably, Mahatma Gandhi was a stretcher-bearer for the British forces at the very same battle and is reported to have done sterling work during and after the slaughter.

General Louis Botha, who led the vastly outnumbered Boers at Spioenkop, would go on to become president of an independent Republic of South Africa!

It is interesting to note that Churchill, Gandhi and Botha were all present at Spioenkop that day and one wonders what the course of history might have been had any one of them not survived.

Kops around the world

At the end of the 1905-06 season, Liverpool Football Club rewarded the loyalty of the fans by building a new stand. It was christened as the 'Spioenkop' in memory of the many scousers who died in battle during the Anglo-Boer War. Leeds United Football Club's mascot, Lucas Kop Cat, is also named after the South African hill, as is the village of Spion Kop in Nottinghamshire. Similarly, in Australia there are numerous hills bearing the name 'Spioenkop' in honour of the battle.

The hill of Spioenkop near Ladysmith in KwaZulu-Natal overlooking the Spioenkop dam in the background.

Photo © Chris Bloom

Our floral Kingdom

South Africa has the third highest level of biodiversity in the world.

South Africa is home to the world's smallest succulent plants (less than 9.9 mm) and the largest (the baobab tree, around 20 m tall).

South Africa is the only country in the world with an entire plant kingdom inside its borders.

The Cape Floral Region contains more plant species per square metre than anywhere else on our planet.

THE BUSHMAN

The San is the most studied anthropological group in the world. The San people were the 'First people of Africa'. They were called Bushmen by the Europeans and were hunter-gatherers. For more than 20 000 years, the Bushmen were the sole inhabitants of southern Africa, until the arrival of the Bantu tribes in the region about 1500 years ago, followed by white colonists, a few hundred years ago.

It is believed that the genes of the San predate the rest of humanity, making the San our original ancestors. We still have much to learn from them.

Although very little is known of Bushman life and culture, what we do know is that they had an incredible knowledge of plants, animals, seasons and climates.

PRESERVING A CULTURE

Considered the oldest culture in the world, and the creators of beautiful rock art that can be seen throughout southern Africa, the San never received the respect they deserved. In the past 2 000 years, the San were slowly pushed to live in the arid sands of the Kalahari Desert by Bantu tribes and white farmers who took the more fertile land for their crops and livestock. They were largely considered to be vermin, continuously evicted and 'relocated' to the point of extinction. Right into the beginning of the twentieth century, it was even considered legal to purchase a licence to hunt these people.

Today the San people number between 30 000 and 55 000. The Richtersveld region in the Northern Cape has been returned to the ownership of the San people under South Africa's land restitution programme, where they still lead a semi-nomadic life.

THE REVERED ELAND

The Eland is the most revered animal amongst the indigenous people of southern Africa, hence its representation in the majority of San rock art. The Eland played a crucial role in saving the Earth Mother known as Ninawatu. As the legend goes, Ninawatu had seen the devastation that humans caused and felt responsible for creating these beings. She approached Ranadu, the pitiless judge, and was sentenced to three months in the underworld. The earth froze and the spirits left. Nature and the animals could not bear these conditions. Imbube, the lion, called a meeting to plan the rescue of Ninawatu. Impofu, the Eland, was chosen above all other animals to rescue the Earth Mother from the underworld because of the strength of his back and his kind nature. As Impofu and Ninawatu escaped the underworld, Impofu was struck by a poisonous arrow. Impofu fell once Ninawatu was safe and as his spirit departed, she gathered it up and threw it into the skies, turning it into stars. The indigenous people know it today as the constellation of the Eland.

> **"** I owe my being to the Khoi and the San whose desolate souls haunt the great expanses of the beautiful Cape – they who fell victim to the most merciless genocide our native land has ever seen, they who were the first to lose their lives in the struggle to defend our freedom and dependence and they who, as a people, perished in the result. **"**
>
> Thabo Mbeki

THE WORLD'S OLDEST JEWELLERY COLLECTION

Jewellery and artistic engravings found in the ancient Blombos cave in the southern Cape date back 77 000 years. The findings are the oldest cultural items to be found anywhere in the world.

HOW TO TAME A LION

The gentle Bushmen had a particular ability for moving among wild animals, specifically lions, with ease. They would sleep in the middle of the open veld, completely exposed to these beasts without a worry in the world.

Some explain this phenomenon as owing to the Bushmen's knowledge of the plant properties which they powdered and sprinkled upon their night fires. Others attributed this keen sense of survival to 'supernatural' powers.

The reality of the situation was that Bushmen studied the behavioural patterns of all animals with which they came into contact. The hallmark of their social attitudes was their utter belief in co-operation. They knew the lions were territorial, and that each pride had a dominant male. When the Bushmen moved into the area, they quickly identified the lion families and their leading males. They kept a close eye on the developments in the pride, waiting to see when the alpha male was getting older or weaker and when the young males were ready to usurp him. The Bushmen knew exactly when the alpha males were overthrown and which young male took his place. The first time the new dominant male had a chance to take a nap, three or four of the best hunters would creep up to him and proceed to give the sleeping lion the beating of his life with their sticks, shrieking and shouting at the top of their voices. The poor, disorientated beast would flee in confusion. Through this act, a tacit and rather fearful understanding developed between the alpha lion and his subjects that these people, who had spared his life, were not to be tangled with.

ASTRONOMERS FROM THE PAST

There is evidence that the Bushmen had been observing the movements of the planet Jupiter and its satellites with the naked eye, long before European astronomers.

Stories as told by Roger Webster in *At the Fireside*

ZOLA BUDD

This barefooted teenage athlete attained fame in the early 1980s when she achieved one incredible record-breaking performance after another. She beat the world-record time for the 5 000 m and ran the fastest ever 3 000 m and 1 500 m by a junior (under 19 years old). However, because of the worldwide sporting ban against South Africa, none of her achievements were officially recognized.

Budd took a drastic step to realise her ambition of competing in the Olympic Games when she applied for British citizenship. She was flown to Amsterdam under an assumed name (Miss Hamilton), then spirited into England in a private plane chartered by the Daily Mail, a London tabloid. Zola Budd was declared a British subject just 10 days after applying for citizenship which caused fury among anti-apartheid campaigners. 'I'm just a runner,' Zola Budd told the press, 'Not a politician.'

Budd was again the centre of controversy during the women's 3 000 m final at the Olympic Games in Los Angeles. An accidental collision between American athlete Mary Decker and Budd caused Decker to stumble and crash dramatically onto the infield. With her left hip injured, Decker was unable to resume the race. Budd finished seventh, and Romanian Maricica Puica went on to win the gold medal. The IAAF jury found that Budd was not responsible for the collision.

To some, Budd symbolised South Africa's determination to overcome global ostracism. Budd, however, never demonstrated any public support for apartheid. In fact, in 1984 she became the only white ever to be voted the Sports Star of the Year by the readers of Bona, a South African magazine with a predominantly black readership. To this day, many blacks in South Africa refer to their taxi vans in which they travel to work as Zola Budds, or Zolas.

SPORTING CONTROVERSY

BASIL D'OLIVIERA

Basil D'Oliviera never played cricket for South Africa, yet he was nominated as one of the country's cricketers of the 20th century. As a Coloured man, D'Oliviera was deprived of the opportunity to play for his country and, in 1960, he left his birthplace of Cape Town and emigrated to England. By the time the England team was to be selected for the tour to South Africa in 1968, D'Oliviera had played 16 tests for England as an all-rounder. However, a political storm was gathering, with Prime Minister John Vorster warning the MCC that D'Oliviera would not be admitted into South Africa if he were selected for the England tour.

In fact, he even secretly discussed bribing D'Oliviera not to come if selected. In the Ashes series prior to the South African tour, D'Oliviera scored 158 at the oval, staking a strong claim for a place in the touring team, however the selectors opted to leave D'Oliviera out of the 16-man squad. England bowler Tom Cartwright was selected, but when a shoulder injury forced him to pull out 20 days later, he was replaced by D'Oliviera. Vorster was furious, and said: 'We are not prepared to receive a team thrust upon us by people whose interests are not in the game but to gain certain political objectives which they do not even attempt to hide. The MCC team is not the team of the MCC but of the anti-apartheid movement.' A week later the MCC called off the tour. Twenty-seven years passed before England would tour South Africa again.

STADIUM STAMPEDE

Kaizer Chiefs and Orlando Pirates played before 62 000 soccer fans on 11 April 2001 at the Ellis Park Football Stadium in Johannesburg. The match initially appeared to be like any derby between the Chiefs and the Pirates. The stadium was full, with no place to stand. There were lots of cheering, happy fans. But things changed after the Pirates equalised. Tens of thousands of fans still outside the gates hoping to get tickets for the game began pushing towards the fence around the field, trying to find a way in. The fence collapsed in four places and the lively crowd lunged forward to disaster. Officials tried in vain to call for calm. 29 people were trampled to death inside the stadium and 14 outside. A further 155 people were injured. The match was tied 1-1 when it was abandoned, 34 minutes after play began.

COMRADES TWINS

For most, 90 kms is a long stretch to run non-stop, but for brothers Sergio and Fika Motsoeneng it was as easy as going to the toilet. The almost identical looking Motsoeneng brothers swapped places in toilet stops along the way. While one ran on, the other would race ahead in a car. At their roadside toilet stops, the brothers changed everything, including their running shoes.

Changing shoes was necessary because microchips in each runner's shoelaces and sensors allowed constant tracking of every entrant. South Africans across the country were able to log on to a web site and find out exactly where their favourite runners were at any moment. Suspicions were raised after Sergio finished ninth in the 1999 Comrades Marathon, a staggering result for an inexperienced athlete. The brothers nearly got away with it had it not been for one minor detail. Sergio and Fika Motsoeneng were caught after a newspaper published photos showing them at different stages of the run wearing identical watches on opposite wrists. They forgot to take time to check where they kept the time.

SEWSUNKER PAPWA SEWGOLUM

They called him Papwa. His real name was Sewsunker Sewgolum. A South African of Indian origin, Papwa could have been a top international professional golfer at the time of Gary Player, however, as a 'non-white', many of the bigger golfing tournaments were out of bounds to him. Born in 1930, Papwa did not attend school, and spent much of his time hitting golf balls on the beach with whatever branches he could find that resembled golf clubs. To make ends meet, he became a caddie at the Beachwood Country Club in Durban. With borrowed clubs and borrowed shoes, he won the Natal Amateur at 16. A loophole in the notorious Group Areas Act enabled Papwa to gain permission to play in a few white tournaments. However, although he was allowed to play the golf course, he was not allowed to use any of the club facilities, including the clubhouse. In 1963, Papwa won the South African Natal Open tournament at the Durban Country Club. Papwa's victory, however, was overshadowed when the prize-giving ceremony was moved indoors as a result of a sudden onset of rain. But since the laws of the country precluded Indians from being allowed inside the Durban Country Club, Papwa stood in the rain whilst being handed his trophy through an open window. Photographs of Sewsunker 'Papwa' Sewgolum receiving his trophy in the rain - while the club's white patrons sat in comfort inside - flashed around the world, prompting an international outcry. A number of countries reacted by imposing sports sanctions on South Africa. Within a year of this victory, Papwa was banned by the South African government from playing in any tournaments and from entering any golf course, even as a spectator. The government withdrew his passport, thereby destroying any possibility of Papwa competing internationally.

HANSIE

Wessel Johannes Cronje, known to the world as Hansie, was a South African sporting hero, a brilliant cricketer and South African cricket captain. Hansie was an inspiration to his nation and his fans around the world.

The country was shocked when Hansie was accused of match-fixing in 2000. Cronje said 'The allegations are completely without substance'. However Cronje was sacked as captain after subsequently confessing that he had not been 'entirely honest'. He admitted accepting between $10 000 and $15 000 from a London-based bookmaker for 'forecasting' results, not match fixing, during a one-day series in India. Cronje was subsequently banned for life from playing or coaching cricket.

Cronje, aged 32, died in 2002 when the private aircraft in which he had hitched a ride home, crashed into the Outeniqua mountains. Despite everything, Hansie was still voted as one of the Great South Africans on a show of the same name in 2004. Thousands of South Africans took part in an informal nationwide poll to determine the '100 Greatest South Africans' of all time. Predictably, Nelson Mandela topped the list. But the once much-loved Hansie was voted the 11th Greatest South African, his name appearing amongst such luminaries as Professor Christiaan Barnard, General Jan Smuts, Shaka Zulu and Mark Shuttleworth. A fitting tribute to a great man who sadly lost his way.

SEA COTTAGE

Many great horses have thundered over the South African turf, but the reputation of Sea Cottage, a highly intelligent and brave horse, towers above them all. In 1966, Sea Cottage was the overwhelming favourite to win the Durban July. It was reported that almost all the bookmakers in Natal would have faced bankruptcy should Sea Cottage have won. On 16 June 1966, while Sea Cottage was taking an early morning trot along Durban's Blue Lagoon Beach, he was shot in the rump. The news shocked the country and all betting was frozen. Just four days after being shot, Sea Cottage was ready to run again. Two weeks later he finished fourth in the Durban July, with the lump of lead still embedded in his rear end. The following year, Sea Cottage won the July in a sensational dead heat with Jollify, It was the only dead-heat in the 110-year history of the Durban July.

THE BIGGEST MAN-MADE FOREST IN THE WORLD

Photo © Martin Heigan

With 10 million trees,
Johannesburg is the biggest
man-made forest in the world.

Johannesburg is also the biggest
city in the world that does not lie
beside a lake, a river or an ocean.

SETTING WORLD RECORDS

HIGHEST NUMBER OF BIRDS

During the summer months, the wetlands and floodplains of the Nylsvley Nature Reserve attract the largest variety of water birds, as well as the highest number of birds in the Southern Hemisphere.

DEEPEST UNDERWATER CAVE

The Boesmansgat is renowned as the second deepest underwater cave (about 299 m) and the largest of its kind in the world.

LARGEST GREEN CANYON IN THE WORLD

The Blyderiver Canyon is the largest green canyon in the world and the third largest overall, after the Grand Canyon in the USA and the Fish River Canyon in Namibia.

OLDEST MOUNTAINS IN THE WORLD

The mountains around Barberton are the oldest in the world, dating back 3.5 billion years. They include the second oldest exposed rocks on the planet (only rocks from the Isua Greenstone belt in Western Greenland are older).

HIGHEST COUNTRY IN THE WORLD

All of Lesotho exceeds 1000 m in altitude, and has the highest 'lowest' point of any country on earth.

WORLD'S SECOND LARGEST CANYON

Fish River Canyon on the South African border with Namibia is the second largest canyon in the world '(Grand Canyon is the largest). The whole gorge measures 160 km in length and is 127 km wide, and the inner canyon is an amazing 550 m deep.

LARGEST CYCAD FOREST IN THE WORLD

The cycad forest near Modjadjifkloof has the most cycads in the world. At 13 m, the cycads are also the world's tallest.

WORLD'S LARGEST CONSERVATION AREA

South Africa, Zimbabwe and Mozambique are tearing down fences between the countries' game parks to create a 35 000 km² game park that will become the largest conservation area in the world.

LARGEST ESTUARINE SYSTEM

The St Lucia estuarine system is the largest estuarine system in Africa and supports five eco-systems.

LARGEST NATURAL FOUNTAIN

Gasegonyana (little water calabash) is commonly called 'The Eye of Kuruman'. It is the largest natural fountain in the Southern Hemisphere. This sweet water spring delivers 20 million litres of water daily to the 71 000 inhabitants of Kuruman.

MOST GEOLOGICALLY STABLE

The star-watching town of Sutherland is one of the most geologically stable places on Earth, despite being on a 6 million year old volcano that is not yet officially extinct.

183

THE SECOND-HIGHEST WATERFALL IN THE WORLD

Photo ©Gallo images

The Tugela Falls in KwaZulu-Natal
is the world's second-highest
waterfall. The falls consist of five
major drops, of which the highest
is a sheer drop of 411 m. The total
drop is 948 m.
(The highest waterfall is Angel Falls
in Venezuela.)

TRIVIA *from the past...*

THE PORTABLE CHURCH

It was after the Anglo Boer War when the town of
Adelaide in the Cape desperately needed to restore its
church, but funds for material were not available.
Out of the blue, a wagon brought in the supplies needed.
These included a beautiful hand-carved pulpit, matching
chair and all the timber they required.
The Boer townsfolk assumed the British had sent
the supplies as an apology.
It was not until a letter was received from a church in
Adelaide, Australia, a few years later that the mystery
of the church material was revealed.
The letter read:
*It is with trepidation that we enquire as to whether a
consignment of oak wood, which we ordered
from England about two years ago for our new church,
has not, perhaps, by mistake been delivered
to your town in South Africa instead of ours.*
To this day the beautiful church in Adelaide,
South Africa, stands as a reminder of the very
fortunate and timely mistake.

AT HOME AT LAST – SARAH BAARTMAN

She was called the 'Hottentot Venus', a Khoisan woman who lived in the early 1800s.
Sarah Baartman was working as a slave in Cape Town when she was 'discovered' by
British ship's doctor William Dunlop. In the early 1800s, Europeans were arrogantly
obsessed with their own superiority and with proving that others, particularly blacks, were
inferior and oversexed. Baartman's physical characteristics, although not unusual for
Khoisan women, created much interest as she had unusually large buttocks and genitals.
We'll never know what Sarah Baartman had in mind when she was persuaded by Dunlop
to travel - of her own free will – with him to England. What Dunlop had in mind was to
display her as a 'freak', a 'scientific curiosity' and make money from these shows, some of
which he promised to give to her. Sarah was put on **exhibition** in London and
then moved to Paris four years later where she continued her degrading round of shows
and exhibitions. Once the Parisians got tired of the Baartman show, she was forced to turn
to prostitution. She died in 1815 at the age of 25, thousands of kilometres from home
and family. She had attracted the attention of French scientist, Georges Cuvier, who made
a plaster cast of her body and displayed her pickled brain and genitals at the Musee de
l'Homme in Paris. Some 160 years later, they were still on display, but were finally removed
from public view in 1974. In 1994, President Nelson Mandela suggested that her remains
be brought home. Eight years later, they were finally returned to South Africa. Sarah
Baartman, displayed as a freak because of her unusual physical features, was laid to rest,
187 years after she left Cape Town for London. Her remains were buried on Women's Day,
9 August 2002, in the area of her birth, the Gamtoos River Valley in the Eastern Cape.
Sarah Baartman finally had her dignity restored by being buried where she belongs -
far away from where her race and gender were so cruelly exploited.

LIVINGSTONE, I PRESUME

Legendary missionary, Dr David Livingstone, was referred to as
'the greatest man of his generation' by Florence Nightingale.
He died a hero in 1874. However, he had a less-than-auspicious start to his
travels in Africa when he began his mission work preaching in English to the
Setswana people. Livingstone did not allow for the fact that direct translations from
English to Setswana might have some strange and hilarious results. For instance,
there is no Setswana word for 'spirit', the closest word means
'vapours rising from a boiling pot'.
In Setswana, 'cow dung' and the concept of mortal sin have the same meaning.
There is also no distinction between various forms of 'love'
(for example, brotherly/godly love and physical/sexual love) in the Setswana language. The concept
of resurrection also caused some alarm and confusion, as Livingstone explained to the chief of the area,
Chief Sechele, that on Resurrection Day all the dead would rise, implying that this Christian God
intended to bring back all the enemy warriors the Chief had successfully disposed of in battle.
Thus **a Livingstone sermon went something along these lines**: '*That the God who lives
in the ground will come down from the sky, accompanied by all the dead warriors that you have killed.
He will then proceed to have sex with everybody because the people have cow dung on the
vapours of their boiling pots.*' Of course the Setswana people thought
Livingstone was a madman. Perhaps he just simply presumed too much.

Source: Roger Webster from 'At the Fireside'.

LEAVING A LEGACY

Jan Smuts was a fighter, philosopher, politician, field marshal , naturalist and an intellectual. Jan Smuts not only helped refine the mechanisms of the future United Nations, he **personally drafted the UN Charter's Declaration of Human Rights**. Although he did not attend school until 12 years old, when he left five years later, he was top of his class. He served two terms as prime minister.
The first from 1919 – 1924 and the second was from 1939 – 1948 when General Hertzog, who refused to participate in World War II, was forced to resign.

THE WAR TIME **HERO**

The year was 1942. While still a prisoner of war he sank a fully laden steamer – an F boat – while moored in Tobruk harbour.
This he did by placing a small tin filled with gun powder in amongst drums of petrol in the hold, leading a fuse from there to the hatch, lighting the fuse and closing the hatch. In carrying out this deliberately planned action, he displayed ingenuity, determination, and complete disregard of personal safety, of punishment by the enemy or from the ensuing explosion which destroyed the vessel.
His name was **Job Masego** – A true South African war hero.

THE WORLD IS **FLAT**

"You don't mean round the world, it is impossible! You mean in the world. Impossible"

These were the words of Paul Kruger, president of South Africa, to a sailor sailing around the world in 1897. Despite being an intelligent man, progressive thinker and visionary, he believed that the earth was flat.

SUNBATHING FOR SINGLES ONLY

In the 1960s it was **illegal** for sunbathers of the opposite sex at the municipal swimming bath to be closer than a specified distance from each other. To ensure the legislation was upheld, the official on duty carried a ruler to assist him with his inspection. Any two persons not adhering to the specified distance were charged accordingly.

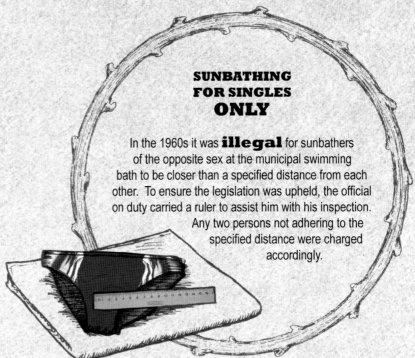

THE PEACEFUL PHILOSOPHER

It was in the early 1700s that Mohlomi, South Africa's greatest philosopher, prophet, healer and pacifist was born. This highly respected chief travelled extensively spreading his beliefs: a chief is a chief through the **grace** of his people. He shared his philosophy that 'it is better to thrash the corn than to shape the spear' with others around the country and as far afield as Zimbabwe and Botswana. His strategy was to marry the daughters of the chiefs he visited and father their children, thus ensuring peaceful relationships with their tribe. It is said he had more than 1 000 wives and children by the time he died. When Mohlomi was asked to treat a young boy to ensure he would become a powerful chief. He responded *'Power is not acquired by medicine: the heart is the medicine.'*
Mohlomi advised the young boy
'One day you will truly be a chief and ruler over men. Learn to understand men and know their ways. Learn to bear with their human weaknesses and shortcomings. Always determine to direct them along the paths of truth and purity. In their disputes, adjudicate with justice and sympathy. You must not allow elements of preferences based on wealth, status or prestige to influence and tarnish any of your decisions.'
The young boy went on to become the great King Moshoeshoe, the founder of the Basotho nation, **the Nelson Mandela of the nineteenth century**.

4 LEGGED CELEBRITIES

JACK THE SIGNALMAN'S ASSISTANT

In the early 1890s in the little town of Uitenhage in the Eastern Cape, Mr James Wide worked as a signalman for the South African Railways at the Uitenhage terminus. Tragically, he was involved in a terrible accident which resulted in both his legs being amputated at the knees. Desperate to retain his job, Mr Wide decided to train a baboon to assist him in his work as a signalman. The baboon's name was Jack. One of Jack's first tasks was to take out the railway car, place it on the rails, push Mr Wide up the tracks to check the points and then push him back to the terminus. Jack was then trained by verbal command to pull down and lift up the correct railway track levers. And so Jack's training as a signalman's assistant progressed. It was recorded that the faithful animal completed his tasks perfectly for over ten years.

ABLE SEAMAN JUST NUISANCE

In 1939 in Simon's Town, a Great Dane was officially inducted into the navy. His trade was listed as 'bone crusher' and his religion 'Canine Divinity League' (i.e. anti-vivisection). His Christian name was a matter of some debate, until finally someone said: 'Leave it out and say Just Nuisance!' And so Just Nuisance it became. A nuisance the big canine certainly was. He travelled on the train without a pass, went AWOL and resisted eviction from local pubs at closing time. The general punishment was no bones for a week. Despite these misdemeanours Just Nuisance did take his duties seriously. With his fellow sailors' best interests at heart, he was helpful in gently breaking up fights and guiding drunken souls home after a heavy night out. Just Nuisance's antics got the better of him when, in 1943, he jumped from a moving truck. He was declared an invalid and subsequently discharged on 1 January 1944. On his seventh birthday, he was laid to rest with full military honours and a firing party on top of Red Hill. His legacy lives on in a proud bronze statue in Jubilee Square, Simon's Town

Huberta the Travelling Hippo

One day, back in 1928, a liberal hippo left the confines of her lagoon near St Lucia in Natal to explore the coastline. She stopped off at a sugar cane estate for padkos, drew crowds of sightseers in Umhlanga and even visited the Durban Country Club. Here the fans proved too much for the independent creature and she bolted across the golf course in a mad getaway, causing mass destruction along the way. After a tour through the city of Durban, Huberta returned to the calm, cool waters of the Umgeni River and was declared 'royal game' which meant she could not be interfered with. Locals on the south coast took this declaration to heart and Lady Huberta was met with many traditional welcomes – local Indian communities beat their drums in her honour, many Zulu tribes thought of her as the spirit of King Shaka, and the Pondo people suggested that she was the reincarnation of a famous sangoma. After a six-month sojourn in Port St Johns, Huberta finally reached East London in March 1931. Keiskamma River, near Peddie, is where her journey ended. A farmer and his two sons sadly wounded Huberta and returned the next morning to finish the job. A public outcry called for the men to be fined a considerable amount.

The AmaThole Museum in King William's Town upholds her legacy. Eighty years later another free-spirited hippo left St Lucia for a trip south. Spotted in Ballito frolicking amongst the waves, Hippy, as some called her, met with as sad an ending as her ancestor did; after much controversy and only three months' travel, she was put down.

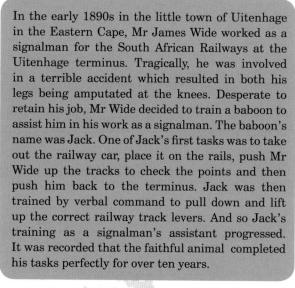

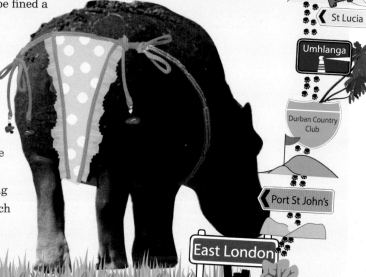

MAXIMUM SECURITY

Max, German-born Mountain Gorilla

Max, a German-born Mountain Gorilla who lived in the Johannesburg Zoo, became a national hero when he apprehended a daring criminal in 1997. Attempting to escape from police by jumping into the gorilla's cage, an armed robber shot Max twice while the crime-fighting gorilla pinned him to the wall and bit him on the bottom. Both criminal and gorilla were taken to hospital after the incident. The man was later convicted of rape, robbery and wounding a gorilla, which secured him a 40-year sentence. Cuddly toys were crafted in Max's image and the police honoured the 200 kg animal with a bullet-proof vest.

'The first thing the gorilla did was rip my jeans and bite me on the buttocks.'
Armed robber Isaac Mofokeng

BOETIE THE BRAVEHEART

On the night of 31 May 1773, one brave stallion faced his worst nightmare – the wrath of the Atlantic waves! Anchored in the protected False Bay, the ship De Jonge Thomas gradually lost ground in the face of strong winds and heavy rain, hitting a sandbank about 500 m from shore and disintegrating. Crew members were flung into the arms of the choppy seas while the cargo made it safely to shore. Ignoring the seamen's plight, soldiers on land were ordered to protect the cargo from being stolen. But one man and his horse felt it inhumane not to help the drowning crew.

Wolraad Woltemade and his horse, Boetie, surfed the backwash seven times – saving fourteen people by pulling them to shore via rope thanks to Boetie's strong horsepower. On their last attempt, the weight of six anxious crew members was too much for brave Boetie to handle and they all disappeared underwater.

WARRIOR AND PROTECTOR

During the 1880s, Jock, an English Staffordshire Bull Terrier, became the famous pup of author Sir Percy Fitzpatrick. The runt of the litter, Jock was saved by Fitzpatrick from being drowned in a bucket. Rewarding his owner with extreme loyalty, Jock showed his bravery in a fight to the death with both a crocodile and a baboon. Towards Fitzpatrick, Jock displayed a playful and loving nature and the remarkable bond between dog and master resulted in the well-known literary classic, Jock of the Bushveld. The plucky Jock was permanently deafened when a Kudu cow kicked him. He was killed by a farmer who shot him when he mistakenly thought Jock was killing his chickens.

NELLIE THE ENTERTAINER

If you were a child in 1948, you would have been celebrating the birthday of Nellie the Elephant with over 20 000 other children in Mitchell Park in Durban. Nellie, who was presented to the park by the Maharaja of Mysore, was a favourite celebrity. She was an accomplished mouth organ player, could crack coconuts, and took children for rides on her back. Then in 1949, Nellie was sent to the Taronga Zoo in Australia.

Not knowing what a people-loving animal she was, she was put in an enclosure surrounded by a moat and a fence. So used to being in close contact with children, Nellie reached over the moat trying to get out, and broke her back.

durban

has the highest number of tall buildings in south africa with **218**

Source: www.emporis.com A building is classified as tall if it is at least 12 storeys, or has a known height of at least 35 m.

followed by cape town with 160 and johannesburg with 132

Photo: Mariola Pawelczyk Editing: Darren Tomkins

191

GOLD

Egoli a name used to refer to Johannesburg means 'place of gold' in isiXhosa and isiZulu.

'Instead of rejoicing you would do better to weep: for this gold will cause our country to be soaked in blood.' Paul Kruger, former president of the Transvaal.

The Rand Refinery is the largest refinery of gold in the world.

South Africa has 40% of the world's known gold resources and, after China, is the world's leader in gold production.

Moab Khutsong Gold-Mine in North West province has the world's longest winding cable, able to lower workers to 3 054 m in one uninterrupted four-minute journey.

Gold is the only metal that does not rust – even if it is buried in the ground for thousands of years.

THE GRUMPY BOER

An old, white-bearded boer called Willem Prinsloo had settled on a farm called Modderfontein. When the gold rush boomed, Prinsloo wanted nothing to do with the gold prospectors. He was swayed, however, when a man offered his wife a cow which would produce more milk than six of their cows combined. After much nagging from his wife, the deal was concluded and Prinsloo exchanged his Modderfontein farm for a cow which filled a bucket of milk twice a day, £30 000 cash and £40 000 in shares in the newly formed gold mining company. The Modderfontein gold company subsequently became one of South Africa's richest gold mines. Prinsloo then moved to a sheep farm near Pretoria. An even grumpier Prinsloo was convinced by Thomas Cullinan to sell half his farm on the condition that the prospectors never touched Prinsloo's half of the farm. The half he sold became the Premier Diamond Mine where the biggest diamond in the world was mined.

Although many people believe gold was only discovered in 1870, Africans had been trading gold with the Arabs since 1450. Ancient writings and manuscripts make reference to the fact that all the alluvial and surface diggings, prospected in the southern part of Africa, had been mined before.

In 1884, a young prospector sunk a shaft in the De Kaap valley and found what appeared to be a gold nugget, six metres below the ground. On closer inspection, it was identified as a gold locket which contained a parchment inscribed with unrecognisable characters and a lock of human hair. To this day, the questions around its origin and how it got to be buried so deep are still unanswered.

A lump of pure gold the size of a matchbox can be flattened into a sheet the size of a tennis court!

BURIED TREASURE

The treasure ship, the Grosvenor, sank in deep waters off Lwambazi Bay in the Eastern Cape in 1782. The majority of the 150 passengers survived and made their way overland to the Cape of Good Hope. The ship had been carrying a cargo of bullion, yet despite numerous attempts to salvage the treasures, only a few coins and artefacts have ever been found.

You can have a drink in the world's deepest pub in the old mine at Gold Reef City. The pub is 226 m below the ground in what was a stable. It housed the 300 donkeys that were used to pull cocopans in the 1920s.

DEEPEST IN THE WORLD

The Mponeng mine is the deepest in the world, closely followed by the TauTona gold mine, west of Johannesburg. The TauTona mine has around 800 km of tunnels and workers in the mine have to travel for up to an hour to reach the rock face, which can reach temperatures of 60°C.

GOLD RUSH ON TABLE MOUNTAIN

1856 saw Cape Town's very own gold rush on the slopes of Table Mountain. The Cape citizens swamped the mountain armed with picks, shovels and sieves. The gold rush started with the servant of a Mr Salem who was rumoured to have found a piece of gold-bearing ore. Mr Salem set up a refreshment stand at the base of the gorge. The food and refreshments, at prices double those in town, sold like crazy and Mr Salem did a roaring trade. With time, the Capetonians realised there was no gold and it later emerged that Mr Salem, who was himself an ex-convict from Van Diemens land in Tasmania, had used a piece of gold-bearing ore that originated from Australia.

Every September in Pilgrim's Rest, Mpumalanga, contestants pay tribute to our gold rush ancestors at the National Gold Panning Championships.

CHEAP LABOUR

A petition in favour of importing cheap Chinese labour to work on the Transvaal gold mines was signed in 1904 by 45 000 supporters. By the end of that year, the first 21 462 Chinese had arrived.

More steel is poured in an hour than all the gold that has been poured since the beginning of time.

IF THERE IS ONE THING IN THIS PLANET THAT HAS THE POWER TO BIND PEOPLE IT IS SOCCER...

Nelson Mandela

ZAKUMI

the mascot with attitude: zakumi is lively, outgoing, adventurous and spontaneous and symbolises south africa through his self-confidence, pride, hospitality and social skills.

VUVUZELA

the beautiful noise: vuvuzela (voo-voo-zeh-lah) large, colourful plastic trumpet with the sound of a foghorn, blown enthusiastically by the crowd at soccer matches. from the zulu word for 'making noise'

LA DOOOOO MAAA

the celebratory cheer: laduma! (la-doo-mah) - used to celebrate when a goal is scored, from the zulu word for 'it thunders'

life is rhythm football is rhythm when i'm in

MAKARAPA

the unmistakable look: makarapa (or makaraba) a miner's helmet modified with figurines and emblems identifying a favourite team or player and familiar phrases. makarapas boast phrases such as 'the time is now', 'bafana bafana' or 'for the love of the game' and figurines or team logos. the first makarapa goes back to 1970 when it was made to prevent spectators from being hit by bottles during soccer matches. if you really want to complete the soccer fan dress code then a pair of oversized sunglasses will finish the look.

football is the only common language of the african continent
danny jordaan

SHO SHOLOZA

the song of encouragement - shosholoza. traditionally sung by all-male work gangs in a call and response style, this song is a favourite at sport events in south africa and has come to represent the banding together of a people, their pride and dignity, and their progression into a new and free world.

albert johanneson was the first south african to play professional football in europe, playing for coventry city, dutch side heracles and torino in italy * stephen kalamazoo mokone was the first black south african to play for a professional european team, has a street in netherlands named after him and inspired the film 'the black meteor', de zwarte meteoor * lucas 'the chief' radebe became the most capped south african footballer with 70 bafana bafana appearances, and became one of the most respected players of the english premier league after being appointed as captain of leeds * zakumi, the 2010 mascot, is modelled on mark fish, who played for arcadia shepherds, jomo cosmos, orlando pirates, lazio of italy, bolton wanderers, ipswich, charlton athletic and even turned down an opportunity to play for manchester united * kaiser motaung was named rookie of the year when he played in the usa for atlanta chiefs * jomo sono was voted 'footballer of the year' in canada, 'south african footballer of the year', and 'north american sportsman of the year' and was the first black person to be inducted into the south african soccer hall of fame * kaiser chiefs' player, pule doe ntsoelengoe, was inducted into the us soccer hall of fame and was one of american soccer league's all-time leaders for both appearances and goals.

rhythm. and i feel the

South Africa

I am an African
Not because I was born there
But because my heart beats with Africa's
I am an African
Not because my skin is black
But because my mind is engaged by Africa
I am an African
Not because I live on its soil
But because my soul is at home in Africa

When Africa weeps for her children
My cheeks are stained with tears
When Africa honours her elders
My head is bowed in respect
When Africa mourns for her victims
My hands are joined in prayer
When Africa celebrates her triumphs
My feet are alive with dancing

I am an African
For her blue skies take my breath away
And my hope for the future is bright
I am an African
For her people greet me as family
And teach me the meaning of community
I am an African
For her wildness quenches my spirit
And brings me closer to the source of life

When the music of Africa beats in the wind
My blood pulses to its rhythm
And I become the essence of music
When the colours of Africa dazzle in the sun
My senses drink in its rainbow
And I become the palette of nature
When the stories of Africa echo round the fire
My feet walk in its pathways
And I become the footprints of history

I am an African
Because she is the cradle of our birth
And nurtures an ancient wisdom
I am an African
Because she lives in the world's shadow
And bursts with a radiant luminosity
I am an African
Because she is the land of tomorrow
And I recognise her gifts as sacred

Wayne Visser

70% of South Africans consult traditional healers.

The World Health Organisation estimates that in sub-Saharan Africa, there is one traditional healer for every 500 people, whereas there is only one medical doctor for every 40 000 people.

SANGOMA

INYANGA

The iNyanga is a HERBALIST and is concerned with medicines made from plants and animals. The medicines are known as 'umuthi'. Although most iziNyanga are trained through apprenticeship to be healers, some may have dreams or visions of umuthi and are guided to the exact place to dig or find a particular umuthi.

Traditional African belief says that all things - animal, vegetable or mineral - have power, and small pieces of the animal or vegetable are used as umuthi for a range of situations including 'warding off evil, providing personal protection and luck, or to ensure the faithfulness of a lover or the defeat of an enemy'.

The sangoma, or diviner, is someone sacredly called to the profession who is in contact with ANCESTRAL spirits. Some illnesses are believed to be caused by unhappy ancestors who haven't been respected or acknowledged sufficiently. The sangoma will throw a set of bones, and give advice to the customer on actions to be taken to appease the ancestors.

Sangoma make their diagnosis with AMATHAMBO, or the throwing of bones. This is the ability to consciously interpret through images or symbols produced by the arrangement of the bones that have been thrown. The sangoma goes into a trance to determine what is ailing the patient by creating an altered state of consciousness brought about by drugs, plants or in many cases self induced, as with autohypnosis.

The sangoma, without having to exchange words, will physically perceive the pain actually experienced by the customer with his ability to see, feel and interpret the various vibrations emitted by the patient.

EVEN FOR SOCCER. When South African soccer star Gary Bailey played goalkeeper for Manchester United in 1983 they went through a difficult patch, conceding more goals than they would have liked. A witchdoctor proposed to Bailey's father that they use some umuthi to remedy the problem. The witchdoctor advised him to lock the goal-post with a padlock before the match, so that no goals could get in. One will never know if it was the umuthi or good play, but Manchester United went on to win the 1983, FA Cup Final and the Charity Shield. When Bailey returned to South Africa, to play for Kaizer Chiefs, he brought with him his padlock and key.

To find a traditional healer in the urban city areas, you need look no further than the classifieds in the newspapers, street billboards or the flyer left on your car windscreen!

HERBALIST, ASTROLOGER & TRADITIONAL HEALER

EXEPART DR MARIAM
CELL: 079 20

ROOM No. 2
IJDOKOTELAWESINTU -
DR. MAMA - AYUBU
+ BACK FROM SSESE
• REMOVE BAD LUCK
• MEN $ WOMEN WITHOUT KIDS
• SEXUAL PROBLEMS
• PENIS ENLARGEMENT
+ IZIFO ZOCANSI
+ UKUTHOLA-ABANTWANA
• CUSTOMER ATTRACTION
+ HELP
CALL: C

UBUNTU-SERGERY
FORTUNE-TELLER
HERBALIST-HEALLER
- BAD LUCK
- SEXUAL PBL'S **DR. BANTU**
- BEWITCHED PEOPLE
- MISUNDERSTANDING
- PREGNANCY PROBLEMS
- LOST LOVER
- SYMPTOMS OF HIV ETC

STREET CHOW

Restaurant

Life moves fast in South Africa, the people are constantly on the go. For those who have hectic jobs, there's no time to prepare food or sit down for a leisurely meal; so food is prepared and eaten on the streets.

Street food or street chow, as it is known, is common in taxi ranks, on street corners, at busy intersections and outside butcheries in the townships, on pavements in the city centre, beaches and markets.

Street chow stands, stalls and grills offer a wide range of food, depending on which region you're in, you're probably more likely to find boeries or boerewors rolls in Jozi than the samoosas and spicy pines that are sold on the Durban beachfront. Chicken dust, however, is pure township – you'll find eKasi, as it is called, right across the country.

CHICKEN DUST

In a typical township, most of the street corners are occupied by people with their braai stands grilling chicken next to taverns, bars and, more commonly, bus stops and taxi ranks. They call it chicken dust because of their locations on dusty streets. Raw chickens are flattened and cooked on a grill over coals. You can choose from a quarter, half and whole chicken (full house). Prices vary from one place to another. You also have a choice of any flavour you want - mild and hot. Chilli sauce is the popular one. The chicken takes about 45 minutes to cook and is probably the most popular take-away street food.

SPICY PINE

Imagine chunks of fresh, juicy pineapple rolled on a bed of curry spices then skewered onto a wooden kebab stick. This Durban Indian delight is a tasty treat when walking down the Durban promenade on a bright, sunny day.

SENSATIONAL SAMOOSAS

These deep-fried, triangular pastries with various spicy fillings are one of the tastiest bites you can eat, a speciality in Durban. Samoosas are made with a variety of fillings ranging from meat to delicious potato or sweet corn. They are the perfect appetisers to tantalise your palate.

BUNNY CHOW!

If it's not hot, it's not a BUNNY CHOW! This hollowed-out quarter, half or full loaf of bread filled with delicious curry then topped with the scooped-out inside of the loaf is one of Durban's claims to fame. Let's just say it's no meal for a rabbit. You can enjoy the bunny in Indian areas or restaurants. Place your order for bean, chicken or mutton in a quarter or half bunny. The traditional way to savour this gargantuan meal is with your hands, so leave your cutlery behind. This is street chow, no need for formalities.

Mopani worms are sold for the same price as the best beef in town. These worms or caterpillars are rich in protein and are found on the mopani tree in the savannahs of Southern Africa. The thorny-bodied worms are boiled, dried and sold in the marketplace. Some people prefer them fried in oil for 15 minutes and salted for taste. Eating mopani worms, however, requires great skill; to chew up the crunchy head and sharp thorns without having your gums stabbed needs careful practice.

BEEF OR CHICKEN WORS ROLL AKA A 'BOERIE'

Choose your size -

mega, medium or regular.

This roll with a grilled sausage centre is a popular hit on the streets of Mzansi. With a choice of your own filling of onion rings, sauce and chicken or beef, the mega roll can be shared because it's so big.

THE GREAT GATSBY

No, not F Scott Fitzgerald's classic book, the ultra-long roll cut lengthwise and stuffed with curried meat, mutton, steak, polony, vienna sausage, calamari or fish together with chips, lettuce, tomato, cucumber and even gravy. It is fare unique to Cape Town and best described as 'cardiac arrest'! The Gatsby is a fantastic ending to a night of drinking and partying and can be bought at most local Cape takeaways.

MAMA'S MIELIES

Gone are the days when you had to wait for a woman who shouts 'mielies' in your neighbourhood to enjoy what the American folk call 'corn on the cob'. Now you can find roasted, boiled and fried mielies at taxi ranks, city centres and in the townships. The wait for a perfectly done mielie hasn't changed though. Boiled mielies take 30 to 45 minutes to cook. Roasted mielies are quick to prepare, taking only 15 to 20 minutes. Fried mielies off the cob are fried in a pan and spiced with chillies and curry powder. Cooking oil is used to fry par-boiled mielies for 20 minutes. The spices are added for flavour and you can find these at the city markets.

HOT SLAP CHIPS

Hot chips, or 'slap tjips' in Afrikaans, are 'limp' oily chips. They have been a popular street chow for years. Thicker in cut than your normal French fries, 'slap tjips' are a local favourite when drenched in salt and vinegar. They are sold on the street with a selection of sauces.

WANDERING WALKIE TALKIE

Boiled chicken heads and feet form the classic street chow combo. Found mainly in the townships, this combo titbit has made its cluck to fame in city centres, markets and taxi ranks. The chicken heads and feet are boiled for 20 minutes, then lightly salted and served when they've cooled. 'Walkie talkies', as they are popularly known, come with an option of traditional steam bread, depending on how far your hunger has travelled.

Photo © Karen Lotter

201

203

HOW BIG IS BIG?

AN EGG TO FEED THE RUGBY TEAM

An ostrich egg is equivalent to 24 hens' eggs.

BABOON SPIDER

(actual size)

FALLING FROM 5 STOREYS

Dungeons, at the mouth of Hout Bay in Cape Town, regularly provides the most perfect and challenging surfing waves of up to 70 ft or 21.3 m. That's higher than a 5-storey building.

AS BIG AS A COUNTRY

The Kruger National Park is the size of a small country. With an area of 18 989 km^2, the park is almost as big as Wales, which is 20 779 km^2 and Israel, which is 20 330 km^2.

THE HEART OF A BLUE WHALE

Not only is the blue whale's heart the same size as a small motor vehicle, but a grown man could swim in its arteries.

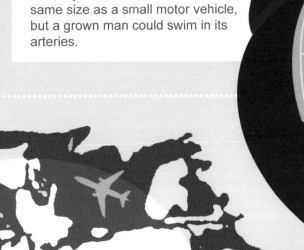

CANGO CAVES

The main chamber of the Cango Caves is 98 m long and 49 m wide. Big enough to have sufficient standing room for 5 000 people or, if you prefer, to park two Boeing 727s.

EARTHWORM

The longest earthworm found near King Williams Town measured 6.7 m (22 ft) - as long as 4 men lying head to toe.

MY, WHAT BIG TEETH YOU HAVE

A hippo can open its mouth 1.2 m wide, that's big enough to fit a nine-year-old child. A hippo's tooth can measure half a metre wide and is 30 cm in length. Its teeth can make up to a third of the animal's weight.

BAOBAB TREE

The 6 000 year old baobab tree in Limpopo has a girth of 47 m. Up to 60 people can fit inside the trunk of this baobab tree and order a drink at the same time at the pub inside.

SOUTH AFRICAN Inventions

ACTION POTENTIAL STIMULATION DEVICE (APSD) - A device for arthritis relief.

ALOE VERA HEALTH CARE PRODUCT - Products made from the juice of local aloes.

BARLOW WADLEY BROADBAND RADIO - The first broadband radio in the world.

BELL ARTICULATED TRUCKS - Over 50 models sold in 80 countries.

HOODIA GORDONII APPETITE SUPPRESSANT - The indigenous hoodia cactus, used by the Khoisan, is now sold worldwide.

COLINDICTOR - The first machine in the world that could record a telephone conversation.

CYBERTRACKER - A handheld database and GPS used by Western and traditional trackers worldwide.

DART AND FLAMINGO SPORTS CARS - Famous for their stylish design and excellent road holding.

DISA PUSH BUTTON TELEPHONE - The first push button phone in the world.

VIBOL FUEL-SAVING EXHAUST SYSTEM - Reduces fuel consumption and pollution.

FIRST USE OF FIRE - One of the most significant technological innovations in the history of the human race.

FOURCADES SPECTROCOPE - The first 3D mapping system in the world.

FREEPLAY RADIOS, TORCHES AND CELLPHONE CHARGERS - The first wind-up appliances which have improved the quality of life of thousands of rural people.

HIPPO DRUM AND Q DRUM - Large rollers of water containers that can be rolled along the ground to transport large quantities of water with minimum effort.

JETMASTER FIREPLACES AND BRAAIS - Their advanced design has made them bestsellers in South Africa, Australia and Europe.

KREEPY KRAULY, BARACUDA AND POOLCOP POOL CLEANING SYSTEMS - South Africa is a world leader in the design of pool cleaning equipment.

PLAYGROUP ROUNDABOUT WATER PUMP - Uses the energy of kids playing to pump water up from the ground.

PLETHYSMOGRAPH - The first instrument in the world for measuring rate of blood flow.

POLICANSKY FISHING REEL - World-class lever reels that rival Penn and other famous makes.

RADAR - South Africans made important improvements to radar during World War 11.

ROOIVALK HELICOPTER - Lethal but innovative weapons of war.

SCHEFFEL BOGIE - A revolutionary railway carriage wheel system that reduced wear and tear.

.SHUTTLE LOW WATTAGE TRANSFORMER - Useful and safe innovation that should be installed in every office and home.

SMARTLOCK SAFETY SYRINGE - Reduces the risk of infection amongst medical staff from needle stick injury.

SMOCKING PLEATER - The first automated device for gathering and pleating clothing for smocking.

SUNSAT TELECOMMUNICATIONS SATELLITE - This micro satellite has sent back superb photographs of planet earth.

TELLUROMETER - A highly accurate distance measuring device that revolutionised surveying worldwide.

TURBOHEAT SOLAR SPIRAL - A new and innovative solar heater that provides hot water and room heating for rural families.

VAN DER BIJL'S PIONEERING VACUUM TUBE - Used for the first transcontinental radio broadcasts in the USA.

VUVUZELA - A horn that has traditional roots and makes an awful lot of noise at soccer matches.

WADLEY LOOP RECEIVER RADIO - Used for radio broadcasts between South Africa and Britain during World War II.

The CAT SCAN was invented by Allan Macleod Cormack, from Cape Town, for which he won a Nobel Physics Prize in 1979. It uses x rays, radiation detectors and computers to produce images of planes through the body

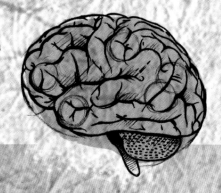

ROOIBOS TEA caffeine—free, high in antioxidants and produced only in South Africa. It was invented at the turn of the century by the locals of the Cedarberg area of the Cape.

COMPUTICKET was the first online ticket booking system in the world

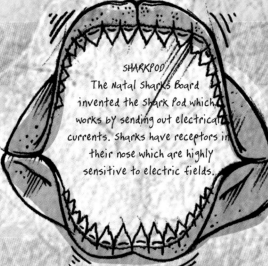

SHARKPOD
The Natal Sharks Board invented the Shark Pod which works by sending out electrical currents. Sharks have receptors in their nose which are highly sensitive to electric fields.

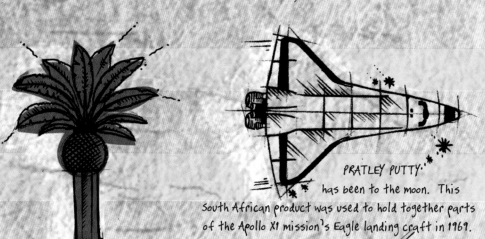

PRATLEY PUTTY has been to the moon. This South African product was used to hold together parts of the Apollo XI mission's Eagle landing craft in 1969.

Telecommunications engineer Ivo Lazic disguised CELL PHONE TOWERS as huge palm trees. The 'trees', made from environmentally—friendly material, are in international demand.

SPEEDGUN for measuring the speed of a cricket ball. It made cricket even more interesting and formally launched at The Oval in England during the 1999 Cricket World Cup.

We are inventive and resourceful. Anybody who has seen a taxi steered by a spanner and held together by wire can be in no doubt that the philosophy of 'n Boer maak 'n plan, is alive and well across the land.
Sarah Britten

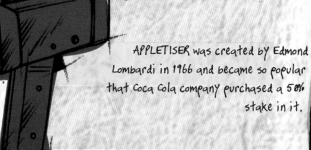

APPLETISER was created by Edmond Lombardi in 1966 and became so popular that Coca Cola company purchased a 50% stake in it.

207

CLIMATE CHANGE

Climate change is not only an environmental phenomenon but an economic, social and political issue that is already affecting every South African.

The effects of climate change extend wider than the impact of natural disasters. Throughout Africa, the resultant lack of food and water will increase the risk of disease, exacerbate violent conflicts and create political instability.

At current supply and demand, South Africa's fresh water resources will be fully utilised by 2025.

The frequency of large flood events in the Southern Cape region rose from once every 12 years between 1967-2002 to once every 1.4 years between 2003-2008.

In a 2006 report, the UN Food and Agriculture Organisation (FAO) concluded that worldwide livestock farming generates 18% of the planet's greenhouse gas emissions. By comparison, all the world's cars, trains, planes and boats accounted for a combined 13% of greenhouse gas emissions.

An increased depletion of the ozone layer has led to an increase in UV-B radiation reaching the earth's surface. South Africa is one of the countries, alongside Australia, New Zealand, Argentina and Chile, that lies exposed to this damaged area of the ozone layer.

South Africans emit carbon dioxide at a rate of ten tons of CO_2 per person per year (above the world average of seven tons per person per year). In 1990, South Africa was rated among the top ten countries in the world for its negative contribution, being responsible for approximately 1.2% of the earth's total global warming effect.

Since 2009, South Africa is no longer on the top ten list of the largest contributors to global warming.

Kalk Bay in the Cape taken during the storms of 2007. Photograph courtesy Independent Newspapers.

WORLD CUP 2010
STAD:UMS

GREENPOINT STADIUM: Cape Town
Capacity: 70 000 seats
Hosting: five first-round, one second-round, one quarter-final and one semi-final.
A particularly impressive stadium, Greenpoint is known as the African Renaissance Stadium. The stadium is an all-weather, multi-purpose, environmentally sustainable, world-class stadium.

ELLIS PARK STADIUM: Johannesburg
Capacity: 61 000 seats
Hosting: five first-round, one second-round and one quarter-final
Ellis Park was host to the 1995 Rugby World Cup final.

MBOMBELA STADIUM: Nelspruit
Capacity: 46 000 seats
Hosting: five first-round
Features 18 roof supports that resemble giraffes, perhaps an enticement for visitors to visit the Kruger National Park situated nearby.

PETER MOKABA STADIUM: Polokwane
Capacity: 46 000 seats
Hosting: four first-round.

LOFTUS VERSFELD STADIUM: Pretoria
Capacity: 50 000 seats
Hosting: five first-round and one second-round.

VODACOM PARK STADIUM: Bloemfontein
Capacity: 48 000 seats
Hosting: five first-round and one second-round.

MOSES MABHIDA STADIUM: Durban
Capacity: 70 000 seats
Hosting: five first-round, one second-round and one semi-final.
At 360 m long, the arch is 33 m longer than the arch at Wembley Stadium and with a height of 106 m is higher than the Statue of Liberty. The Sky Car ferries visitors to the stadium arch's highest point, where they can enjoy a breathtaking 360-degree view of the city. The energetic can try the adventure walk up the arch's 550 steps, and those wanting some excitement can take the stadium bungee swing across the pitch.

SOCCER CITY STADIUM: Johannesburg
Capacity: 96 000 seats
Hosting: Five first-round, one second-round, one quarter-final and the final match.
The stadium design is based on a calabash, or African pot, and symbolises the melting pot of African cultures.

ROYAL BAFOKENG STADIUM: Rustenburg
Capacity: 42 000 seats
Hosting: four first-round and one second-round
The Royal Bafokeng Sports Palace was opened in 1999 and completely funded by the Royal Bafokeng Nation, an administrative entity presiding over the world's richest platinum mines.

NELSON MANDELA BAY STADIUM: Port Elizabeth
Capacity: 50 000 seats
Hosting: five first-round, one second-round, one quarter-final, and the third-place play-off.

SOUTH AFRICA'S IMPRESSIVE WORLD CUP STADIUMS PROVIDE AN ARSENAL OF WORLD-CLASS ARENAS, FULLY LOADED WITH THE BEST TECHNOLOGY IN WORLD SPORT, DRAPED WITH A GENEROUS HELPING OF LOCAL INFLUENCE AND CULTURE. THE TEN STADIUMS ARE HOST TO 64 MATCHES AND WILL SEAT MORE THAN 570 000 PEOPLE DURING THE 2010 SOCCER WORLD CUP.

mmm... dis lekker!

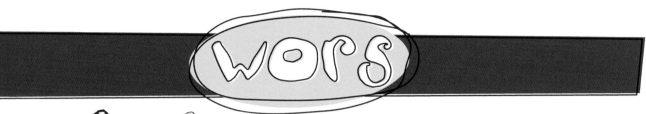

braai 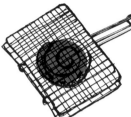 boerewors until brown but **JUICY**

SAUCE {or sous in Afrikaans}

in a  potjie --  **2**  chopped  onions

ADD **2** tomatoes  ~SIMMER~ for **30** mins

ADD **1** tablespoon Worcestershire Sauce  **1/3** cup chutney  and a **dash** vinegar

 **Pap** {Putu in Zulu}

Boil **2** litres of WATER ADD salt **+ 2** cups  Mielie Meal STIR

COOK on a **LOW** heat for **1hr**

ENJOY with a cold  or **2**

YUM! DESSERT YUM! YUM!

melt **4**  ADD a teaspoon brandy **+** 1 cream pour over vanilla ice cream

SLIGHTLY USED TOILET ROLLS
10s R8.95
24s R20.99
STILL IN GOOD CONDITION

The LOO with a VIEW
The longest 'Long Drop' in Africa!

Enjoy the view at Oribi Gorge

Celebrating April Fools' day in the Sunday Times

 NATIONAL SKIRT EXTENSION PROJECT (NSEP)

NATIONAL SKIRT EXTENSION PROJECT (NSEP) CALL CENTRE: 0860 111 412.

THE NATIONAL SKIRT EXTENSION PROJECT

After extensive consultation it has been determined that the current skirt length on the majority of ladies restroom signs is too short. As such, a new figure, bearing a longer skirt length, has been recommended for use nationwide.

Compliance will be mandatory. Pending approval, the National Skirt Extension Project will mean that all owners of public restroom facilities will be required to install the new, approved ladies signage as a matter of urgency.

 As a temporary solution, the public may utilise one of the temporary stickers to cover over their existing signs until such time as they have the correct signage installed.

ACCEPTABLE MEASUREMENTS

If the distance from the base of the foot to the base of the skirt is more than one tenth (1/10) of the overall height of the figure then the sign is not compliant. Existing signs that fall within the aforementioned measurements will be seen as compliant and will not need to be changed.

Examples of compliant/non-compliant signs:

PLEASE NOTE
ONLY ONE (1) PIECE OF TOILET PAPER TO BE TAKEN PER PERSON

UXOLO
IPHEPHA ITOLETHE ELILODWA OLITHATHILE UMUNTU NGAMUNYE

Things are changing...

but to remain so, we need your cooperation.

USAGE INSTRUCTIONS

PLEASE CLOSE TAP AFTER FLASHING!!! (REMEMBER TO FLASH)

NOW YOU ARE ALLOWED TO LEAVE

THANK YOU FOR CO-OPERATING

Sign in Greater Marble Hall Municipality Buildings

Photo by Alton Doller courtesy www.getaway.co.za

The ladies' toilet at this Kakamas farm stall says 'drip dry' Photo courtesy www.getaway.co.za

TALKING KAK

Please Remember:

1. Urine only in the front section of the toilet.
2. EVERYTHING except urine (crap, toilet paper, sand, tampons, whatever...) goes into the back (main) section.
3. After crapping, put two scoops of soil on top of your deposit.
4. You MUST NOT put soil in the front (urine) section – it will block the pipe.
5. Guys, either sit and piss or use the urinals.
6. Feed the pig, vomit in the bush. Do not vomit in these toilets!

This is a sign with instructions on how to use the long drop at Bulungula Backpackers Lodge in the Transkei

SMIT MOTORS

LADIES	GENTS
ABAFAZI	AMADODA
DAMES	MANS
GIRLS	BOYS
INBOARDS	OUTBOARDS
AMATITI	AMATOTI
WATERPLAS	WATERSTRAAL
EVE	ADAM
E-HLALA	E-HIMA
SOWS	BOARS
GEESE	GANDERS
HEN TROUTS	COCK TROUTS
HUNTED	HUNTERS
TANNIES	OOMS

Covering all options to remain politically correct in Volksrust

TEST YOUR KNOWLEDGE

CAN YOU GUESS WHO I AM?

1. After Shakespeare, which playwright has had the most plays performed in the world?

2. Who won 'The World Mayor Award' in 2008?

3. Who sold his company, Thawte Consulting, for R3.5 billion at the age of 26?

4. Who was named South African sportsman of the twentieth century?

5. Who was the only woman to visit Nelson Mandela in prison during his 27 years of imprisonment?

6. Whose life is portrayed in Richard Attenborough's movie, Cry Freedom?

7. Who used soccer as part of an anti-discrimination campaign, naming the teams in Johannesburg, Pretoria and Durban 'The Passive Resisters'?

8. Who was South Africa's five-year-old HIV-positive TV celebrity?

9. Who was the first person killed in the Soweto Riots of 1976?

10. Who is the most productive novelist of all times, with a total of 906 books written under different names?

What am I?

1. I stand 2 m tall and am the largest carnivore of my kind, and can even capture a small bird.

2. From my hind legs to my antennae I am 160 mm long and I can jump as high as 1 m.

3. My good looks are featured in the photograph on the right, can you guess what I am?

Photo courtesy Matthew Harvey

MATCH ME TO MY SPOTS

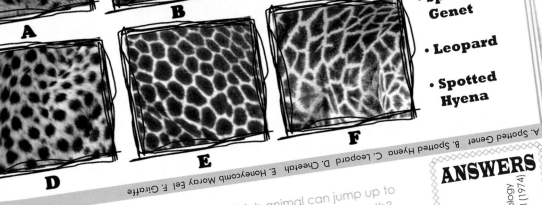

- **Honeycomb Moray Eel**
- **Giraffe**
- **Cheetah**
- **Spotted Genet**
- **Leopard**
- **Spotted Hyena**

A. Spotted Genet B. Spotted Hyena C. Cheetah D. Leopard E. Honeycomb Moray Eel F. Giraffe

15 Questions

1. Where in the world will you find the only game reserve in a city centre?
2. What word does not exist in any of the South African indigenous languages?
3. Of the 400 000 South Africans who signed up for World War II, what percentage of them were black, Coloured and Indian?
4. Which South African battle resulted in more Victoria Crosses being awarded than any other day in British history?
5. Which area in the world has the highest concentration of endangered species, with a total of 15 species per km² being in danger of extinction?
6. What record breaking event occurred in Johannesburg on 14 August 1909?
7. Which animal can jump up to 4 m high and 15 m in length?
8. What game is played by 40% of the population and attracted 36 000 people to a tournament organised in KwaZulu Natal?
9. Where was author of the Lord of the Rings, JRR Tolkien, born?
10. An event occurred in the Valley of Ceres in 1969, in which 12 people were killed. What was the event?
11. What, dating back 77 000 years, was found in the Blombos cave near Stilbaai in the Southern Cape?
12. Which Springbok player's surname is best represented in South African sport?
13. What would you be describing if you said in blazons, 'per pall fesswise gules, sable and azure, a fesswise pall vert fimbriated argent, or an argent'?
14. Which South African women have won the Miss World title?
15. Which creatures have 160 species found in South Africa, of which 50 are found nowhere else?

ANSWERS

1. The Franklin Game Reserve on Naval Hill in Bloemfontein
2. Stranger
3. 40%
4. The Battle of Rorke's Drift
5. The Cape Flats
6. The heaviest recorded snow storm
7. The springbok when it is pronking
8. The indigenous game called Morabaraba
9. Bloemfontein, 1892
10. Earthquake, felt 1 175 km away, measuring 6.3 on the Richter Scale
11. Jewellery and artefacts
12. du Plessis
13. The South African flag using flag terminology
14. Penny Coelen (1958) and Anneline Kriel (1974)
15. Frogs

TRUE/FALSE

1. An owl's eyes are almost half the size of its brain.
2. Fossil records found in South Africa indicate that sharks are older than dinosaurs.
3. A lion's roar can be heard 8 km away.
4. The world's longest millipede (or Shongololo), the African Giant Black millipede, reaches a length of over 380 mm and has over 1 000 legs.
5. African Black-footed Penguins can swim faster than the Atlantic Bottlenose Dolphin, and can attain speeds of 29-37 km/h.

When you live in fear,

You fear living.

When you live freely,

You are free to live.

Derryn Campbell

REFERENCES

The information sourced for the book was not taken from academic records or encyclopaedias, but rather from the vast array of interesting and informative non-fiction books which are available in South African bookstores and libraries. The information presented in the book represents the tip of the iceberg and readers will find any one of the books listed entertaining and enjoyable. They come highly recommended!

CULTURE
Barbara Elion with Mercia Strieman. *Clues to Culture*. One Life Media.
Charles Mitchley. *South African Heritage*. Mill Street Publications.
Dee Rissik. *Culture Shock*. Times Edition, Marshall Cavendish.
Marianne Thamm and Toby Newsome. *How to be a South African Handbook*. Double Storey Books.
Denis Beckett. *Flying with Pride*. WildNet Africa.

QUOTATIONS AND PROVERBS
Jennifer Crwys-Williams. *The Penguin Dictionary of South African Quotations*. Penguin Books.
Julia Stewart. *Stewart's Quotable Africa* and *Stewart's Quotable African Women*. Penguin Books.
Dianne Stewart. *Wisdom from Africa*. Struik Publishers.
Bridget Hilton-Barber & Pat Hopkins. *Place*. Zebra Press.
Mokgadi Pela and Mike Lipkin. *Phila*.

ABOUT SOUTH AFRICA
Dawid Van Lill. *Van Lill's South African Miscellany* and *Van Lill's South African Sports Trivia*. Zebra Press.
Bill Malkin. *It's a Fact*. Jonathan Ball Publishers.
Ian Harrison & Peter Joyce. *The Book of Firsts*. Jonathan Ball Publishers.
Guy Lundy and Wayne Visser. *South Africa Reasons to Believe*. Aardvark Press.
Pat Hopkins, Denise Slabbert & Jabulile Bongiwe Ngwenya. *The South African Fact Book*. Penguin Books.
Bridget Hilton-Barber. *Weekends with Legends*. The Spearhead Press.
Editors Inc. *South Africa at a glance 2009/2010*.
South Africa Yearbook 2008/2009. www.gcis.co.za.

HISTORY
Roger Webster. *At the Fireside Series*. Spearhead.
Max du Preez. *Of warriors, lovers and prophets* and *Of tricksters, tyrants and turncoats*. Zebra Press.
Rob Marsh. *South Africa, Weird and Wonderful*. Tafelberg.
Rob Marsh. *Unsolved Mysteries of Southern Africa*. Striuk Publishers.
Ben Maclennan. *The Wind Makes Dust*. Tafelberg.
Lauren Beukes. *Maverick*. Oshun Books.
John Cameron-Dow. *A Newspaper History of South Africa*. Don Nelson Publishers.
Reader's Digest. *South Africa's Yesterdays*. The Reader's Digest Association of South Africa.

SUBJECT SPECIFIC
Arthur Goldstuck. *Ink in the Porridge* and *The Leopard in the Luggage*. Penguin Books.
Astronomical Society of Southern Africa. *Sky Guide, Africa South*.
Anusuya Chinsamy-Turan. *Famous Dinosaurs of Africa*. Struik Publishers.
Jay Heale & Diane Stewart. *African Myths & Legends*. Struik Publishers.
Shaun Tomson. *Surfer's Code*. Gibbs Smith Publishers.
Dawid van Lill. *African Wildlife Trivia*. Struik Publishers.

ON THE LIGHTER SIDE
Sarah Britten. *The Art of the South African Insult*. 30° South Publishers.
Jill Ritchie. *Ag Shame!* Papillon Press.
Chris Marais and Pat Hopkins. *101 Beloved Bars*. Zebra Press.
Norman Nel. *Would you please say a few words?* Executive Living.
Helen Boardman. *A Matter of Facts*. Zebra Press.
Richard George, Denise Slabbert, Kim Wildman. *Offbeat South Africa*. Struik Publishers.

WEBSITES
Those websites which were used extensively and
are of particular interest are listed below. The full
list of website references is available on request
from the publishers.

www.southafrica.info
www.southafrica.net
www.ZAR.co.za
www.sahistory.org.za
www.emailjokes.co.za
www.GPSA.co.za
www.getaway.co.za
www.sagoodnews.co.za

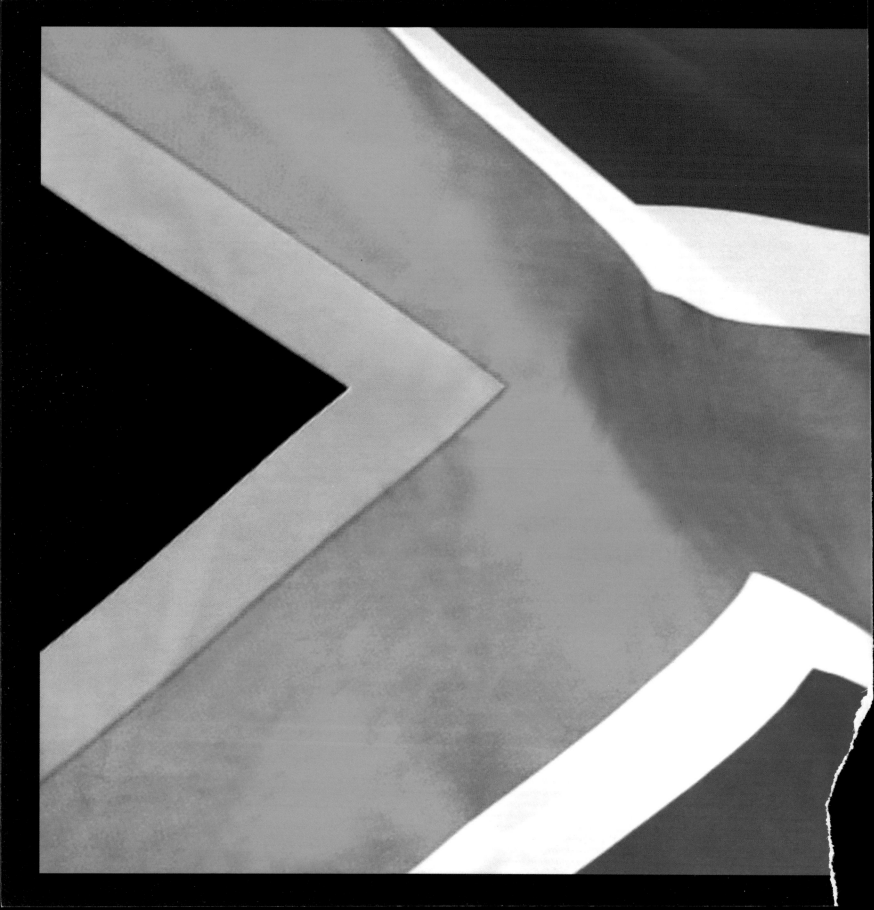

The **FLAG** MUST be treated with **DIGNITY** and **RESPECT**.

It may never be allowed to touch the ground or floor; be used as a table cloth, or draped in front of a platform; be used to cover a statue, plaque, corner stone etc. at unveiling or similar ceremonies; be used to start or finish any competition, race, or similar event; be manufactured or used as underclothes, bath and floor mats or any similar demeaning application; be used for any commercial advertising in a manner that will distort or show disrespect to the flag.

The flag was flown for the first time on the 10th of May 1994 when **NELSON MANDELA** became **President**

Not only is the flag one of the **youngest** in the world, but it is also the **only** flag in the world with **6 colours** The flag was originally commissioned as an interim flag but was embraced with such **PASSION** and **PATRIOTISM** that it has become permanent.

Few would have imagined – almost a decade ago – that this collection of colourful shapes could become such a potent **SYMBOL** of **UNITY** and **PROGRESS**. But then fewer still would have thought that a country torn apart by decades of racial oppression could **TRANSFORM** itself into a beacon of **DEMOCRACY** and **HOPE**.

If the **red band** is at the bottom, you're flying your flag **upside down** – the traditional sign of **surrender** (or if you're at sea, the international maritime signal of **distress**). Unless you're Mark Shuttleworth floating in space, in which case there is **NO** top or bottom!

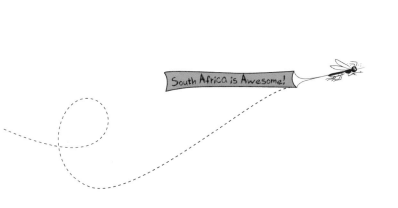

This book is dedicated to South Africa's future.....
- To those who believe in it,
- To those who are a part of it,
- And to those who are determined to positively improve it.

To order copies of this book, or to send us your interesting South African information, photographs or suggestions

Email
info@awesomesa.co.za

Visit our website
www.awesomesa.co.za

Phone
+27 (0)82 786 8450